Temperature Conversion Table

American Oven Temperature Terms	Degrees Fahrenheit	Degrees Centigrade (Celsius)
	160 170	71 77
	200 212	93 100
Very Slow	225 230 250	107 110 121
Slow	275 300 302	135 149 150
Moderately Slow.	320 325	160 163
Moderate	350 356 375	177 180 190
Hot	390 400	200 205
	425 428	218 220
	437 450	225 232
Very Hot	475 500	246 260
Broil.	525 550	274 288

TEMPERATURE

Volume 11

Haw — Jam

WOMAN'S DAY ENCYCLOPEDIA OF COOKERY

1979 Edition
For WOMAN'S DAY

JEANNE VOLTZ, *Food Editor*

For FUNK & WAGNALLS, INC.

Supervising Editor—**NORMA H. DICKEY**
Production Editor—**KATHIE L. ATTLEE**
Production Executive—**EDWARD HAAS**
Editorial Staff—**DONNA L. AMOS, JUNE V. ROOK**
Art Director—**MURRAY KESHNER**
Layout Artists—**HERBERT ASCHER, MARTIN GORDON,
ERLA SIGURDARDOTTIR**

Special Project Staff:

Contributing Editors—**INEZ M. KRECH, JAMES W. TRAGER**

Original Edition

Prepared and edited by the Editors of WOMAN'S DAY
GLENNA MCGINNIS, *Food Editor*

Special Project Staff:

Editor—**NIKA STANDEN HAZELTON**
Associates—**L. GERALDINE MARSTELLER, HELEN FEINGOLD,
SUSAN J. KNOX**

First Revised Edition

Special Project Staff:
Editor—**MARIE ROBERSON HAMM**
Associate Editor—**ISABEL CORNELL**

Volume 11

Hawaiian — Jambalaya

Arranged alphabetically, the articles in this volume fall between the two words listed above. Among the interesting and informative entries found in this volume, several sections are worthy of special attention. We have listed these below for your convenience.

How to use the Woman's Day Encyclopedia of Cookery

The twenty-two volumes of the Woman's Day Encyclopedia contain a wealth of alphabetically arranged information. If you wish to prepare Apple Pie, look under Apple in volume 1. But to find all of the information in all of the volumes, you should use the twenty-third volume, the Index. Composed of five separate indexes, volume 23 includes: meal and menu planning; information on nutrition and diet; techniques of cookery and equipment use; a listing by author; and an alphabetical listing by ingredients.

This Encyclopedia contains many individual entries that supplement one another. Meal and Menu Planning, for instance, is treated throughout the Encyclopedia in many different entries. The first index in volume 23 collects these entries and lists volume and page numbers for such diverse items as Busy Day Dinners and Low Cost Meals. How to entertain or cook in different national styles will be simplified by consulting such items as Parties or Mexican Cookery. If you want to cook for a crowd or make up a Christmas menu, this index shows you where to find Quantity Cooking and three separate styles of Christmas meals.

If you are learning to cook or beginning to plan diets for a family, two other indexes offer assistance. The Encyclopedia entries that contain information on nutrition and diet are listed in one index, and techniques of cookery and equipment are listed in the other. If you want to know which foods are necessary in your child's diet or how to cut down on cholesterol, see the second index. If you want to find out which pan is appropriate for a layer cake, see Bake in the third index.

The fourth index in volume 23 is a listing by author of all the special articles in the Encyclopedia. Here you will find titles and location of articles by noted cookbook authors and food and health authorities.

A major part of volume 23 is the listing of all the recipes contained in the Encyclopedia, arranged alphabetically by main ingredient and by one or more menu categories. Thus, an Abalone Chowder recipe in volume 1 is listed in this Index under ABALONE and under SOUPS. A Crabmeat Dip recipe appears under CRABS, under DIPS, APPETIZER, and under APPETIZERS.

These volumes offer helpful advice on cooking, meal planning, food budgeting, and entertaining. Brimming with tempting recipes, mouthwatering photos, and interesting tid-bits about the origin and history of some of the ingredients, the Woman's Day Encyclopedia of Cookery is indeed a browsing library for food lovers.

HAWAIIAN COOKERY

HAWAIIAN COOKERY

Portuguese, Chinese, Japanese, Koreans, Filipinos, Americans and native Hawaiians have all left their mark on Hawaiian cuisine. Island housewives have not only adopted traditional dishes of the various settlers but have become adept at combining foreign foods with native products. You will find here a generous sampling of some of their most notable dishes, slightly adapted to the foods available on the "mainland."

Glossary of Hawaiian Foods

AKU—*bonito*
ALANI—*orange*
HAUPIA—*thick coconut pudding*
I'A—*fish*
I'A MAKA—*raw fish*
IPU PU—*squash*
IPU-HAOLE—*watermelon*
KI—*tea*
KOPAA—*sugar*
KOPE—*coffee*
LAIKI—*rice*
LAULAU—*package of luau, pork and salt fish, tied in ti leaves and steamed*
LUAU—*feast, leaves of taro*
MAHIMAHI—*dolphin*
MAIA—*banana*
MOA—*chicken*
NIOI—*red peppers*
NIU—*coconut*
OPAE—*shrimp*
PAA KAI—*salt*
PELEHU—*turkey*
POI—*pasty staple food from taro root*
PUPU—*appetizer*
UALA—*sweet potato*
ULA—*lobster*
WAI—*fresh water*
WAIU—*milk*
WAIUPAA—*cheese*
WAINA—*grapes*

APPETIZER AND SOUP

WATER-CHESTNUT AND PINEAPPLE ROLL-UPS

Cut bacon slices in thirds, slice water chestnuts and drain canned pineapple chunks. Wrap a bacon slice around a chunk of pineapple and a slice of water chestnut. Secure with a toothpick. Broil until bacon is crisp, turning

once or twice. Drain on paper towel. Put on rack in shallow baking pan, and just before serving, reheat in preheated moderate oven (350°F.) about 5 minutes.

POLYNESIAN WATERCRESS SOUP

- 3 tablespoons butter or margarine
- 3 tablespoons all-purpose flour
  Salt
- ½ teaspoon curry powder
- 3 cups milk
- 1½ cups coarsely shredded carrots
- 1 cup water
- 1 cup chopped watercress
  Diced papaya, fresh or canned
  Chopped macadamia nuts
  Shredded coconut

Melt butter and blend in flour, ¾ teaspoon salt and curry powder. Gradually add milk and cook, stirring, until thickened. Cook carrots, covered, in water until tender. Add watercress and cook ½ minute. Add to hot milk mixture and bring to simmering point. Add a little more salt if necessary. Serve at once with last 3 ingredients as garnishes. Makes 6 servings.

MAIN DISHES

MAINLAND LUAU

A luau is a very special Hawaiian feast whose main attraction is a fat young pig steamed in an underground oven. For mainlanders we've put together a mock luau menu using recipes given in this section.

Fresh-Vegetable Sticks
Mock Kalua Roast
Coconut Sweet Potatoes
Glazed Pineapple Wedges
Korean Bean-Sprout Salad
Macadamia-Nut Pie
Minted Iced Tea

MOCK KALUA ROAST

Kalua means "to bake underground."
A suckling pig is traditional.

- 1 pork shoulder (boneless butt portion, about 5 pounds)
- ½ garlic clove
  Salt
- ¼ cup guava jelly
- 2 tablespoons firmly packed brown sugar
  Coconut Sweet Potatoes
  Glazed Pineapple Wedges

Rub meat with garlic and sprinkle with salt. Wrap tightly in foil. Put in shallow roasting pan and roast in preheated moderate oven (350°F.) 4 hours. Uncover, spread with guava jelly mixed with brown sugar and brown in preheated hot oven (425°F.) 10 to 15 minutes, or until well glazed. Surround with sweet potatoes and pineapple wedges. Makes 6 servings.

NOTE: Hawaiians mince the garlic and mix it with ¼ cup vegetable oil, then rub the meat with the mixture before wrapping in foil. When meat is done it is uncovered and browned in a very hot oven or put under the broiler until browned. It is then cut in serving portions and eaten sprinkled with Hawaiian salt (coarse salt).

Coconut Sweet Potatoes

Peel sweet potatoes and wrap each in foil. Bake in preheated moderate oven (350°F.) 1 hour, or until tender. Open foil, pour a little melted butter or margarine over each and sprinkle with flaked coconut. Bake 10 minutes longer, or until coconut is browned. Or put canned sweet potatoes in a shallow baking dish. Heat, butter, sprinkle with coconut and brown.

Glazed Pineapple Wedges

Pare a fresh pineapple, cut in quarters and remove center core. Cut each quarter in 3 wedges. Melt 2 tablespoons butter or margarine in skillet. Add pineapple and sprinkle with brown sugar. Heat.

CHINESE SWEET PORK

In Hawaii this can be bought, already cooked, in most meat markets.

2½ pounds lean boneless fresh pork in one piece
½ cup Chinese barbecue sauce for making sweet pork
   Salt and pepper

Cut meat in thin strips about 1½ inches wide. Marinate in barbecue sauce 3 to 4 hours. Place on a rack in a roasting pan and sprinkle with salt and pepper. Roast in preheated moderate oven (350°F.) 1 hour, turning once and basting occasionally. Makes 6 to 8 servings.

LAULAUS

In Hawaii taro leaves (luau) are used for wrapping the meat and fish but spinach can be substituted. Foil is used instead of ti leaves.

1 pound spinach
1¾ pounds pork, cut in 6 pieces
1 tablespoon coarse salt
1 pound butterfish or other fish, cut in 6 pieces

Wash spinach and remove stems and fibrous part. Put pork in bowl, add salt and work in thoroughly. Arrange 5 or more spinach leaves on palm of hand, add a piece each of pork and fish and fold to form a bundle. Make 6 bundles and wrap each tightly in foil. Steam in steamer or on rack in skillet or kettle 4 to 6 hours. Makes 6 servings.

BARBECUED BEEF

Sesame seed suggests Korean origin.

1 cup soy sauce
¼ cup sugar
2 tablespoons vegetable oil
1 green onion, thinly sliced
1 garlic clove, minced
1 teaspoon monosodium glutamate
½ teaspoon coarsely ground pepper
2 tablespoons sesame seed, toasted and crushed
3 pounds steak (round or sirloin), sliced ½ inch thick

Mix together all ingredients, except steak, and marinate steak in mixture 1 to 2 hours, turning occasionally. Broil quickly, preferably over charcoal. Makes 6 to 8 servings. **NOTE:** Toast sesame seed in a dry pan over moderate heat until golden, then crush.

KOREAN FRIED RICE

Koreans do not use egg to bind their fried rice and they add sesame seed, which gives their rice a distinctive taste and texture.

1 pound boneless pork
   Soy sauce
1 teaspoon sugar
2 teaspoons sesame seed, toasted and crushed
1 garlic clove, minced
4 green onions, finely sliced
1 ounce dried mushrooms
¼ cup vegetable oil
⅓ cup chicken broth
1 pound fresh bean sprouts or 1 can (1 pound), drained and rinsed
½ pound Chinese peas in pods or 1 box (10 ounces) frozen peas
½ pound fresh water chestnuts, cooked and sliced, or 1 can (5 ounces), drained
4 cups cooked rice

Cut pork in small cubes. Combine ⅓ cup soy sauce, sugar, sesame seed, garlic and onions. Marinate pork in the mixture 1 hour. Meanwhile, soak mushrooms in warm water 1 hour, then squeeze out water and cut mushrooms in thin slices. Cook pork in oil 5 to 8 minutes, stirring occasionally. Add chicken broth, 2 tablespoons soy sauce, bean sprouts, Chinese peas (remove strings and cut pods in 1-inch diagonal slices), water chestnuts, mushrooms and rice. Steam 5 minutes, stirring several times. Makes 8 servings.

BANANA-CHICKEN CURRY

Bake this in a dish that can go to the table. To serve, spoon it over steamed rice.

¼ cup butter or margarine
¼ cup all-purpose flour
2 teaspoons curry powder
½ teaspoon salt
¼ teaspoon pepper
2 cups chicken broth
3 green-tipped bananas
2 cups diced cooked chicken
Grated coconut (optional)
Hot steamed rice

Melt butter; add flour, curry powder, salt and pepper, and stir until smooth. Gradually add chicken broth and cook, stirring constantly, until smooth and thickened. Peel bananas and cut in 1-inch lengths. Arrange in greased 1½-quart casserole. Pour half of the curry sauce over bananas and bake in preheated moderate oven (350°F.) 15 minutes. Arrange chicken on top and add remaining sauce. Bake 5 minutes until heated through. Sprinkle with grated coconut, if desired, and serve on rice. Makes 4 servings.

CHICKEN MACADAMIA

Macadamia trees are named for John Macadam, an Australian chemist.

3 pounds chicken breasts
Salted water
2 eggs
½ cup all-purpose flour
¼ cup cornstarch
½ cup water
1 teaspoon ginger juice or ½ teaspoon powdered ginger
1 small onion, minced
¼ teaspoon pepper
2 tablespoons vegetable oil
2 tablespoons soy sauce
2 tablespoons white wine
Fat for deep-frying
1½ cups raw rice, steamed
Sweet-Sour Sauce
½ cup toasted chopped macadamia nuts

Remove bones and skin from chicken breasts; simmer bones and skin in salted water at least 30 minutes; drain, reserving stock; add water to make 2 cups for Sweet-Sour Sauce. Cut raw chicken meat in bite-size pieces. Beat together or whirl in blender remaining ingredients, except last 4. Marinate chicken meat in mixture ½ hour. Drain, then fry in hot deep fat (375°F. on a frying thermometer) until golden brown and done; drain. To serve, spread rice on platter and arrange chicken pieces on top. Pour sauce over chicken and sprinkle with macadamia nuts. Makes 6 to 8 servings.

Sweet-Sour Sauce

Mix ¼ cup cornstarch, ¼ cup packed brown sugar, ⅓ cup soy sauce and ½ cup vinegar. Gradually add 2 cups reserved hot chicken stock and cook, stirring constantly, until thick and clear.

TERIYAKI MEATBALLS

These can be made bite-size for pupus ("appetizers").

2 eggs
2 pounds ground round steak
½ cup cornflake crumbs
½ cup milk
2 tablespoons grated onion
1 teaspoon salt
¼ teaspoon pepper
Teriyaki Sauce

Beat eggs and mix thoroughly with remaining ingredients, except sauce. Shape in balls about 1½ inch in diameter and arrange in a layer in greased shallow baking pan. Pour sauce over balls and bake in preheated slow oven (300°F.) about 45 minutes, turning and basting every 15 minutes. Makes about 3 dozen balls.

Teriyaki Sauce Mix 1 cup soy sauce, ½ cup water, 2 teaspoons ginger juice (or 1 teaspoon powdered ginger), 2 cloves garlic, minced, and 1 teaspoon sugar.

PINEAPPLE TERIYAKI

1 slice boneless beef sirloin, cut 1 inch thick (about 1¼ pounds)
1 can (13½ ounces) pineapple chunks
¼ cup soy sauce
1 garlic clove, crushed
¾ teaspoon ground ginger
Stuffed olives
Hot cooked rice (optional)

Cut meat in 1 to 1¼-inch cubes. Drain ½ cup syrup from pineapple. Mix syrup, soy sauce, garlic and ginger; pour over meat cubes. Stir and let stand at room temperature at least 1 hour, then thread olives, meat and pineapple chunks on skewers, beginning with olives. Broil, turning once, cooking to desired doneness, 8 to 10 minutes for rare. Baste once with drippings in pan. Serve with rice, if desired. Makes 4 or 5 servings.

CHICKEN KAMAAINA

Kamaaina means "old-timer" in Hawaiian.

6 halves of chicken breast
6 pineapple spears
   All-purpose flour
   Salt and pepper
1 cup coconut milk (see Sweet-Potato Poi)
2 tablespoons butter or margarine
2 tablespoons shortening
½ cup grated coconut
   Hot cooked rice

Bone chicken breasts, leaving skin on. Roll each half around a pineapple spear and fasten with small skewers or toothpicks. Then roll in flour seasoned with salt and pepper, dip into coconut milk and roll again in flour; chill. Melt butter and shortening together in skillet and brown chicken breasts on both sides. Transfer to a buttered shallow baking dish, sprinkle with grated coconut and bake in preheated hot oven (400°F.) 15 to 20 minutes, or until tender. Meanwhile, add 1 tablespoon flour to pan drippings and stir in remaining coconut milk. Cook, stirring, until smooth and thickened. Serve with chicken and rice. Makes 6 servings.

CHICKEN LONG RICE

Long rice is also known as bean thread or cellophane noodles. It can be bought wherever Chinese foods are sold.

1 fryer, 2½ to 3 pounds, cut up
2 tablespoons vegetable oil
2 cups boiling water
1 teaspoon salt
4 ounces long rice
1 cup thinly sliced green onions with tops
1 tomato, cut in wedges

Brown chicken in oil. Add water and salt and simmer ½ hour, or until tender. Meanwhile, soak long rice ½ hour in warm water to cover. Drain and add to chicken. Simmer 10 minutes. Add onion and tomato and simmer 5 minutes. Makes 4 servings.

GRILLED MAHIMAHI

Mahimahi is "dolphin," but halibut is a good substitute.

¼ cup butter
1 teaspoon vegetable oil
⅛ teaspoon garlic salt
1 teaspoon soy sauce
½ teaspoon lemon juice
1½ pounds mahimahi or halibut steak
   Lemon wedges

Melt butter and add remaining ingredients, except fish and lemon wedges. Add fish and marinate 30 minutes. Grill over charcoal or broil 5 to 6 minutes on each side, or until fish flakes easily with a fork. Serve with lemon wedges. Makes 4 servings.

SHRIMPS TEMPURA

1½ pounds large shrimps
½ cup cornstarch
½ cup all-purpose flour
1 teaspoon salt
¼ teaspoon monosodium glutamate
1 egg
½ cup water
   Vegetable oil for frying
   Chinese mustard or sweet-sour sauce

Shell and clean shrimps, leaving tails on. Split shrimps through back, cutting almost through. Open to butterfly shape. Mix dry ingredients. Add egg and water and beat until smooth. Heat oil 1½ inches deep to 375°F. on a frying thermometer. Holding shrimps by tail, dip in batter and drop gently, a few at a time, into the hot oil. When shrimps rise to surface, turn and continue cooking until golden brown. Serve with the mustard. Makes 3 or 4 servings.

SIDE DISHES

SWEET-POTATO POI

Boil sweet potatoes in their jackets until tender. Peel and mash, beating until smooth. Season to taste with salt and pepper. Gradually beat in enough coconut milk to make the desired consistency—one-finger, two-finger or three-finger poi. (The consistency of poi varies with the amount of liquid used. It is called one-finger, two-finger or three-finger poi according to the number of fingers needed to get it from the serving dish to the mouth without dribbling it on the chin.) Keep hot in top part of double boiler. Serve in individual bowls.
NOTE: To make coconut milk, heat 1 can (3½ ounces) flaked coconut (or 1 cup fresh or frozen grated coconut) and 1 cup milk to the boiling point. Allow to cool at room temperature. Strain through 2 thicknesses of cheesecloth, squeezing out as much liquid as possible. Discard coconut.

SPICED BANANAS

4 green-tipped bananas
2 cups sugar
¾ cup cider vinegar
¼ cup lemon juice
2 tablespoons butter
2 sticks cinnamon
1½ teaspoons whole cloves
1 teaspoon chopped fresh ginger
½ teaspoon salt
¼ teaspoon each ground nutmeg and mace

Peel bananas and cut in 1-inch pieces. Combine remaining ingredients and bring to boil. Add bananas and simmer 5 minutes. Remove bananas from syrup before serving, hot or cold, with meat. Makes 4 to 6 servings.

NOTE: Any leftover syrup can be used in cooking ham or pork chops.

GREEN BEANS ORIENTALE

1 can (5 ounces) water chestnuts, sliced
2 tablespoons vegetable oil
2 tablespoons soy sauce
1 package (9 ounces) frozen French-cut green beans
1 teaspoon sugar
  Salt and pepper

Sauté water chestnuts in oil until golden brown. Add soy sauce, beans and sugar and cook over low heat until beans are just tender-crisp and still bright green, separating them with a fork as they defrost. Add salt and pepper to taste. Makes 4 servings.

CURRIED RICE

1 cup raw rice
1 medium onion, quartered and sliced
6 tablespoons butter
1 tablespoon curry powder
2 cups chicken broth
1½ teaspoons salt
½ cup raisins
½ bay leaf

Cook rice and onion in butter, stirring constantly, until golden. Add curry powder and mix well. Add remaining ingredients and bring to boil. Reduce heat, cover and cook without stirring 20 minutes. Remove bay leaf. Serves 4.

CRUNCHY BEAN SPROUTS

3 slices bacon
1 package (10 ounces) fresh bean sprouts or 1 can (1 pound), drained
1 green onion, thinly sliced (include top)
1 to 2 tablespoons soy sauce
½ teaspoon ginger juice or ¼ teaspoon ground ginger
½ teaspoon monosodium glutamate

Cook bacon until crisp and remove from skillet. To fat remaining in pan, add remaining ingredients. Stir-fry 3 minutes. Drain and top with crumbled bacon. Makes 4 servings.

HAWAIIAN FRIED SANDWICHES

1 package (3 ounces) cream cheese
1 medium banana, sliced
1 can (8¼ ounces) crushed pineapple, well drained
¼ cup chopped macadamia nuts, pecans or walnuts
8 slices firm bread
¼ cup milk
1 egg, beaten
  Dash of salt
  Butter

Soften cream cheese with fork, then add banana and

mash together. Stir in pineapple and nuts. Use as filling for 4 sandwiches. Cut each sandwich in half diagonally. Combine milk, egg and salt in shallow dish. Dip each side of sandwich into egg mixture. Melt 2 tablespoons butter in skillet, add sandwiches and brown slowly on both sides, adding a little more butter if necessary. Makes 4 servings.

SALADS

CHINESE CHICKEN SALAD

2 pounds chicken breasts
1 cup water
  Salt , pepper and monosodium glutamate
1 teaspoon ginger juice or ½ teaspoon powdered ginger
1 tablespoon soy sauce
2 cups shredded lettuce
½ cup shredded watercress or other salad greens
¼ cup celery, thinly sliced on the diagonal
2 tablespoons thinly sliced green onions and tops
  Lettuce leaves

Cut chicken meat from skin and bones and place skin and bones in saucepan with water. Lay meat on top of bones and sprinkle with salt, pepper and monosodium glutamate. Steam 15 minutes, turn meat over and again sprinkle with salt, pepper and monosodium glutamate; steam another 15 minutes. Remove chicken and cut into julienne strips while continuing to simmer skin and bones 2 more hours. Strain stock and cool. Remove congealed fat from top. Heat stock with ginger and soy sauce and pour over chicken. Cool until it jellies. Stir with a fork and add lettuce, watercress, celery and onion. Serve on lettuce leaves. Makes 6 servings.

PAPAYA-MACADAMIA SALAD

Mix diced papaya with shredded lettuce and chopped macadamias. Moisten with French dressing or mayonnaise.

KOREAN BEAN-SPROUT SALAD

1 pound (4 cups) fresh bean sprouts or 2 cans (1 pound each), drained
1½ tablespoons finely chopped green onions and tops
2 tablespoons soy sauce
1 tablespoon sesame-seed or vegetable oil
2 teaspoons sesame seed, toasted and crushed
½ teaspoon sugar
¼ teaspoon garlic salt
  Dash of cayenne

Cook bean sprouts in boiling salted water 2 to 3 minutes. Drain and chill. (If using canned bean sprouts, rinse in cold water but do not cook.) Combine all ingredients and chill. Drain and serve. Makes 6 to 8 servings.

ORIENTAL SHRIMP SALAD

2 cups fresh bean sprouts or 1 can (1 pound), drained
2 cups cooked shrimps (1 pound) raw shelled
1 cup crisp chow-mein noodles
1 can (5 ounces) water chestnuts, drained, minced
¼ cup minced green onion
¼ cup minced celery
  Soy Mayonnaise
  Lettuce

Cook bean sprouts in boiling salted water 2 to 3 minutes. Drain and chill. (If using canned bean sprouts, rinse in cold water but do not cook.) Combine all ingredients, except last 2, and mix with Soy Mayonnaise. Serve on lettuce. Makes 4 to 6 servings.
Soy Mayonnaise Mix thoroughly ¾ cup mayonnaise, 1 tablespoon each lemon juice and soy sauce, ¾ teaspoon ginger juice (or ⅜ teaspoon ground), and ½ teaspoon monosodium glutamate.

DESSERTS

MANGO SHERBET SPECIAL

Put half a ripe mango in each sherbet glass. Top with pineapple sherbet and fill glasses with chilled champagne.

PINEAPPLE-GINGER SAUCE

1 can (8¼ ounces) crushed pineapple
¾ cup pineapple juice
½ cup sugar
¼ cup light corn syrup
2 dashes angostura bitters
2 tablespoons chopped preserved ginger
½ cup coarsely chopped macadamia nuts

Combine all ingredients, except nuts. Bring to boil and simmer about 15 minutes. Cool and add nuts. Serve on ice cream, cake, pancakes or waffles. Makes about 2 cups.

PORTUGUESE SWEET BREAD

  Sugar
2 packages active dry yeast
½ cup lukewarm potato water (105°F. to 115°F.)
1 cup warm mashed potato
⅛ teaspoon ginger
½ cup milk
2 teaspoons salt
7 eggs
½ cup butter or margarine, melted and cooled
7 to 8 cups all-purpose flour

Add 3 tablespoons sugar and yeast to potato water and stir until dissolved. Blend in potato and ginger. Set aside

in warm place until doubled in bulk. Scald milk and salt and cool to lukewarm. Beat 6 eggs until light. Gradually beat in 1¾ cups sugar. Stir in butter. Combine yeast and egg mixtures and blend well. Stir in 2 cups flour, add milk and beat until well blended. Add 2 more cups flour and beat 5 minutes. Gradually stir in more flour until dough is stiff enough to knead. Turn out on floured board and knead about 10 minutes, adding only enough flour to prevent sticking. Put dough in an oiled large bowl, cover and let rise until doubled in bulk. Punch down, put on floured board and divide in 4 pieces. Shape in round loaves and put on oiled cookie sheets or into 8½ x 4½ x 2-inch loaf pans. Let rise in warm place until doubled. Beat remaining egg with a few drops of water and brush on loaves. Bake in moderate oven (350°F.) 40 to 50 minutes. Makes 4 round loaves.

MACADAMIA-NUT PIE

Similar to the traditional southern pecan pie.

1 tablespoon all-purpose flour
⅔ cup sugar
3 eggs, slightly beaten
1 cup dark corn syrup
1 cup coarsely chopped macadamia nuts
3 tablespoons butter or margarine, melted
  Pastry for 1-crust 9-inch pie, chilled

Mix flour and sugar. Add eggs, corn syrup, nuts and butter. Pour into pastry shell. Bake in preheated hot oven (400°F.) 10 minutes. Reduce heat to 300°F. and bake 35 to 40 minutes longer, or until filling is set and outside edges are firm.
NOTE: Macadamia nuts are usually sold salted. Shake off as much salt as possible before using.

PINEAPPLE ANGEL PIE

3 eggs, separated
  Salt
1½ cups granulated sugar
1 teaspoon vanilla extract
1½ teaspoons cider vinegar
2 teaspoons cornstarch
1 tablespoon lemon juice
1 can (8¼ ounces) crushed pineapple
1 cup heavy cream
2 tablespoons sifted confectioners' sugar
½ cup grated coconut

Beat egg whites with ⅛ teaspoon salt until stiff but not dry. Gradually beat in ½ cup granulated sugar. Add ½ teaspoon vanilla. Gradually add ½ cup more sugar alternately with vinegar, beating well after each addition until stiff and glossy. Put in greased and floured 9-inch piepan, leaving a depression in center. Bake in preheated slow oven (275°F.) 30 minutes. Increase heat to 300°F. and bake 30 minutes longer. Cool. Meanwhile, in top of double boiler, beat egg yolks, cornstarch and dash of salt until thick and lemon-colored. Gradually beat in remaining ½ cup sugar alternately with lemon juice. Fold in undrained pineapple and cook over hot water, stirring constantly, 10 minutes, or until thick. Pour into bowl and cover with waxed paper, pressing paper flat against mixture to prevent a skin from forming. Chill. When ready to serve, whip cream with confectioners' sugar and remaining vanilla until stiff. Fill meringue shell with pineapple mixture and spread cream on top. Sprinkle with coconut.

HAWAIIAN TREATS

A candy featuring four Hawaiian favorites: pineapple, macadamia nuts, ginger and coconut.

    ½ cup firmly packed light-brown sugar
    1 cup granulated sugar
    ½ cup drained crushed pineapple
    1 cup light cream
    1 teaspoon vanilla extract
    ½ cup coarsely chopped macadamia nuts
    ¼ cup finely chopped preserved ginger
    1 tablespoon butter or margarine
    1 cup flaked coconut

Combine sugars, pineapple and cream. Cook, stirring, until a small amount of mixture forms a soft ball when dropped in very cold water (236°F. on a candy thermometer). Remove from heat. Add vanilla, nuts, ginger and butter and cool slightly. Beat until creamy. When mixture begins to hold its shape, turn out on waxed paper and shape in a long roll about 1 inch in diameter. Coat outside with coconut. Chill and slice about ½ inch thick. Makes about 3½ dozen slices.

PINEAPPLE MILK SHERBET

    1¾ cups milk
    ½ cup sugar
    1 can (8¼ ounces) crushed pineapple
    2 tablespoons lemon juice
    ¼ cup orange juice

Combine milk and sugar. Add remaining ingredients and stir until sugar is dissolved. Pour into 9 x 5 x 3-inch loaf pan and freeze. Stir twice during freezing. Makes 6 servings.

PINEAPPLETS

A jellied confection somewhat resembling Turkish paste.

    1 can (1 pound, 4 ounces) crushed pineapple
    2 envelopes unflavored gelatin
    2 cups granulated sugar
    1 tablespoon lemon juice
    1 cup chopped walnuts or pecans
    Confectioners' sugar

Drain ½ cup syrup from pineapple, sprinkle with gelatin and stir. In heavy saucepan, add granulated sugar to pineapple and remaining syrup and cook 20 minutes, stirring often, or until thick (224°F. on a candy thermometer). Remove from heat, add gelatin and stir until dis-

solved. Stir in lemon juice and nuts. Pour into buttered 8-inch square pan. Cool and chill until firm. Cut in 1½-inch squares and roll in confectioners' sugar just before serving. Makes 2 dozen.
NOTE: Keep candy refrigerated since it will soften at room temperature.

ROYAL HAWAIIAN DELIGHT

    1 cup heavy cream
    ¼ cup sifted confectioners' sugar
    ½ cup miniature marshmallows
    1 can (1 pound) tropical fruit salad, drained
    ¾ cup flaked coconut
    Maraschino cherries

Whip cream until stiff. Add sugar and whip gently until mixed. Fold in marshmallows, Hawaiian fruits, and coconut, reserving a little for the top. Chill. Sprinkle with reserved coconut and the cherries. Makes 6 servings.

FRESH-COCONUT CREAM PIE

    1 fresh coconut, grated (see Note)
    2 cups milk
    Sugar
    ¼ teaspoon salt
    3 tablespoons cornstarch
    4 eggs, separated
    1 tablespoon butter or margarine
    1 teaspoon vanilla extract
    1 baked 9-inch pie shell
    ¼ teaspoon cream of tartar

Reserve 2 cups grated coconut. Add milk to remaining coconut (there should be about 1 cup). Bring to boil, stirring, and let stand 20 minutes. Strain through fine sieve, pressing to extract all liquid. Add more milk if necessary to make 2 cups. Mix ⅓ cup sugar, salt and cornstarch; add to beaten egg yolks. Stir in milk, add butter and cook over low heat, stirring constantly, until mixture thickens; let bubble a little. Cool. Stir in vanilla and 1 cup reserved coconut. Pour into pie shell. Beat egg whites until frothy, add cream of tartar and continue beating until stiff. Gradually add ½ cup sugar, beating constantly. Spread on pie filling. Sprinkle with remaining coconut. Bake in preheated slow oven (325°F.) 15 minutes, or until coconut is lightly browned. Turn off heat, open oven door and let pie stand in oven 10 minutes. Remove from oven and let pie stand until it reaches room temperature before serving. Leftover pie should be refrigerated.
NOTE: To prepare fresh coconut, pierce holes in end of coconut and drain off liquid. Put coconut in shallow pan in preheated moderate oven (350°F.) 20 to 30 minutes, or until shell cracks in several places. Remove from oven and pound with hammer to crack shell open. Remove coconut meat and cut off black outer shell. Grate meat on grater or whirl a few small pieces at a time in blender until finely grated or shredded. If fresh coconut is not available, substitute 2 cans (3½ ounces each) flaked coconut and proceed as directed.

PINEAPPLE-COCONUT CREAM

1 envelope unflavored gelatin
  Water
1 can (13¼ ounces) pineapple tidbits
¼ cup sugar
¼ teaspoon salt
2 eggs, separated
2 tablespoons lemon juice
½ teaspoon vanilla extract
1 cup heavy cream, whipped
¼ cup toasted flaked or shredded coconut

Sprinkle gelatin on ¼ cup cold water. Drain pineapple and add enough water to syrup to make 1 cup. Heat with sugar and salt in top of double boiler over hot water until sugar is dissolved. Pour over slightly beaten egg yolks and return to double boiler. Cook, stirring, until very hot. Add gelatin and stir until dissolved. Chill until slightly thickened, then stir in lemon juice and vanilla. Fold in stiffly beaten egg whites and whipped cream. When mixture holds its shape, fold in pineapple tidbits and pour into serving bowl. At serving time, sprinkle with coconut. Makes about 6 servings.

HAZELNUT—This grape-size, smooth-shelled nut grows on shrubs and trees belonging to the genus *Corylus*. The nuts grow in clusters and each is wrapped in a fuzzy outer husk that opens as the nut ripens. The hazelnut is also known as a cobnut or filbert.

Hazelnuts are an essential nut in European dessert cookery and baking. The nuts are often toasted for a browner color and a better flavor; they are seldom blanched.

Whole hazelnuts can be salted, or sugared, or eaten as is. Chopped hazelnuts can be used in candies, baked goods, and desserts. Sliced hazelnuts can be added to salads and to main dishes for texture.

Availability and Purchasing Guide—Hazelnuts are sold in the shell, in bulk or by the pound. Look for nuts with clean shells that are free from scars, cracks, or holes. The shells should be well filled so that the kernel does not rattle.

Shelled salted hazelnuts are sold in bulk and packaged in film bags. Fresh-shelled kernels should be plump, meaty, crisp, and brittle.
2¼ pounds in-shell = 1 pound shelled = 3½ cups

Storage—Keep tightly covered and away from light.
Kitchen shelf: 1 month
Refrigerator shelf: 3 to 4 months
Refrigerator frozen-food compartment, prepared for freezing: 6 months
Freezer, prepared for freezing: 1 year

Nutritive Food Values—Hazelnuts provide protein, fat, iron, and thiamine.
3½ ounces = 634 calories

Basic Preparation—To shell hazelnuts, use a nutcracker as the shell is brittle. Remove the kernel intact. To slice or chop nuts, use a long sharp knife and a cutting board.
To Toast—Place nuts on a cookie sheet in preheated moderate oven (350°F.) for 5 to 6 minutes, stirring once. Turn them out on a rough cloth and rub them briskly in the cloth. This will remove fine skin fibers. The nuts must then be picked over. They can be ground in a blender or a nut mill, and used like other nuts.
To Roast in Oven—Spread nutmeats in a shallow pan and place in preheated hot oven (400°F.) about 7 minutes, or in preheated slow oven (275°F.) for 20 minutes. Stir nuts frequently to prevent scorching. For salted nuts, add 1 teaspoon salt per cup of nutmeats. If desired, while nutmeats are warm, rub off skins with cloth or between fingers.
To Skillet-Roast—Heat 2 teaspoons cooking oil in a skillet over low heat. Add nutmeats and 1 teaspoon salt per cup of nuts. Stir constantly until thoroughly heated. Drain well on paper towels.
To Grind—Use a special nut grinder or an electric blender; when butter or paste is desired, use a meat grinder. Hazelnuts are excellent when ground, with a dry grain that is not oily.

HAZELNUT AND MUSHROOM SAUCE

½ cup sliced hazelnuts
½ onion, minced
¼ cup sliced mushrooms
¼ cup butter or margarine
2 tablespoons all-purpose flour
1 teaspoon salt
¼ teaspoon pepper
2 chicken bouillon cubes
2 cups hot water

Brown hazelnuts, onion, and mushrooms in butter; remove from skillet. To fat, add flour and seasonings, mixing well. Add bouillon cubes which have been dissolved in the hot water; cool until thickened. Return hazelnuts, onion, and mushrooms to sauce; serve hot over rice. Makes about 2½ cups.

HAZELNUT CREAM

½ cup shelled hazelnuts
1 cup milk or light cream
2 egg yolks
¼ cup sugar
1 teaspoon vanilla extract
1½ teaspoons unflavored gelatin
1 tablespoon water
½ cup heavy cream, whipped

Spread hazelnuts in pie pan and toast in preheated moderate oven (350°F.) until skins are coming loose. Place in towel and rub to remove skins. Grind in nut grinder or blender. Combine with milk, egg yolks, and sugar. Cook over lowest possible heat, stirring constantly, until *almost* boiling. Remove from heat. Add vanilla. Soften gelatin in water. Stir into hot custard until completely dissolved. Cool; fold in whipped cream. Pour into glass serving dish and chill until set. Makes 3 large servings.

HAZELNUT TARTS

Pastry (2-cups flour recipe), unbaked
½ cup firmly packed brown sugar
1 tablespoon all-purpose flour
⅛ teaspoon salt
1 cup dark corn syrup
2 eggs, well beaten
2 tablespoons melted butter or margarine
1 teaspoon vanilla extract
1 cup chopped hazelnuts
Undiluted evaporated milk

Line tart shells with pastry. Mix sugar, flour, and salt; add syrup, eggs, butter, and vanilla; pour into pastry. Sprinkle nuts over top and brush edges of tarts with evaporated milk. Bake in preheated moderate oven (350°F.) for 10 minutes; reduce heat to slow (325°F.) and bake for 25 minutes longer. Makes 8 tarts.

CHOCOLATE DIAMONDS WITH HAZELNUTS

2 squares (2 ounces) unsweetened chocolate
½ cup butter
1 cup sugar
2 eggs
½ cup sifted all-purpose flour
¼ teaspoon salt
½ teaspoon vanilla extract
⅔ cup chopped hazelnuts

Melt chocolate and butter over hot water. Add remaining ingredients except nuts and mix well. Spread in greased pan, 1 x 10 x 15 inches. Sprinkle with nuts. Bake in preheated hot oven (400°F.) about 12 minutes. Cool slightly in pans and cut into 1½-inch diamonds. Makes about 4 dozen.

HAZELNUT CINNAMON BUNS

2 cups sifted all-purpose flour
2 teaspoons baking powder
½ teaspoon salt
5 tablespoons shortening
⅔ cup milk
¼ cup butter or margarine, softened
¼ cup firmly packed brown sugar
1 teaspoon ground cinnamon
½ cup sliced hazelnuts
¾ cup light corn syrup

Sift flour, baking powder and salt together; cut in shortening. Add milk and knead for 1 minute. Roll out on floured board into a sheet 12 x 6 inches. Spread with butter, brown sugar, cinnamon, and nuts. Roll as for jelly roll. Cut into 1-inch slices. Pour 1 tablespoon syrup into each greased muffin pan; put slice of dough in each. Bake in preheated very hot oven (450°F.) for 12 minutes. Makes 1 dozen.

HEAD CHEESE—Head cheese is a well-seasoned cold cut made of the edible parts of a calf's or a pig's head such as the cheeks, snouts, and underlips, to which sometimes brains, hearts, tongues, and feet are added. The meat is boiled, stripped from the bones, skinned, cut into pieces, and seasoned with onions, herbs, and spices. Then it is put into a mold and pressed into a firm, jellied mass.

Head cheese is named so misleadingly because, at one time, cheese was added to the meat. It is available in food stores, as are other cold cuts, but it can also be made at home.

Head cheese is used in Scandinavian *smörgåsbord*, in French hors d'oeuvre, and in German, Swiss, and Austrian sandwiches. Every country where farm people butcher meat has its own version of head cheese.

HEAD CHEESE

1 calf's or pig's head
Water
White wine
1 onion, studded with 4 cloves
6 celery stalks with leaves
4 parsley sprigs
1 carrot, sliced
1 bay leaf
12 peppercorns
2 teaspoons salt
Cayenne, ground nutmeg, and dried sage

Have the butcher clean the head and remove the snout. Reserve tongue and brains. Wash head well and place in a kettle large enough to cover the head with equal parts of water and wine. Add tongue and onion studded with cloves. Tie celery, parsley, carrot, bay leaf, and peppercorns in a cheesecloth bag; add. Bring water to a boil and simmer for about 4 hours, skimming the surface as it cooks. Remove tongue from water after 1½ hours. Skin tongue and cut into 1-inch cubes. Remove head from water and reserve cooking liquid. Remove meat from head and cut into 1-inch cubes. Drop brains into cooking liquid and simmer for 15 minutes. Remove membrane from brains, and cut into 1-inch cubes. Toss with tongue and meat from head; season to taste with salt, cayenne, nutmeg, and sage. Spoon mixture into a loaf pan or mold, pressing firmly. Pour ½ cup of the cooking liquid into the pan. Cover pan and weight to keep meats under the liquid. Cool, and then chill for 48 hours. Serve chilled and cut into slices. Makes 8 servings.

HEART

—The hearts of beef, veal, lamb, and pork are used in cookery, especially in Scandinavia and in central Europe. Poultry hearts are usually used as giblets.

Hearts are tasty meat when properly cooked. Since they are less tender cuts, they must be cooked slowly in moist heat, by braising and stewing. Stuffing adds to the interest of the dish.

Hearts are nutritious and inexpensive; and when seasoned with thyme, marjoram, or other herbs, and cooked in a good sauce, make a good family dish.

Hearts can be used in many recipes calling for sliced, diced, or ground meat.

Availability and Purchasing Guide—Beef heart is the largest and averages 3 to 3½ pounds; it may weigh as much as 5 pounds. One heart makes about 8 servings. Veal (calf's heart) is smaller and more tender. It weighs ¾ to 1 pound and makes 2 or 3 servings. Pork heart averages ½ pound and makes 1 or 2 servings. Lamb heart is the smallest and weighs ⅛ to ½ pound; usually one heart is allowed per serving. Occasionally two very small lamb hearts are served as a single portion

Storage—Keep in refrigerator loosely wrapped. Maximum storage time is 3 to 4 days as heart spoils rapidly. Quality is best when used within 24 hours.
Refrigerator shelf, raw: 3 to 4 days
Refrigerator shelf, cooked: 5 to 6 days
Refrigerator frozen-food compartment, prepared for freezing: 2 to 3 weeks
Freezer, prepared for freezing: 6 months to 1 year

Nutritive Food Values—Heart is high in protein, iron, riboflavin, and niacin, and has fair amounts of thiamine.
Beef, 4 ounces, braised = 213 calories
Veal (calf), 4 ounces, braised = 236 calories
Pork, 4 ounces, braised = 221 calories
Lamb, 4 ounces, braised = 295 calories

Basic Preparation—Wash heart. Cut out fat, veins, and arteries. Use whole, sliced, or ground. Braise or cook in liquid.

TIMETABLE FOR COOKING HEARTS

	BRAISED (After Browning) (Hours)	COOKED IN LIQUID (Hours)
Beef		
Whole	3 to 4	3 to 4
Sliced	1½ to 2	
Veal (calf)		
Whole	2½ to 3	2½ to 3
Pork	2½ to 3	2½ to 3
Lamb	2½ to 3	2½ to 3

Cooking times are based on top of the range or cooking in a slow oven (300°F. TO 325°F.).
A pressure cooker shortens the cooking time to about 1 hour. Follow manufacturer's directions for accurate cooking times.

To Braise—If desired, stuff heart before braising. Brown the heart on all sides in a small amount of shortening. Add about ½ cup of liquid. Season with salt and pepper. Simmer, covered, over low heat on top of the range or in preheated slow oven (300°F. to 325°F.). Check occasionally for moisture; if necessary, add a little more hot liquid to prevent scorching.

To Cook in Liquid—Add 1 teaspoon salt for each quart of water to be used. Place heart in deep heavy saucepan. Add water to cover and any desired seasonings. Simmer, covered, until tender.

SAVORY STUFFED HEART

1¼ cups raw rice, cooked
    Few celery leaves, chopped
3 onions, chopped
1 teaspoon poultry seasoning or ½ teaspoon each dried thyme and sage
    Salt and pepper
1 beef heart
2 tablespoons fat
2 cups beef bouillon or water

Mix rice and next 3 ingredients; season to taste with salt and pepper. Trim heart and remove large tubes, excess fat, and blood vessels. Season well inside and out with salt and pepper. Fill with some of rice mixture and sew edges together. Brown well in hot fat in heavy kettle. Cover; cook slowly without added water for 2 hours. Remove meat and pour off all fat. Put remaining rice mixture in kettle; add bouillon and season to taste. Put heart on top, cover, and simmer for 1 hour longer, or until meat is tender. Makes 8 servings.

BEEF HEART WITH VEGETABLES

1 beef heart
    Water
2 teaspoons salt
¼ teaspoon pepper
1 teaspoon mixed pickling spice
1 celery stalk
4 carrots, sliced
4 onions, sliced
4 raw potatoes, sliced
    Bottled gravy sauce

Trim heart; remove large tubes, excess fat, and blood vessels. Cover with water. Add salt, pepper, pickling spice, and celery. Cover and simmer for 2 hours, or until tender. Remove heart, reserving stock, and slice. Put vegetables in bottom of casserole and cover with sliced heart. Add strained stock and a little gravy sauce. Cover, bake in preheated moderate oven (375°F.) for 1 hour. Makes 4 servings.

HEART STEW

1½ pounds beef or veal heart
2 tablespoons all-purpose flour
1 teaspoon salt
  Dash of pepper
2 tablespoons cooking oil
2 onions, sliced
1½ cups water
  Hot mashed potatoes

Trim heart; remove large tubes, excess fat, and blood vessels. Cut meat into thin slices. Dredge with flour, salt, and pepper. Brown lightly in hot oil. Add onion and water. Cover and simmer for 45 minutes. Serve with potatoes. Makes 4 servings.

DANISH VEAL HEARTS

2 veal hearts (about 1½ pounds)
6 parsley sprigs, chopped
2 onions, sliced thin
1 tablespoon fat
½ bay leaf
4 peppercorns
1 teaspoon salt
  Dash of pepper
2 small carrots, diced
1 celery stalk, diced
1 cup water
¼ cup heavy cream

Trim hearts and split lengthwise. Remove large tubes, excess fat, and blood vessels. Stuff hearts with parsley and half of onion; close with skewers or sew with string. Brown on all sides in fat in heavy kettle. Add remaining onion, seasonings, carrots, celery, and water. Cover; simmer for 2 hours, or until hearts are very tender. Remove to hot serving platter. Strain broth, add cream, and pour over hearts. Makes 4 servings.
NOTE: Pork or lamb hearts may be substituted for the veal (calf) heart.

VEAL HEARTS WITH FRUIT STUFFING

2 veal hearts (about 1½ pounds)
  Salt and pepper to taste
8 pitted dried prunes
2 tart apples, peeled and sliced
3 tablespoons butter or margarine
1 cup water
¾ cup light cream

Trim hearts and split lengthwise. Remove large tubes, excess fat, and blood vessels. Sprinkle hearts inside and out with salt and pepper. Stuff hearts with prunes and apple slices. Skewer or sew opening together. Brown hearts on all sides in butter. Gradually add water and

1 teaspoon salt. Bring to a boil, cover, and simmer for 1½ hours, or until hearts are tender. Remove hearts and slice. Stir cream into pan juices. Reheat but do not boil. Serve over heart slices. Makes 6 servings.

HERB—An aromatic plant used to add flavor to food. These plants usually owe their flavoring qualities to essential oils which are readily soluble or easily volatized by heat and quickly permeate the foods with which they are mixed. For culinary use the seeds of some of these plants are the seasoning agent, in others it is the foliage. The herbs most used in American kitchens are parsley, sage, thyme, marjoram, dill, fennel, tarragon, basil, chives, oregano, and savory.

Strictly speaking, only seed plants which do not develop woody persistent tissue can be considered herbs, but certain plants which do not qualify botanically have long histories of use in cooking as flavoring agents. These include such flowers as the rose, marigold, violet, and scented geranium.

From the earliest times herbs have been used in cooking and medicine and for their sweet scent. They have played a large part in folklore and all sorts of magical properties have been accredited to them. The Assyrians, shapers of one of the earliest of recorded civilizations, who settled along the Tigris in what now is Iraq about 3000 B.C., used herbs. Among the 200 plants they were familiar with were dill, fennel, origanum, and thyme. The Egyptians sprinkled parsley on the graves of their dead, and both Greeks and Romans put sweet marjoram in funeral wreaths.

The Greeks and Romans also believed in love potions made from various herbs, including anise, basil, fennel, and garlic. It was thought that anise made one's face young, that basil attracted scorpions (especially if pounded together with crabs), and that thyme could not grow unless it was blown upon by sea winds. Herbs were also used for all sorts of medical cures, and of course, in cookery.

The Middle Ages continued the use of culinary herbs and the herb gardens of monasteries and castles were lovely to behold. Anise, mint, and parsley were favorites for gravies, sauces, and relishes. Dill added flavor to vegetables. Puddings, tarts, pastries, cakes, and conserves were made with the addition of sweet marjoram, thyme, savory, and anise. Some more unusual culinary preparations included marigolds for soup and drinks (as well as for "angry words"), and cumin for roasted peacock. Borage flowers were used as a garnish, and rue was much more popular than it is now. Basil was "for potage," and also to "make a woman shall not eat of anything that is set on the table." This feat was accomplished by serving the food on a hidden bed of basil, because "men say that she will eat none of that which is on the dish whereunder the basil lieth."

Herbs have always been used for beverages, both alcoholic and nonalcoholic. Today, country people and herbalists are still fervent supporters of herb teas and wines. Woodruff is a traditional and continuing ingredient in the *Maibowle* of the Germans, while wormwood is used for absinthe.

Many herbs, including geranium leaves and mint, were said to have healing powers for wounds, and various common and unpleasant ailments have been thought to be curable by herbs. Present-day herbalists continue the tradition, and modern pharmacists use herbs in preparation of some medicines. The type of herb for the type of ailment has differed in different times and different countries. Baldness, a problem throughout the ages, has been thought to be stopped by onions, parsley, and southernwood.

Queen Victoria's mother, a demanding woman, recommended a violet drink to "soothe the system" in case of bronchitis, fevers, and catarrhs.

Herbs have long been used for a cosmetic effect. Sir Hugh Platt, an Englishman writing in 1609, claims they "relieue," or relieve, for ladies, "The wrongs that Nature on their person wrought/Or parching sun with his hot firie rayes." Sir Hugh recommends sorrel "to take staines out of ones hands presently." "To take away the freckles in the face," according to Sir Hugh, you must "wash your face in the wane of the moone with a spunge, morninge and euening with the distilled water of Elder Leaues, letting the same drie into the skiine. Your water must be distilled in Maie."

The careful instructions as to the time of day and year which are necessary for this herbal remedy to be efficient are not uncommon in herb lore. Herbs have always been connected with magic and superstitution, and have sometimes been explained in terms of astrology. From earliest times the influence of the moon upon plants has been considered important. The 17th-century astrologers had complicated charts where they reckoned that each disease was caused by a planet. The illness could be cured either by use of herbs belonging to an opposite sign, or by sympthay, with the herb of the same sign.

Garlic has been worn in an amulet or carried in the pocket or eaten, to ward off all sorts of evil, including vampires, the evil eye, and witches. The plant is used in many spells and charms, and was thought, because of its humanlike form, to screech when it was uprooted. There was also a belief that whoever pulled up the root would himself die. Its juice acted as an anesthetic, as a love potion, to help abscesses, and to soften ivory, as well as "for devil sickness or insanity," "sterility," or "heavy mischief in the home." In fact, it was claimed that it "cures every infirmity except only death where there is no help."

The smell of the aromatic leaves of the herbs, as well as the flowers of some of them, contributes to their flavor and probably accounts for some of the magical properties given to them. But they have long been used for their smell alone. Today the essential oils from roses and sweet calamus are used commercially in perfume, scented soaps, and other sweet-smelling preparations. The early burning of aromatics for the gods was to unleash their smell. In medieval days lavender and sweet flag were often strewn on the floor. Sweet woodruff, which smells like new-mown hay, lent its fragrance to floors and was put among clothes in chests. Costmary and bay scented the medieval version of finger bowls at tables. Potpourris, a mixture of dried flower leaves, are improved with the addition of herbs now, as they have been for years.

Considering the wide uses of herbs, it is not surprising that rulers throughout the ages have been interested in information about them. The Roman Emperors had botanists all over the empire sending back herbs to the capital. Physicians in the later Middle Ages and Renaissance constantly checked herbal experiments in an attempt to keep them up-to-date and free from error. Partly because of the great financial value of herbs and spices in the Middle Ages, when they were used extensively by the rich to flavor and preserve food in those days of nonrefrigeration, Columbus was allowed to set forth on his famous voyage to the New World by Ferdinand and Isabella, who hoped he would discover the spice islands of the East.

Our colonial ancestors set great store by herbs and used them much as they had in the old country. All gardens had their corner where herbs were grown, if not an herb garden proper. Many of these herb gardens of the old colonial mansions were ravishingly planted in formal designs in the English fashion. We can still see them in colonial Williamsburg, for instance, filling the air with their sweet scent. The Indians of America used many of the weeds growing in the fields and forests for herb teas and medicines. The colonial housewife often had to consult her Indian squaw neighbor to find out if an interesting-looking and smelling plant was poisonous.

Today, herbs have become once more part of daily living. They are easy to cultivate, in a backyard garden or in pots or a box on a kitchen window sill. They prefer light, moderately rich, well drained soil, and a sunny exposure. The great majority of culinary herb plants are annuals which are replaced each spring with new fresh plants. The perennials such as sage and tarragon are propagated by stem cuttings. Few gardening efforts are less troublesome or more rewarding than growing herbs of one's own, for nothing adds such zest and flavor to one's cooking as a pinch of a favorite herb.

When cooking with herbs, here is a word of caution: Be selective about the kinds of herbs used and conservative about the amounts. Use preferably only one herb to flavor a dish if the herb has a pronounced flavor, and don't use too many different herbs in the course of a meal, or the palate will be confused. How little or how much of an herb to use is essentially a question of personal taste, arrived at by experimentation. But remember that a little goes a long way when it comes to herbs, and that not everybody likes the same herbs.

Use ⅓ to ½ teaspoon dried herbs for every tablespoon fresh herbs. This proportion depends on the age of the dried herbs as the flavor of dried herbs deteriorates on standing. Crumble herbs before using to release flavor.

The leaves and/or roots of some herbs, called "potherbs," are themselves cooked and served as vegetables. These include the leaves of borage, chervil, chicory, Good-King-Henry, lovage, orach, rampion, and sorrel; the leaves and roots of sweet cicely and rampion; the roots of skirret. When cooking potherbs, boil leaves as you would spinach, roots as you would turnips.

A CHART OF THE BEST-KNOWN HERBS AND THEIR CULINARY USES

NAME	ORIGIN AND DESCRIPTION	PART USED— FORM AND FLAVOR	CULINARY USES Appetizers & Soups	Meat & Poultry
ANGELICA (Angelica archangelica)	Grows in northern Europe, western Asia, but is not grown in this country now except in a few private gardens. Usually biennial, with care it is a weak perennial. It grows to about 7 ft. high on hollow stems. The leaves are large, yellow-green, and serrated; roots are long and fleshy; small flowers are greenish-white.	Leaves, leafstalks, and stems, dried or fresh roots, and dried seeds are used. The stems are imported from France. The leaves are not available here. The flavor is bitter and aromatic, resembling juniper berries.	Use chopped fresh leaves as garnish for fish canapés. Flavor vegetable or bean soup with cut-up root and seeds.	Use whole leaves as garnish for meat dishes, stews.
ANISE (Pimpinella anisum)	Grows in southern Europe, Asia Minor, India, Mexico, South America, and other temperate and hot countries. An annual, it reaches up to 2 ft. high with light-green leaves, notched 3 times, and yellowish-white flowers. The seeds are downy and ridged, brown with tan stripes when dried.	Fresh and dried leaves, and powdered flowers are used. Also seeds, whole and ground. All have sweetish licorice flavor.	Refreshing flavor for lobster or shrimp cocktail, for cream-of-cabbage or cauliflower soup.	Add to beef or veal stew for a subtly sweet taste and aroma.
BASIL, SWEET (Ocimum basilicum) **BASIL, DWARF** (O. minimum) **BASIL, ITALIAN** (O. crispum) Also called Curly Basil **BASIL, LEMON** (O. citriodora)	Native to Near East; grown throughout the world. Sweet basil is an annual plant growing 1 to 2 ft. tall. The leaves are large (up to 2 in.), glossy and purplish. Bush basil is shorter, growing up to 10 in. with smaller leaves.	Leaves with leaf stems, fresh, dried, or ground, are used. The flavor of the standard sweet basil is like spicy cloves. The smaller varieties have much the same taste.	A pinch gives variety to seafood cocktails and dips; or to bean, pea, beef, tomato, or turtle soups.	Sweetly fragrant with hamburger, sausage, veal, beef, pork, duck, and lamb or beef stews. Rub hare or venison lightly with basil before roasting.
BAY LEAF (Laurus nobilis) Also called Sweet Bay or Laurel	Mediterranean, Asia Minor, Portugal, Central America, southern United States. Leaf of a small evergreen tree with spreading branches. The leaves are smooth, waxy, and from 1 to 3 in. long and 1 in. or more wide. When fresh, only the underside is pale yellowish-green but the brittle dried leaf is yellowish-green all over, shiny on top and dull underneath.	The dried leaf, whole or ground, is used in cooking. Its bitter pungent flavor is even stronger when the leaf is crushed.	A tempting seasoning in tomato juice, chowders, and beef, lamb, mutton, or game soups, either alone or in an herb bouquet.	Add it to game, pot roasts, stews, tripe, or shish kabobs. Try with chicken or duck, roasted or in pies.
BORAGE (Borago officinalis)	Grows widely throughout the world, including Europe, Asia, and eastern United States. An annual. It is over 2 ft. tall, and is covered with grayish hairs which make it look grayish-green and fuzzy. Some of the oval leaves are as long as 6 in. The bright blue flowers are star-shape.	Leaves and flowers, dried or fresh, can be used. The foliage has the flavor and aroma of cucumber.	Dried or fresh leaves add a pleasant flavor to soups. May take the place of parsley.	
BURNET (Sanguisorba minor)	Asia, North America. Leaflets are very long and deeply toothed. This gives them a fernlike effect. There are 10 varieties of this herb, but this is the one used in cooking.	Fresh or dried leaves have delicate odor and flavor like cucumber. Seeds, dried and pounded, have limited use for vinegar.	Place fresh or dried leaves in soups at beginning of cooking. Goes well in asparagus, celery, Lima-bean, or mushroom soups.	Use in stews.

CULINARY USES

Fish & Seafood	Cheese & Eggs	Breads & Stuffings	Sauces & Gravies	Vegetables & Salads	Desserts & Beverages
Add fresh or dried leaves to water in which fish is poached. Use fresh whole leaves as garnish for baked and broiled fish.		Use chopped dried leaves sparingly in poultry stuffing.		The blanched stalk may be eaten like celery, cooked as a vegetable, or prepared with sugar and eaten like rhubarb. The stems may be cooked with sugar, rhubarb, and a little lemon. Add leaves, whole or chopped, to green salads. Cook fresh leaf shoots like spinach, although they have a somewhat bitter flavor. Roast or boil roots.	Leaflets and stems are good candied in sugar syrup with lemon or lime added, and, if desired, green food coloring. Use as decoration for cakes, confections. Sprinkle chopped fresh leaves on fruit salad; add whole leaves as garnish to cold drinks. Dried roots and fruits flavor cakes and candy; cooked stems flavor rhubarb jam.
A sprinkling in fish stuffings gives subtle flavor.	Add a little to cottage cheese as a lunch salad.	Gives an unusual taste to rolls, scones, or to stuffing for fish.	Use a little to give an elusive, licoricelike flavor to pudding sauce.	Add to beets, carrots, pickles, sauerkraut; to apple, beet, cucumber salad.	Sprinkle seeds over a coffeecake; mix into cookies, fruit compote, preserved fruit.
Try it with crab, lobster, mackerel, shrimps, swordfish, eel, or in fish dressings and butters.	A pungent addition to rarebits, omelets, scrambled eggs, soufflés.	Its clovelike flavor is delectable stirred into corn bread or muffins. Try adding to other herbs or alone in stuffing for duck.	Add to herb butters, in stuffings, marinades, tomato sauces, and pesto.	Use it with eggplant, onions, rutabaga, squash, tomatoes, for sure, and in green, or seafood, carrot, cauliflower, cucumber, or tomato salads. Sprinkle over boiled potatoes or peas.	Its sweet, warm quality adds to the deliciousness of fruit compotes.
Gives fine flavor to fish stews, pickled fish, or to steamed lobster, shrimps.		Tasty in poultry stuffings.	Pleasant bitter taste to spark meat or tomato sauce, marinades, or gravies.	Cook with artichokes, beets, carrots, tomatoes, or crumble into fish or potato salad. Delicious in salad dressing for tomato salad or in jellied seafood.	Consider using a bit when making custards.
				The young leaves are similar to spinach and may be cooked with other greens or used alone as a vegetable. Add a few fresh leaves to water in which green peas, beans, or salsify (oyster plant) are cooked. In salads, leaves may be combined with cabbage, cucumber, lettuce, or mixed greens.	The beautiful star-shape borage flowers may be candied and used to decorate cakes and cookies. Sprigs of flowers and leafy tips gave fragrance and elegance to iced tea, fruit and wine drinks, and to lemonades.
		Use chopped leaves like parsley in stuffings.	Leaves or dried and pounded seeds used as flavoring for salad dressings and vinegar.	Toss fresh young leaves in beet, cabbage, carrot, celery, lettuce, mixed-green, or tomato salad; or mix dry herb with dressing. Fresh or dried leaves may be added to mayonnaise dressing before serving. Boil fresh young leaves like spinach, or place leaves in water in which vegetables are cooking.	Use leaves for tea, and fresh sprigs to garnish iced drinks.

A CHART OF THE BEST-KNOWN HERBS AND THEIR CULINARY USES

NAME	ORIGIN AND DESCRIPTION	PART USED— FORM AND FLAVOR	CULINARY USES	
			Appetizers & Soups	Meat & Poultry
CAPER (Capparis spinosa)	A native of the Mediterranean, now cultivated in southern Europe and North Africa as well as in southern United States. The caper plant is a low (about 3 ft.) straggling, spiny shrub with white flowers and roundish or oval green leaves.	Capers are small unopened flower buds, gathered in the early morning before they have opened. They are usually pickled in brine, but are also available dried in bulk.	Add capers to canapés in place of olives.	Use as a garnish for leftovers, especially cold roasts.
CARAWAY (Carum carvi)	Grows in Europe, temperate Asia, Japan, and parts of United States and Canada. Usually a biennial, it grows to about 1 ft., with feathery bright-green leaves like a carrot and with small flowers, usually white, growing like Queen Anne's Lace in umbrellalike clusters.	The dried fruit, caraway seed, is often used whole or ground, as are the fresh young leaves, leaf stems, and roots. Seeds have a sharp flavor like a mixture of anise and dill; leaves are milder in taste. The sweet root has a much more delicate flavor than parsnips.	Chopped leaves and young shoots, as well as seeds, give a distinctive flavor to bean or cabbage soups or to clam chowder.	Adds subtly pungent quality to beef à la mode, goulash, or sauerbraten. Place sprigs in bottom of pan for roast goose or pork. Use leaves as garnish for meat.
CELERY, CULTIVATED (Apium graveolens, var. dulce) **CELERY, WILD** (A. graveolens) Sometimes called Smallage	Celery grows in temperate zones throughout the world. Usually biennial, although sometimes annual, it has wrinkled pale-green leaves and tiny white flowers which grow in large umbrella-shape clusters. Golden Heart celery has bleached white stalk; Pascal, a green stalk. The seeds which form on the flower stalks are less than ⅟₁₆ in. long. Wild celery is a lower plant that resembles lovage, with which it has sometimes been confused.	All parts: root, stalk, leaves (fresh and dried), and seeds (dried, whole, or ground) can be used in cooking. All parts have a somewhat sweet flavor. The root is considerably sweeter than the stalk, which has a mildly sweet aromatic flavor. The leaves are more sharp and pungent. The seeds have the flavor of the fresh celery, but the seed covering provides a somewhat bitter taste.	Canapés, cheese, fish, shellfish may be sprinkled lightly with seed just before serving. Or add chopped celery to ingredients and garnish with stalk and leaves. Fresh leaves especially good in soups.	Add to meat loaves, stews, and pot roasts.
CHERVIL (Anthriscus cerefolium)	Native of Europe; naturalized in northeast United States. An annual growing up to 2 ft., it has delicate, fernlike bright-green leaves, much like parsley. The flowers are small and white and grow in clusters.	Leaves, fresh or dried, as well as whole sprigs, are used in cooking and as a garnish. The root of the tuberous variety may be cooked and eaten like a carrot. The leaves and stalk have a mild parsley flavor, sometimes with a whiff of licorice or tarragon. A curly-leafed variety has a definite anise-like flavor and smell.	The tender leaves garnish a dish, or season asparagus, chicken, spinach, or sorrel soups.	Is friendly with beef, game, lamb, pork, veal, poultry. Good in meat loaf.
CHIVES (Allium schoenoprasum)	Grows in Europe and temperate Asia, as well as extensively in United States. A relative of the onion, chives grow in clumps, with a tiny bulb under the ground and tubular green leaves rising above to a height of 10 in. The thin flowers are lavender.	The tiny bulb and the freshly picked flowers can be used as well as the fresh, frozen, freeze-dried, or dried leaves. The green leaves and the bulb have a mild onion flavor.	Garnish for dips, soups, or appetizers; happy addition to seafood cocktails or to Vichyssoise.	Chop the slender leaves over beef, game, lamb, pork, veal, or poultry dishes. The bulbs are used in sausage.
CLARY SAGE (Salvia sclarea)	Native to southern Europe and Mediterranean countries. This 3- to 4-ft. biennial has unusually large leaves (about 9 in.) at its base. They are gray-green and quite broad. The leaves at the top are smaller. Although a member of the sage family, it is commonly referred to as Clary.	Leaves, fresh or dried, ground or whole, have a lavenderlike odor, and taste, naturally enough, like sage.	Try a teaspoon of chopped dried leaves in meat soups.	A fresh or dried leaf in the roasting pan; use dried powdered leaf in sausage.
COSTMARY (Chrysanthemum balsamita) Also called Bible Leaf or Alecost	A native of western Asia, it grows wild in some parts of North America. A perennial, it grows over 3 ft., with shrubby stems, and light-green, slightly downy leaves. The flowers are like small daisies, although sometimes there are no white petals.	Leaves, fresh and dried, are used and have a lemony mint odor.		Crushed fresh leaves or dried leaves flavor beef and hamburgers. Place a costmary leaf in the bottom of the roasting pan for chicken, wild duck, or venison.

CULINARY USES

Fish & Seafood	Cheese & Eggs	Breads & Stuffings	Sauces & Gravies	Vegetables & Salads	Desserts & Beverages
Capers are an excellent garnish to hot or cold fish. They are a tasty addition to tartar sauce. Along with lemon, they are the base of nicoise dressing.			Most fish and meat sauces are enhanced by the addition of capers. Use with oily sauces, dressings and tartar sauce.	Always use in antipasto. Use as a garnish for other green and vegetable salads.	
	A pleasant smooth taste in cheese spreads, cream or cottage cheese, creamed eggs.	Seeds, of course, in rye bread. Also widely used in muffins, rolls, and scones.	Add a little to give zest to sour-cream dressing for salads.	Add sprigs of leaves to water in which cabbage, cauliflower, potatoes, or turnips are boiled. Combine seeds with beets, sauerkraut, potatoes, noodles, creamed onions, turnips, or cabbage. Use fresh herb in cabbage, cucumber, lettuce, potato, and tomato salads. Cook leaves like spinach or use as salad green; boil roots as vegetable and eat plain or with cream sauce.	Use seeds in baked pears, baked apples, applesauce, spice cake, poundcake, sugar cookies, and pumpkin pie, or sugar-coated as candy.
Shredded codfish and salmon croquettes are good flavored with seed. Use in chowders and stews. Add a stalk to water in which fish is poached.	Scrambled eggs, cream and cottage cheese pep up with seed. Add chopped celery to creamed or deviled eggs or omelets.	Biscuits and salty bread are enhanced by celery seed.		Put seed in cauliflower, cabbage, and stewed tomatoes. Mix chopped celery with carrots, onions, peas, tomatoes, green peppers. Use with fish, potato, and vegetable salads; seeds especially good with cabbage salad. For fruit salads add seed to your favorite dressing and serve; or mix chopped celery in with ingredients. Serve cooked celery plain or with sauce.	
Goes well with all kinds of fish.	Stir some into cream or cottage cheese, omelets, or scrambled eggs.		Mild parsleylike flavor for Béarnaise and butter sauces and French dressing.	Try a little chopped leaf with asparagus, beets, carrots, eggplant, or spinach. Green or potato salads are sparked by this parsleylike herb. Cook the herbage as a potherb, or use as salad green.	
Less pungent than the onion, this is a happy seasoning for any fish.	Chop the leaves fine and mix with cottage or cream cheese or into omelets. Use dried leaves in fondues.		Chop them into sour-cream dressing or try some in vinaigrette sauce.	Chopped leaves are good in creamed vegetables, with potatoes, green salads. For an exotic touch, add some of the flowers to a green or cucumber salad. Try pickling the tiny bulbs like onions.	
	Chopped fresh leaves are good in omelets and for flavoring bland cheeses.	May be used like sage in stuffings.	Use leaves in salad dressing and in spice-hot sauce for barbecue.	Add a touch to the water in which yellow vegetables are cooking.	
					Place a leaf in the bottom of the baking pan when baking poundcake. The flavor is very dominant, so take care to use only 1 leaf. It is an ingredient in herb teas. Use in eggnog, or to garnish strawberry shrub.

A CHART OF THE BEST-KNOWN HERBS AND THEIR CULINARY USES

NAME	ORIGIN AND DESCRIPTION	PART USED— FORM AND FLAVOR	CULINARY USES	
			Appetizers & Soups	Meat & Poultry
DILL (Anethum graveolens)	Native to Europe; naturalized in North America. This 2- or 3-ft. high plant, grown as an annual, has fine wispy bluish-green leaves and a hollow gummy stem. The yellow flowers are in large umbrella-shape clusters. The seeds are very tiny.	The leaves and stems, fresh and dried (the fresh are better), as well as the seed of this herb are used. Leaves are quite pungent and stems are bitter; both should be finely chopped for use. The aromatic seeds are available whole or ground; have a sharp taste.	Sprinkle in avocado or fish cocktails, or into bean, borscht, split-pea or tomato soup.	Fresh pungent flavor for lamb chops, stew, or a bowl of rich creamed chicken. Sprinkle over broiled steak or cook with corned beef.
FENNEL, WILD (Foeniculum vulgare) **FENNEL, SWEET** (F. vulgare, var. dulce) Also called Finocchio or Florence Fennel **CAROSELLA** (F. vulgare, var. piperitum)	Wild fennel and the form cultivated in gardens (sweet) are known primarily for their wispy bright-green leaves. Both are erect perennials, the wild variety growing over 4 ft. high. The stems are smooth and glossy and thin in comparison to those of the Carosella, a variety of the garden-grown fennel. It has thickened stalks like celery and grows to the height of about 2 ft. Finocchio is considerably shorter than the wild, and the base of the stems is very thick, overlapping like celery.	Seeds (fresh, as well as dried whole or ground); leaves; stems; bulbous bases and roots of finocchio and carosella are all edible and used in cooking. Flavor is sweet, like anise. Finocchio is especially sweet.	Try this to give a faint sweet quality to fish or seafood cocktails; or try in cabbage or fish soup.	Liver, pork, lamb stew, duck, or goose gain new flavor from this herb. Especially flavorful in certain hot or sweet Italian sausages.
FENUGREEK (Trigonella foenum-graecum)	Grows in Europe and the Orient as well as in United States. An annual, it grows, usually not branching, to about 2 ft. The leaves are as long as 1 in. and the plant has white flowers, growing alone or in pairs.	Dried seeds, available whole, suggest a burnt-sugar or maple taste. The fresh leaves and stems are also used. Ground seeds are used in curry.	Use in meat and vegetable soups.	Good in moderation with beef, lamb, pork, and veal dishes.
HORSERADISH (Armoracia lapathifolia or Radicula armoracia)	Although there is no agreement on the botanical name for this perennial, native to southeastern Europe, it is widely known for its long thick branching wrinkled white root, which grows deep into the ground. The flowering stem above the ground is as high as 3 ft.; the leaves are of 2 kinds: the early ones are comb-like, the later (lower) ones are oblong, shiny and green, with scalloped edges.	Root and leaves are used. Whole fresh root has no odor; the sharp familiar horseradish aroma is only unloosed when it is grated or ground. It is available fresh or preserved in vinegar. The early leaves taste of bitter herbs, with a biting after-taste.	Use ground root with cream cheese and sour cream for a pleasing dip for fresh vegetables.	Good to accompany roast or boiled beef, tongue, lamb, or mutton.
HYSSOP (Hyssopus officinalis)	This perennial, 1 to 2 ft. tall, has long stems with narrow pointed stalkless dark-green leaves, 1 to 2 in. long. Variations of hyssops may have different leaf formations, and flower colors.	Leaves, flowers, stems, and young shoots, fresh or dried, have a bitter aromatic flavor.	Crush 1 or 2 tender young leaves in bottom of bowl for fruit cocktail; particularly good with cranberries. Add a little freshly minced or dried leaves to sweet vegetable soups while cooking.	Minced herb cuts grease on all fatty meats. Sprinkle duck or pheasant lightly with minced herb before roasting. Fresh or dried leaves give additional flavor to game, kidney, or lamb stews.
LEMON BALM (Melissa officinalis)	Native to southern Europe; now in all temperate climates, including eastern United States. It is a very leafy perennial which grows to 2 ft. tall. The leaves, which are up to 3 in. long, are almost round, dark green, and slightly hairy. The flowers are pale yellow and grow in clusters.	Leaves, fresh or dried, are used for their lemon-minty smell and flavor.	Cream soups may be sprinkled lightly with minced leaves just before serving.	Rub roast lamb lightly with crushed fresh or dried leaves before you place it in the oven.

CULINARY USES

Fish & Seafood	Cheese & Eggs	Breads & Stuffings	Sauces & Gravies	Vegetables & Salads	Desserts & Beverages
Add a few seeds to water in which fish is boiled or use chopped dill as compliment to poached salmon and other fish.	Both leaves and seeds excellent for cheese spreads, cottage or cream cheese.	Sprinkle a few seeds in rye or other dark-bread dough to give carawaylike flavor.	Warm, sharp taste to liven drawn butter or sour-cream dressings; good in vinegars. Beef gravy peps up with addition of a few chopped leaves of dill.	A few seeds improve beets, cabbage, carrots, cauliflower, peas, snap beans, potato salad. Leaves flavor cabbage, cauliflower, or turnips. Seeds, with some stems and leaves, used, of course, to pickle cucumbers.	Slightly sharp flavor of seeds adds savor to apple dumplings or stewed pears, and is tasty in cake.
A delicious sweet flavor to add to fish puddings.	It adds importance to omelets or to scrambled eggs.	Italian bakers stud bread and rolls with it. It is good in muffins, too.	Try it in egg or fish sauces.	Delightful seasoning for beets, celery, lentils; mixed in rice or squash; added to sweet pickles. Use leaves in salad, or boil them as potherb. Eat raw stems like celery. Try seeds to spice beets, or put them in sauerkraut.	Adds unusually good flavor to apple dishes, to coffee-cakes, and to sugar cookies. Flavor wine with base of finocchio. Seeds are used in European liqueurs.
				Try with blackeye peas.	Cookies, gingerbread, and rice puddings are flavored with this herb.
Freshly ground root good with tomato sauces for shrimp, clams, oysters, and other seafood.			Cream sauces for beef, fish, ham, and other meats are livened with ground root. Gives dash to cocktail sauces for fish and shellfish. Good in salad dressings, flavored mayonnaise, and mustard.	Fresh young leaves, finely chopped, may be added to green salads. Frequently used in making of pickles.	
Garnish any fatty fish sparingly with minced fresh leaves.				Toss freshly minced herb in vegetable salads.	Use with sweet fruit in pies such as apricot or peach.
		Crushed dried leaves may be added to traditional stuffings; especially good for pork or turkey.	Delicious in cream sauces and those served with fish. Add chopped fresh leaves just before serving.	Chopped fresh leaves may be added to fruit, mixed, or tossed green salad. Or try cooking leaves with chard.	This herb is a welcome addition to tea, fruit drinks, lemonades, or wine cups. If the drink is cold, garnish with a sprig of balm; if the drink is hot, crush 1 or 2 leaves in the bottom of the cup.

A CHART OF THE BEST-KNOWN HERBS AND THEIR CULINARY USES

NAME	ORIGIN AND DESCRIPTION	PART USED— FORM AND FLAVOR	CULINARY USES	
			Appetizers & Soups	Meat & Poultry
LEMON VERBENA (Lippia citriodora)	Originally from Argentina and Chile; now is found in many mild climates. A perennial shrub which grows to about 10 ft. in warm climates and to 10 in. in pots. The yellow-green leaves are long, narrow, and pointed at the end and grow in whorls of 3 or 4 on woody branches.	Dried or fresh leaves of this plant are used; they have a delicate lemony flavor and smell.	Garnish fruit cups with a tiny leaf.	
LOVAGE (Levisticum officinale)	Native of southern Europe; United States' North Atlantic seaboard also grows wild Scotch Lovage, used for medicinal purposes. True lovage is a tall (5 to 6 ft.) plant, with large heavy dark-green leaves like celery, and with clusters of yellowish flowers.	Fresh and dried leaves, stem bases, leafstalks, root, and seeds are used. Greens have celerylike flavor; root tastes and smells strong.	Add a few leaves to tomato-juice cocktail. Leaves give celery flavor to soups.	Cook beef, lamb, mutton, veal, rabbit, or venison stews with seeds in cheesecloth bag. Leaves give celery flavor to stews.
MARIGOLD (Calendula officinalis) Also called Pot Marigold	Native to southern Europe and eastern Asia. A hardy annual, growing from 1 to 2 ft. tall, it has curling green pinnate leaves and bright golden flowers. Flowers, which can be as large as small sunflowers, have oval golden-yellow and orange petals around circular heads.	Dried heads and petals pulverized into powder are used as well as fresh ones. They have a somewhat bitter taste, but lend a subtle flavor and golden color to foods if they are added in moderation. A very little goes a long way.	Try adding 2 or 3 petals to your favorite fish-chowder recipe. A very little powder may be added in cooking chicken broth. Flowers added to vegetable soup is a good idea, too.	Add ½ teaspoon powder to venison stew. Try flavoring braised beef or pot roast with ½ teaspoon powder.
MARJORAM (Majorana hortensis) More exactly, Sweet or Annual Marjoram	Native to Mediterranean area as a perennial, but usually grown as an annual in cooler regions such as northern United States. It grows over 1 ft. tall and the leaves are downy light-green ovals of up to 1 in. The minute flowers sometimes are pinkish or lilac. An aromatic herb, marjoram belongs to the mint family. It resembles sage in flavor although it is considerably less strong. A smaller species, M. onites, resembles M. hortensis, except it has milder flavor. Pot marjoram is usually only sweet marjoram under another name.	Although flowering tips are used in medicine and industry, the leaves are the only part employed in cooking. They have a fragrant aroma and a spicy taste, somewhat resembling sage although considerably less strong.	Add a pinch to avocados, mushrooms, pâtés, to clam chowder or onion soup.	Delightful seasoning for beef, pork, veal, pot roasts, and savory stews.
MINT (Mentha)	There are 25 to 30 species of mint, and about a dozen cultivated in the United States. Those listed below, the most useful for culinary purposes, are found in temperate zones throughout the world. Other mints, not listed here because their use is limited, include Corn Mint and Water Mint. The mints differ somewhat in appearance, but all have square red-tinged stems and purple flowers, in whorls or spikes.	The fresh leaves of all the mints listed can be used for flavoring. Tastes vary slightly, but all mints have aromatic refreshing aroma. The oil from leaves is used commercially. Spearmint is widely available dried and powdered as "mint." Uses for "mint," fresh or dried, follow. Some experimentation with substitution of different types is possible, for most members of the mint family mix well.	Aromatic addition to cranberry juice, fruit cup, or to soups such as pea.	Delicate flavoring for lamb, ham, veal, ragouts.
MINT, AMERICAN APPLE (M. gentilis)	The only one of 2 varieties of apple mint used for cooking (the other has woolly leaves). A hardy perennial with smooth grayish-green leaves with yellow streaks. Shorter than some mints, as it is low growing with a tendency to spread. Its purple flowers blossom in whorls and there are almost square stems.	Leaves have a delicate fruit aroma and taste, refreshing and with a trace of apple.		
MINT, BERGAMOT (M. citrata) Also called Orange and Lemon Mint	Smooth oval leaves, edged with purple, up to 2 in. long. The leaves are broader than those of the more familiar peppermint.	The leaves have a fragrance mixed with lavender, although orange predominates after they have been smelled for a while.		

CULINARY USES

Fish & Seafood	Cheese & Eggs	Breads & Stuffings	Sauces & Gravies	Vegetables & Salads	Desserts & Beverages
				Fresh or canned fruit salads may be garnished with a small leaf.	A crushed leaf may be placed at the bottom of the cup or glass before pouring drink. Delicious for making jellies. Lemon Verbena tea is one of the most popular of the herb teas.
				Blanched root can be served like celery. Boil leaves as a potherb. Add a few seeds to salad dressing and serve over mixed fruit. To give a celery flavor to salads rub inside of bowl with a few leaves.	Candy the root, or, for an even more adventurous sweet, candy the leaf stalks and stem bases. Use lovage seeds as a garnish or ingredient as you would caraway seeds.
Add a few petals to other vegetables in a seafood stew.	A little powder will give color to butter and cheese.	Color buns with a dash of powder.		Cook rice with ¼ teaspoon marigold powder instead of saffron.	Add a few crushed petals to baked or boiled custard or to custard sauce. Color cakes with a dash of powder. Try making marigold cordial.
Sprinkle it over fish before baking or into a cream sauce for fish.	Gives subtle variety of flavor to omelets, scrambled eggs, soufflés.	Delicious in poultry stuffing, or added to biscuit dough or herb breads.	Delicate flavoring for spaghetti sauce or your favorite gravy.	Adds interest to corn, beans, carrots, eggplant, Lima beans, peas, spinach, beans, or to a crisp green salad.	
Refreshing change when cooked with any fish.	Tantalizing flavor for cream or cottage cheese.		Make it into mint sauce to serve with roast lamb. Add to French dressing for green salads. Make flavored vinegar.	Add to cabbage, carrots, celery, potatoes, snap beans, or to jellied salads.	Sweet and tangy in custards, fruit compotes, ice cream, in fruit punch, juleps, mint tea. Make a sugar syrup to add flavor to beverages. Make your own mint jelly or add to currant jelly.
				Preferred with cabbage to spearmint because it is more delicate.	Especially recommended in applesauce and pie.
				Used with chopped cabbage instead of spearmint, as Bergamot is more delicate.	Especially recommended for jelly.

A CHART OF THE BEST-KNOWN HERBS AND THEIR CULINARY USES

NAME	ORIGIN AND DESCRIPTION	PART USED— FORM AND FLAVOR	CULINARY USES	
			Appetizers & Soups	Meat & Poultry
CURLEY MINT (M. spicata, var. crispa)	The mint has dull-green crinkly wide leaves and grows 2 ft. at its tallest. As it has long weak stems and many slender branches, it has tendency to sprawl during summer. The spikes are tipped with violet flowers.	Leaves have piny-resinous odor.		
PEPPERMINT (M. piperita)	There are 2 varieties: Black (var. vulgaris) and White (var. officinalis). Both have pointed leaves 1 to 3 in. long and ½ in. wide, with toothed edges. The flower spikes are thick and blunt. Black has dark-green leaves tinged with purple, and purple flowers tinged with red. It is taller than white variety. The white has light-green leaves.	One of the most popular mints. The oil from white mint is considered of best quality, as the black's is stronger. Largely used commercially, but fresh leaves can be employed by the home cook for an aromatic pungent flavor.		
SPEARMINT (M. spicata, var. viridis)	The most popular of the culinary mints, it resembles peppermint, but the lance-shape leaves are stemless and longer. The flower spikes are long and narrow and pointed. Pale-purple flowers.	Fresh leaves, as well as dried and powdered ones, are used. Recommended for all uses of mint. Very sweet aromatic, one of best mints for flavorings.	See Mint.	See Mint.
MUSTARD, BLACK (Brassica nigra) **MUSTARD, WHITE** (B. alba or B. hirta)	Native to Europe and western Asia and cultivated in western United States, this mustard grows wild throughout country. Black mustard is a hardy annual, growing up to 4 ft., with yellowish-green smooth leaves and the bright yellow flowers characteristic of mustard. The white mustard is a small 18-in. plant, with tender green leaves that spread very quickly.	Both mustards are grown for their seed, which is commercially prepared as mustard flour, the basis of prepared mustard; available also as powdered mustard. Whole seeds of both varieties can be used, but only the leaves of the white are eaten. The black seeds are smaller and considerably more pungent than those of the white.	Tender young white-mustard leaves may be used sparingly in sorrel or lettuce soup.	Season roasts lightly with powdered mustard. Use a bit to flavor creamed chicken or turkey.
NASTURTIUM (Tropaeolum majus or minus)	These annuals, one tall and climbing (T. majus) and one low and bushy (T. minus), have flowers and leaves used in cooking. The small plant, native to Peru, has more flowers and in brighter hues. The leaves are almost circular; the flowers all shades of yellow, orange, and dark red. The light-green seeds turn light brown, and are ridged and wrinkled.	Young stems, leaves and flowers have peppery taste. Pickled seeds and pods used in place of capers.		
ORÉGANO (Origanum vulgare) Often called Wild Marjoram	Native to Eurasia, also grows widely in northeast United States and Canada. There are many varieties of this plant, differing in appearance. In general, an erect perennial, growing up to 3 ft., with branching hairy stems (sometimes purplish) and dark-green leaves shaped like a roundish egg.	Fresh or dried leaves and tops are used, and have sweet aromatic flavor like sweet marjoram or thyme. Oregano is stronger than these two and should be used with care.	Try a pinch in vegetable-juice cocktails, in bean, beef, game, or tomato soup.	It's pungent, so use with care to season beef, lamb, pork, veal, sausages, Swiss steak, or any poultry.
PARSLEY (Petroselinum crispum)	There are more than 30 forms of this carrot-type plant. The main varieties include double-curled, moss-leaved, fern-leaved, and turnip-rooted, whose names describe their leaves or roots. A small green plant, its leaves and flowers vary according to kind.	Leaves have familiar refreshing taste and aroma.	Use it as a garnish, as an ingredient in soup bouquets.	A nutritious flavorful addition to beef, lamb, pork, veal, poultry.

CULINARY USES

Fish & Seafood	Cheese & Eggs	Breads & Stuffings	Sauces & Gravies	Vegetables & Salads	Desserts & Beverages
					Especially recommended in juleps and punches.
					Try making your own peppermint wafers instead of buying them. Or boil leaves and add marmalade for an unusual dessert sauce.
See Mint.	See Mint.	See Mint.	Best kind for traditional mint sauce, chopped leaves in sweetened vinegar.	Adds strong sweet flavor to cabbage, carrots, potatoes, snap beans, or to jellied salads.	Add to sugar syrup to flavor iced beverages.
Add powdered mustard to other ingredients in making deviled crab.	Use powdered mustard in deviled eggs. Flavor cottage cheese and cream cheese with a pinch of powdered mustard.			Cook greens as potherb. Use 1 teaspoon chopped fresh leaves in salad or add ½ to 1 teaspoon seed with mixed green-vegetable salad. A bit of seeds peps up coleslaw. Sprinkle a few seeds onto hot boiled beets, or boil cabbage with a few seeds. White seeds are used in preparing pickles.	
	Chopped fresh leaves and stems are good, like watercress, with cream- or cottage-cheese spreads.		Use pickled seeds in sauces in place of capers. Especially good with brown sauce for mutton.	Toss chopped young stems and leaves or whole leaves into mixed-green or vegetable salads. Use flowers as edible garnish.	For an exotic and pretty touch float flowers in tea.
Adds intriguing taste to any fish, but it's pungent, so take care.	Aromatic flavor to give distinction to cheese spreads or omelets.	A favorite with Mexican, Spanish, and Italian cooks. Good in pizzas, rolls, stuffings.	Sprinkle it in fish butter sauce; in cream, meat, spaghetti, or tomato sauces. Add to marinades for game.	Use a little with broccoli, beans, carrots, Lima beans, mushrooms, onions, peas, potatoes, tomatoes. Add to aspics or potato salad. On its own can be boiled as potherb.	
Exciting flavor for fish stuffings, creamed seafood, or for salmon.	Add a pinch to cheese sauces, deviled or scrambled eggs, or to omelets.	Mild and good in biscuits, herb breads, muffins, stuffings, or added to butter for toast.	Seasoning for butters, marinades.	Seasoning and garnish for most vegetables and salads.	

A CHART OF THE BEST-KNOWN HERBS AND THEIR CULINARY USES

NAME	ORIGIN AND DESCRIPTION	PART USED— FORM AND FLAVOR	CULINARY USES	
			Appetizers & Soups	Meat & Poultry
ROSE (Rosa, various species)	Roses originated in Persia. At present, there are countless varieties of the rose. Some of the most well known include the Damask rose, the Cabbage rose, and the China rose. The beautiful petaled flowers growing from thorny stems are known to gardeners throughout the world.	Petals, preferably fresh with the base cut off, and hips, fresh or dried, are used. (Hips are the small berries left after the flowers dry, and are the rosebush's fruit.) Rosewater is available commercially, although it may be made at home. The heavily perfumed rose varieties used in cooking have a honeyed scent.	Crush a rose petal into fruit cups. Try making rose-hip soup.	For an exotic delight, glaze baked chicken with rosewater and honey. Rub deer and venison with dried hips, mashed and blended with seasonings and marjoram, before baking. Add hips to rabbit stews.
ROSEMARY (Rosmarinus officinalis)	Grows wild in southern Europe, cultivated in Europe and United States. It grows slowly, but reaches height of 2 or 4 ft. Not hardy in the north. An evergreen shrub, has branching stems which bear long (up to 1½ in.) thin dark-green leaves, curving a bit like pine needles. The undersides are grayish and slightly hairy. The flowers are bluish.	Leaves, fresh and dried, and the fresh tops are used in cooking and garnishing. They have a pungent spicy flavor.	Fresh or dried, it gives exciting flavor to fruit cups, chicken, pea, spinach, and turtle soups.	Its affinity for hearty foods fits it well to blend with beef, game, lamb, pork, veal, poultry.
RUE (Ruta graveolens)	Southern Europe was its home. The little perennial, growing up to 3 ft., has evergreen deeply cut grayish-green leaves, which are thick and covered with a nonhairy bloom which rubs off when touched. The pretty four-petaled flowers are yellow.	Leaves, fresh and dried, are used but are very bitter and should be used sparingly.	Blend into chicken broth. Gives a delightfully different flavor to minced chicken or mushroom canapés. Try a few minced (or if you're feeling adventurous, whole) leaves between buttered brown bread for different sandwiches.	Add a few leaves to beef, lamb, chicken, or kidney stews, during or before cooking.
SAGE (Salvia officinalis)	Native to northern Mediterranean countries, but grows now in all temperate zones. Yugoslavia raises one of the best varieties of sage, Dalmatian sage, which is imported by United States. There are over 500 species of this popular herb. Besides the imported Dalmatian sage and the Garden sage (Salvia officinalis), there are White sage, Cyprus sage, a garden variety known as S. horminum, Meadow sage, Pineapple sage (with pineapple fragrance) and Clary sage (see Clary). Most are perennial shrubs with grayish leaves. Garden sage grows 1 to 2 ft. high and has bluish or purplish flowers.	Leaves, fresh and dried, chopped or powdered, are used. The flavor is aromatically bitter; the Pineapple and Dalmatian sages are milder.	A pinch adds extra flavor to cheese dips, pâté, chowders, consommé, and bland cream soups.	It's vital for sausage, and a happy thought for use in stews. Sage is especially good as a seasoning for poultry, pork, veal, and rabbit.
SAVORY, SUMMER (Satureia hortensis) **SAVORY, WINTER** (S. montana)	Summer savory is native to Mediterranean; now cultivated throughout Europe and United States. Bushy, with many branches, this annual grows up to 18 in. on its weak stems, but falls down easily. The leaves are dark green, and the bush has a great mass of pinkish, bluish, or purplish flowers. Winter savory is similar, but is an annual, somewhat shorter and woodier and falling down and spreading. Its leaves are stiffer than those of summer savory.	Leaves, fresh and dried, are used and have a somewhat resinous aroma. Winter savory has a stronger flavor, but can be used with discretion where summer savory is used.	A piquant touch for pâté, vegetable juices, consommés, chowders, bean or lentil soups.	Adds a deliciousness to a chicken loaf, hamburger, lamb, veal, to stews and poultry stuffing.

CULINARY USES

Fish & Seafood	Cheese & Eggs	Breads & Stuffings	Sauces & Gravies	Vegetables & Salads	Desserts & Beverages
Try poaching fish in milk with a little rosewater sprinkled over fish.	Add a few chopped fresh petals to scrambled eggs.	Coffeecakes flavored with rosewater or syrup are good.	Rose petals in sauces and gravies for game help remove "gamy" taste.	Fresh or canned fruit salads may be spiced with 1 or 2 fresh petals.	Rose-petal syrup, made with petals and sugar, or rosewater, deliciously flavors custards, puddings, cookies, cakes, chiffon pies, fruit jello, dessert pancakes, and ice creams. Blend crushed rose leaves with orange-blossom honey, or add to fruit and mint jellies and jams.
Exciting flavor for fish stuffings, creamed seafood, or for salmon.	Add a pinch to cheese sauces, deviled or scrambled eggs, or to omelets.	Sweet fresh-tasting herb to crumble into herb breads, stuffings, dumplings and biscuits.	Sweet fresh-tasting herb to add to cheese, cream, jelly, or game sauces, or to use in marinades.	Tonic addition to lentils, mushrooms, peas, potatoes, spinach, squash, fruit salads.	
	Mix finely minced leaf with cottage or cream cheese for a delicious spread.			Sprinkle a little minced rue over boiled potatoes. Or add to dressing for chicken, veal, tuna-fish, or vegetable salad.	
Belongs in fish stuffings, where it adds appetizing flavor, a faint fragrance. Put a sage leaf inside mild-flavored fish when baking or add to the water in which you boil fish.	Warm astringent taste to give variety to Cheddar cheese, or to your cheese spreads.	Especially good in cheese bread, and, of course, in stuffings.	Appetizing seasoning for brown sauce, French dressing, or for meat gravies.	Try with Brussels sprouts, carrots, eggplant, Lima beans, onions, peas, or tomatoes.	
Happy with baked or broiled fish.	Its aromatic flavor will improve cream cheese. Try it with scrambled eggs.	Fragrant flavorful addition to herb bread and to meat or poultry stuffings.	Aromatic flavoring for barbecue, fish, seafood, or poultry sauces and gravies.	Add a bit when cooking artichokes, beets, cabbage, peas, rice, sauerkraut. Classic with green beans. Fresh leaves are good tossed into salad. Excellent in any dish whose base is peas, beans, or lentils.	Tastes good in stewed pears, or used with quinces.

A CHART OF THE BEST-KNOWN HERBS AND THEIR CULINARY USES

NAME	ORIGIN AND DESCRIPTION	PART USED— FORM AND FLAVOR	CULINARY USES Appetizers & Soups	Meat & Poultry
SWEET CICELY (Myrrhis odorata) Also called Sweet Chervil and Myrrh	Native to Europe, this perennial's hairy stems grow 2 to 3 ft. high. The leaves are fernlike, the flowers small and whitish. The long fruit (up to 1 in.) is narrow and ribbed.	Fresh leaves and seeds are used. Seeds should be sliced and eaten with other herbs. All have an anise-like flavor, although the leaves are weak in taste.	Chopped leaves flavor cream soups with faint anise flavor.	Good in stews.
SWEET FLAG (Acorus calamus) Often called Calamus	Grows in North Temperate Zone throughout world. The plant has yellow-green sword-shape leaves rising from base up to 4 ft. The flower is a dry spike. It grows from a large underground rhizome into a smaller underground stem. Not to be confused with the poisonous blue flag, which has dark-green leaves with no smell.	Leaves, stem, roots, and rhizome, fresh and dried, have strong spicy ginger-like aroma. Rhizome is apt to be tough and requires long boiling.	Young leaves are good addition to chicken soup. Or for winter, use dried and ground leaves or root.	Add to chicken stew young leaves, dried and ground or fresh.
TARRAGON (Artemisia dracunculus) Often called Estragon	Native to western and southern Asia, now grows in temperate and cold United States and southern Europe. A perennial, it grows somewhat like a shrub to a height of above 18 in. The dark-green leaves are long, narrow, and pointed, and occur along the woody stems at intervals.	Leaves, fresh and dried, are used in cooking. Their flavor is somewhat like anise.	Piquant addition to chicken livers, vegetable juices, chowders, consommés.	Highly valued for use with pheasant, sweetbreads, tongue, veal, chicken, or turkey dishes.
THYME, COMMON (Thymus vulgaris) Also called English Thyme **THYME, WILD** (T. serpyllum) Also called Creeping Thyme and Mother-of-Thyme	Garden thyme grows widely in Europe, United States, and Canada; wild thyme, a native to Europe, temperate Asia, and North Africa, grows in North America from southeastern Canada to North Carolina. Garden thyme is a bushy little perennial, about 1 ft. tall, with gray-green leaves, ½ to 1 in. long. English thyme is a variety with broad leaves. There are many varieties of the wild thyme, which, as its name implies, creeps along the ground, rising to varying heights. It becomes firmly matted and its leaves are of many colors as well as green, according to the variety. Some are striped white, some greenish-yellow; flowers may be bluish, purplish, white, or red.	Leaves and the leafy and flowering tops, fresh or dried, of both thymes are used. Both wild and garden thyme have pungent flavor and a sweet fragrance. Leaves and flowers of certain varieties of thyme have particular aromas which are distinctive. Of the creeping thymes, Lemon thyme (T. citriodorus) has lemony scent; Caraway thyme (T. Herbabarona) smells and tastes as name implies; Thymus azoricus has fruity citrus aroma. The chart indicates where a certain variety is especially recommended for use.	Sprinkle a little in seafood or vegetable-juice cocktails; in a gumbo or fish chowder, stew, or ragout.	Use with restraint with beef, game, lamb, pork, veal, or in meat loaf. Rub caraway thyme over meat to preserve it and flavor it.
WATERCRESS (Nasturtium officinale)	Native to temperate Europe. Naturalized in North America in brooks and ponds. A short perennial, it has very small round shiny dark-green leaves, paler green stems, and small white flowers.	The fresh leaves and stems have a slightly peppery flavor and are crisp.	Garnish canapés and seafood appetizers with chopped leaves. Or mix into fruit and vegetable-juice cocktails. Try minced watercress in cheese, fish, and meat sandwich fillings. Add a half bunch of minced sprigs to fish chowders, and creamed potato or vegetable soups. Or use as sorrel.	A pretty garnish for broiled, boiled, or roasted meats and poultry.

CULINARY USES

Fish & Seafood	Cheese & Eggs	Breads & Stuffings	Sauces & Gravies	Vegetables & Salads	Desserts & Beverages
				Root, raw or boiled, can be eaten with oil and vinegar alone or in salads. Fresh leaves add to salads.	Use seeds like cloves or caraway in dessert flavoring.
Use dried root as substitute for ginger in a fish dish.			Young leaves flavor fish sauce.	Slice tiny unborn leaves in center of the young stalk into green salads.	Candied root makes a delicious confection alone or to flavor cream, custard, or rice pudding.
Delicious seasoning for baked or broiled fish, especially for lobster.	Sprinkle it over scrambled eggs or omelets.		Best known in tarragon vinegar; good, too, in butters, marinades, and added to mustards, flavored mayonnaise and tartar sauce. A must for Sauce Béarnaise.	Has an almost spicy taste which adds to asparagus, beans, beets, broccoli, cabbage; tossed green, tomato, fish or jellied salads.	
Pungent warm addition to any type of fish.	Mix it with cream or cottage cheeses, sprinkle on shirred or creamed eggs.	Important in poultry and vegetable stuffings; adds taste to biscuits, herb breads, or waffles.	Delightful addition to an herb bouquet or to seafood sauce.	Try with beans, beets, carrots, potatoes, or in aspics. Delicious when used with creamed onions.	Use T. azoricus in creams and custards. Lemon thyme especially good in jellies.
Minced or whole, garnishes whole fish.	Blend into cottage or cream-cheese spread or into omelets and scrambled eggs.	Minced cress added to biscuit dough or piecrust is delicious and nutritious.		Use as sorrel in your favorite recipe. Sprinkle minced leaves over carrots, cauliflower, potatoes, green beans, and sweet vegetables. Or boil as potherb and serve with your favorite sauce.	

HERMIT

HERMIT—A dark, spicy cookie filled with fruits and nuts. The dark color comes from molasses or brown sugar and ground spices. Hermits may be served plain or with a glaze.

Hermits are early American cookies that originated in New England. They are also found in the South and other parts of the country. Their origin is as obscure as their name. They belong to the group of spicy cookies of the clippership and the spice-trade days. They bear enchanting names like Snickerdoodles, Kinkawoodles, Brambles, Tangled Britches and they all resemble each other; the difference is that one may contain cinnamon, but not other spices, the other raisins and no citron, etc.

MINCEMEAT HERMITS

1 cup sifted all-purpose flour
¼ teaspoon each of salt, baking soda, and ground nutmeg
½ teaspoon ground cinnamon
⅓ cup butter
⅓ cup firmly packed light brown sugar
1 egg
½ cup mincemeat
1 tablespoon dairy sour cream
   Vanilla Glaze

Sift first 5 ingredients and set aside. Cream butter, sugar and egg. Add to flour mixture. Add mincemeat and cream, mixing by hand. Drop by heaping teaspoonfuls in mounds onto ungreased cookie sheet, leaving 2 inches between mounds. Bake in preheated hot oven (400°F.) for 10 to 12 minutes. Remove from oven and frost with Vanilla Glaze while hot. Makes 20.
Vanilla Glaze. Mix 1½ cups sifted confectioners' sugar, dash of salt, 1 teaspoon vanilla extract, 2 tablespoons melted butter, and 2 tablespoons heavy cream.

MOLASSES HERMITS

¾ cup soft butter or margarine
1½ cups firmly packed light brown sugar
½ cup molasses
3 eggs
4 cups sifted cake flour
1 teaspoon each of salt, ground cinnamon, and nutmeg
½ teaspoon each of ground cloves, allspice, and mace
¼ cup strong coffee
1 cup chopped nuts
1 cup each of raisins and currants
   Sifted confectioners' sugar

Cream butter and sugar until light. Beat in molasses. Add eggs, one at a time, beating thoroughly after each addition. Sift flour, salt, and spices and add to first mixture alternately with coffee, beating until smooth. Fold in nuts and fruit. Pour into pan, 15 x 10 x 1 inches, lined with wax paper. Bake in preheated moderate oven (350°F.) about 20 minutes. Turn out on rack and peel off paper. Slip onto cutting board and cut in 35 bars about 3 x 1½ inches. Sprinkle with confectioners' sugar. Makes about 3 dozen bars.
NOTE: These will stay moist a long time.

BROWN-SUGAR HERMITS

½ cup soft butter
1 cup firmly packed brown sugar
2 eggs
2 cups sifted cake flour
1 teaspoon baking powder
½ teaspoon salt
1 teaspoon ground cinnamon
¼ teaspoon each of ground cloves and nutmeg
2 cups seeded raisins, chopped
½ cup chopped nuts

Cream butter and sugar; add eggs, one at a time, beating until light after each addition. Add sifted dry ingredients, raisins, and nuts; mix well. Drop by teaspoonfuls onto greased cookie sheets. Bake in preheated moderate oven (350°F.) about 10 minutes. Makes about 4 dozen.

HERRING

HERRING—These small, saltwater fish belong to the family Clupeidae, related to the shad, alewife, and sardine. The freshwater fish called "lake herring" is a cisco, which is not related to the true herring. Herring is an important food fish, both for human consumption and as the basic diet of other food fishes.

Herring have small heads; they are streamlined and covered with silvery, iridescent scales. Mature herrings measure around ten inches, but they can be larger. They

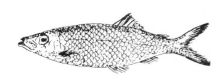

are migratory fish, and appear to spend most of their lives in the deep waters offshore. In the spring they come to the beaches in enormous numbers in order to spawn. The sight of schools of herring, several miles wide, shimmering in the moonlight like an iridescent tapestry as they progress to the shore, is an unforgettable one. Their migrations are uncertain, and no one knows why sometimes they stay away from some shores for years.

Herring females lay an average of 10,000 to 60,000 eggs at each spawning. At spawning time, the female rubs herself against rocks, sand, or seaweed, on which she drops her eggs. These can be seen floating on top of the sea, resembling sawdust. Both eggs and herring are preyed upon by other fish and gulls, porpoises, and sharks.

The economics of many nations were based upon herring. The spawning ground influenced the location of cities, and the capricious habits of the herring often brought disaster, for when the fish did not come, there was no food. Herring have always been fished commercially on a vast scale. Holland's great foreign trade was built upon her successful herring fisheries. One of the reasons why Charles I of England (1600-1649) was overthrown by his subjects (and eventually lost his head) was because he interfered with their free fishing rights. He wanted to tax the fishing rights to get money to fight the Dutch herring trade of the time.

In Europe, especially in Great Britain and in the countries that border on the North Sea, fresh herring is greatly appreciated.

Preserved herring in many varieties is a staple food of Holland and the Scandinavian countries. The herring is salted, pickled, or smoked and dressed with sauces. Many of these herring delicacies are imported into the United States and, along with our own preserved herring, can add considerable variety to a budget diet.

Kippers and bloaters are two herring specialties of England. The fish are cured by salting and smoking. They are baked or broiled just long enough to heat them through. Kippers (a contraction of "kippered herring" referring to the method and ingredients used in the process of curing them) and bloaters (larger herring), are tasty English breakfast food and are served also at high teas and suppers.

Rollmops, the favorite German herring dish, is a rolled-up pickled herring. Like other pickled herring, it can be bought in food stores.

Availability and Purchasing Guide—All year round, although the supply fluctuates depending upon the catch.

Herring is sold fresh, salted in brine, mild-smoked, pickled in wine sauce or other seasoned sauces or with sour cream, and kippered.

Canned herring is available pickled in tomato or wine sauce, as grilled fillets, and rolled with anchovies. Pickled herring in wine sauce or with sour cream is available in jars.

Storage—Fresh and mild-smoked, refrigerator shelf: 1 to 2 days
Fresh and mild-smoked, refrigerator frozen-food compartment, prepared for freezing: 2 to 3 weeks
Fresh and mild-smoked, freezer, prepared for freezing: 1 year
Salted in brine, refrigerator shelf: 1 week
Hard-smoked, pickled, and kippered, refrigerator shelf: 2 to 3 months
Canned, kitchen shelf, unopened: 6 months to 1 year
Canned, kitchen shelf, opened and covered: 3 to 4 days

Nutritive Food Values—Good source of protein and fat. Fresh herring is high in phosphorus. The caloric value of 3½ ounces of fresh salt-water herring can vary from 98 to 176 calories depending on the variety. The value of 3½ ounces of smoked herring varies from 196 to 300 calories depending on variety and method of smoking.
Fresh-water herring (cisco), 3½ ounces, raw = 96 calories
Salad in brine, 3½ ounces = 218 calories
Kippered, 3½ ounces = 211 calories

Basic Preparation—*Fresh herring* is prepared as is any other fresh fish.

Herring in brine should be soaked in fresh water for 24 hours. Water should be changed several times. After soaking, remove head, split, fillet, and skin fish. Prepare as desired.

Smoked herring should be soaked in water or in half milk and half water for several hours. The longer it is soaked the less smoky it will taste.

Kippers and bloaters, if heavily salted, may have to be soaked as other smoked herring is. They should be just heated through or they will be dry. Serve as a breakfast dish with eggs and toast.

Pickled herring is eaten as is and can be chopped and mixed with other foods, with salads, sandwich spreads, etc.

PICKLED HERRING

```
6 herring in brine
1 onion, sliced
½ lemon, sliced
1½ cups cider vinegar
3 bay leaves
⅛ teaspoon crushed red pepper
1½ teaspoons mustard seeds
½ teaspoon sugar
```

Clean herring and soak in cold water for 24 hours, changing water several times. Remove head and bones; rinse and drain. Arrange in covered refrigerator dish in layers with onion and lemon. Combine vinegar with remaining ingredients. Bring to boil; cool; pour over herring. Store, covered, in refrigerator for 3 to 4 days before serving. Makes 6 servings.

ROLLMOPS

```
6 herring in brine
  Prepared mustard
2 small sour pickles, sliced
2 onions, thinly sliced
1 tablespoon capers
1 red pepper, cut up
6 peppercorns
2 bay leaves
1½ cups cider vinegar
1 cup water
```

Clean herring and soak in cold water for 24 hours, changing water several times. Remove head and bones. Rinse and drain. Spread herring with prepared mustard, pickle slices, onion slices, and capers. Roll up each herring and secure with toothpicks. Place in small container with red pepper, peppercorns, and bay leaves. Do not use a metal container, Boil together vinegar and water. Cool; pour over herring. Cover and let stand for 3 to 6 days. Drain before serving. Serve with sour cream, if desired. Makes 6 servings.

GRILLED ENGLISH HERRING

Cut heads, tails, and fins off washed and gutted herrings. Split open along the backbone; draw out the backbone with as many fine bones as possible. Wipe fish and sprinkle with pepper and salt. Dip fish into fine oatmeal, coating it both inside and out. Place fish on broiler rack. Dot each with 1 teaspoon bacon fat. Broil in preheated broiler for 10 minutes on each side, or until crisp and golden brown. Serve immediately with mustard sauce or with lemon.

HERRING IN SOUR CREAM

    5 herring in brine
    1 cup dairy sour cream
    2 tablespoons cider vinegar
    1 teaspoon Worcestershire
    ½ teaspoon dry mustard
    2 onions, sliced
      Dash of cayenne
      Chopped parsley

Clean herring and soak in cold water for 24 hours, changing water several times. Remove head, skin, and bones. Rinse and drain. Cut into 1-inch pieces. Combine remaining ingredients; add herring and mix lightly. Place in glass jar; cover. Let stand in refrigerator for about 12 hours before serving. Makes 6 servings.

BROILED KIPPERED HERRING

    8 mild kippers
    ¼ cup melted butter
      Juice of 1 lemon
      Paprika
    1 tablespoon chopped scallions

Without breaking the skin along the back, split kippers and spread butterfly-style, skin side down in greased shallow baking dish. Brush with butter and lemon juice, sprinkle with paprika, and bake in preheated moderate oven (350°F.) for 10 minutes. Garnish with scallions. Makes 4 servings.

FRIED SMOKED HERRING

    8 smoked herring
      Pepper
    1 cup cornmeal
      Fat for cooking

Wash herring and soak in cold water for 24 hours, changing water twice. Rinse and dry. Sprinkle with pepper and roll in cornmeal. Fry in shallow fat (⅛ to ¼ inch) in skillet for about 12 to 15 minutes or until brown and crisp, turning once. Makes 4 servings.

HERRING BUTTER

Cream ¼ cup butter with 2 teaspoons ground smoked herring or herring paste, and a few drops of fresh lemon juice. May be spread on bread for canapés, alone, or as a base for another food.

HIBACHI—A small brazier with an adjustable grill, varying in size from 4 to 5 inches (for table models) to a full-sized double grill for cooking many items at one time.

The brazier is usually of cast iron, rectangular, and fueled by charcoal. Directly above the fire are the adjustable grill shelves on which food is placed, either in pans or directly on the grill.

Cooking time can be varied by raising or lowering the grills, by varying the amount of charcoal used, or by placing food at different locations on the grill. For example, a steak may be placed in the center of the grill directly over the coals and a pot of vegetables or rice at the grill's edge, further away from the heat.

The best time to put food on the grill is when the burning coals are grey-white in color, when the fire is at its hottest.

Originally the Japanese used the hibachi to heat their homes, in addition to using it for cooking. In modern times, however, we use it almost exclusively for barbecuing and other outdoor purposes. *See* Charcoal Grill Cookbook, Volume 2.

HICKORY—A large family of American trees of the genus *Carya,* all of which have hard wood suitable for timber. Many have rich green leaves in summer which turn a brilliant yellow in fall. Some hickory varieties are raised commercially.

The extremely hard wood of the tree has made hickory a synonym for firmness. Andrew Jackson who was elected president of the United States in 1828, was known as Old Hickory to point up his toughness in war or peace.

Pecan and pignut trees are both members of the hickory family. The thin-shelled nuts of these trees are known as pecans and pignuts. The "hickory" nuts available commercially come from the shagbark or shellbark hickories and have a hard shell.

The hickory nut was eaten by the Indians before the first American colonists arrived in the new country. The name pohickery, mentioned as early as 1653, is a shortened form of the word used by the Virginians to describe an Indian food of water and pounded nuts.

The Indians in Florida used hickory nuts to make a milky liquor which they called "milk of nuts." A contemporary observer, writing in 1775, reported that "this milk they are fond of and eat it with sweet potatoes in it."

Modern cooks find hickory nuts more useful in cakes, cookies, sweet breads, and candies. They can also be used in any recipe calling for pecans.

The shells of hickory nuts are so hard that it is usually necessary to use a hammer to crack them in order to remove the nutmeats.

Availability and Purchasing Guide—Hickory nuts are available only in certain localities. They are sold by the pound in bulk, unshelled; they are rarely available shelled.
3 pounds hickory nuts = 1 pound shelled meats

Storage—Store, in a covered container, in a cool dry place, refrigerate or freeze.
In shell, kitchen shelf, covered: 1 year
Shelled, kitchen shelf, covered: 2 to 3 months

Shelled, refrigerator shelf: 4 months
Shelled, refrigerator frozen-food compartment: 6 months
Shelled, freezer: 6 months to 1 year

Nutritive Food Values—Hickory nuts are high in fat.
3½ ounces = 673 calories

HICKORY NUT CAKE

      1 cup butter or margarine
      2 cups sugar
      3 cups sifted all-purpose flour
      3 teaspoons baking powder
      1 cup milk
      ½ teaspoon each vanilla and orange extracts
      1 tablespoon grated lemon rind
      7 egg whites, beaten until very stiff
      1 cup chopped hickory nuts

Cream butter until soft; gradually beat in sugar, a little at a time. Beat until fluffy. Sift together flour and baking powder. Add flour and milk alternately to butter mixture, beginning and ending with flour. Stir in vanilla and orange extracts and grated lemon rind. Fold in beaten egg whites. Pour into greased 9-inch angel-food pan. Scatter hickory nuts on top of batter. Bake in preheated moderate oven (350°F.) about 1 hour. Cool in pan. Makes one 9-inch cake.

HICKORY NUT CREAMS

      3 cups firmly packed light brown sugar or maple sugar
      1 cup light cream or undiluted evaporated milk
      ½ teaspoon vanilla extract
      1 tablespoon butter
      2 cups hickory nuts

Mix sugar with cream until sugar is dissolved. Bring to a boil and boil until a small amount dropped into cold water forms a soft ball. (234°F. on a candy thermometer.) Cool mixture to 110°F., or lukewarm. Add vanilla, butter, and nuts. Beat with a spoon until creamy. Drop by teaspoons onto wax paper. Makes about 36 creams.

NUT BREAD

      3 cups sifted all-purpose flour
      1 cup sugar
      1½ teaspoons salt
      4 teaspoons baking powder
      ¼ cup shortening
      1 egg, well beaten
      1¼ cups milk
      1 cup coarsely chopped hickory nuts

Sift flour with sugar, salt, and baking powder. Cut in shortening until mixture resembles coarse cornmeal. Beat egg with milk and add liquid all at once to dry ingredients. Stir until just blended. Stir in nuts. Pour mixture into a well-greased pan, 9 x 5 x 3 inches. Cool on a rack and slice while warm.

HICKORY CRESCENTS

      1 cup ground hickory nuts
      1 cup butter
      ¾ cup sugar
      2½ cups sifted all-purpose flour
      1½ teaspoons vanilla extract
         Vanilla Sugar

Combine nuts, butter, sugar, flour, and vanilla. Knead to a smooth dough and shape about 1 teaspoon of dough at a time into a small crescent about 1½ inches long. Bake on ungreased cookie sheets in preheated moderate oven (350°F.) until slightly browned, about 15 to 17 minutes. Cool for 1 minute. While still warm, roll cookies in Vanilla Sugar. Cool completely, and roll again in Vanilla Sugar. Makes about 6 dozen.

Vanilla Sugar. Cut 2 or 3 vanilla beans into 1-inch pieces. Put in jar with 1 pound sifted confectioners' sugar. Let stand for 3 days. The longer the sugar stands, the more fragrant it becomes.

HIGHBALL—An American drink made from whisky or other hard liquor, mixed with water, soda water, or ginger ale and served with ice in a tall glass.

HOECAKE—This is the cornmeal cake of the early American settlers, which often served as bread. The cooking facilities of colonial households were generally primitive, and ovens, even when existing, could not be heated easily. The inventive settlers baked a cornmeal and water mixture on the blades of their hoes on hot coals in front of a wood fire and called them "hoecakes."

Today's hoecakes are baked in a frying pan or on a griddle like any other hot cake.

OLD-FASHIONED HOECAKE

      1 cup white cornmeal
      ½ teaspoon salt
         Boiling water

Mix meal and salt and add enough boiling water to make a dough that is soft, but not thin enough to be a batter. Heat a well-greased 6- or 8-inch frying pan, and spread the dough on it in one cake, flattening with a spoon or spatula. Cook until very brown on one side, then turn with a pancake turner and let brown as long as can be done without burning.

HOLIDAY DRINKS—These beverages will banish Winter's chill and provide the perfect accompaniment to a lovely evening beside a cozy fire.

HOT TOMATO BOUILLON

Use 1 beef bouillon cube for each cup of tomato juice. Heat until steaming hot and cube is dissolved. Sprinkle with chopped parsley, and serve with a lemon wedge, if desired.

SPICY PARTY COFFEE

1 cup heavy cream
2 tablespoons coffee liqueur
1 teaspoon sugar
  Cinnamon
  Hot double-strength coffee

Whip cream with coffee liqueur, sugar and ⅛ teaspoon cinnamon until stiff peaks form. Pour coffee into cups and top with cream mixture, and additional cinnamon, if desired. Makes 6 servings.

CHOCOLATE COFFEE

4 cups hot strong coffee
6 tablespoons canned chocolate syrup
1 teaspoon grated orange rind
½ teaspoon ground cinnamon
  Dash of nutmeg
  Whipped cream flavored with chocolate syrup

Combine all ingredients, except cream, and keep hot until ready to serve. Then pour mixture into small cups (about 4-ounce) and top each with a dollop of flavored whipped cream. Makes about 8 servings.

CAFÉ BRÛLOT

A famous New Year's drink in old New Orleans, where special brûlot cups were used.

4 ounces (½ cup) cognac
2 small cinnamon sticks
8 whole cloves
10 small lumps sugar
2 tablespoons canned chocolate syrup
2 long strips orange peel
2 strips lemon peel
2 cups hot demitasse-strength coffee

Heat cognac gently in top pan of chafing dish. Add remaining ingredients, except coffee, and ignite with match. Stir until sugar is melted and blended. Then slowly stir in coffee. Strain into demitasse cups. Makes 4 servings.

LOW-CALORIE SPICED COFFEE

2 cups hot strong coffee
¼ teaspoon caraway seed
6 whole allspice
1 cinnamon stick
⅛ teaspoon ground nutmeg
6 whole cloves
⅔ cup dry nonfat milk powder
  Non-caloric sweetener equal to 3 tablespoons sugar
  Low-calorie whipped topping

Combine first 6 ingredients. Simmer 15 minutes, strain and chill. Pour over dry milk powder and mix well. Stir in sweetener and pour over ice in tall glasses. Put a spoonful of whipped topping on each glass. Makes 2 servings.

SPICED MULLED ORANGE DRINK

10 to 12 cardamom pods
1 can (1 quart 14 ounces) orange drink
1 cinnamon stick
4 whole cloves
4 whole allspice
¼ teaspoon freshly ground nutmeg

Crush cardamom pods and remove seed (there should be about ¼ teaspoon). Put, with remaining ingredients, in saucepan. Bring to boil and simmer 10 minutes. Strain and serve piping hot. Makes about 1½ quarts.
NOTE: Grape or apple juice can be substituted for the orange drink.

HOT BUTTERED RUM

1 quart apple juice
¼ cup firmly packed light-brown sugar
2 tablespoons butter or margarine
  Rum

Heat apple juice and brown sugar until mixture comes to a boil. Add butter. Pour into mugs and add 1 jigger (or to taste) rum to each. Makes 4 servings.

Punches

HOLIDAY RED PUNCH

This delicious nonalcoholic punch is so pretty, and absolutely no bother to put together in 5 minutes.

1 bottle (28 ounces) carbonated collins mixer
1 bottle (32 ounces) apple juice
1 can (6 ounces) frozen pink lemonade, thawed
3 cans (6 ounces) frozen lemon juice, thawed
  Food coloring

Mix all ingredients in a punch bowl, adding red and a bit of yellow liquid food colorings to make punch bright red. Add ice cubes or an ice ring made by freezing carbonated water in a 9-inch ring mold. Makes 34 four-ounce servings.

CITRUS PUNCH

1 can (6 ounces) each frozen orange-juice concentrate, lemonade and limeade
  Water
1 bottle (28 ounces) ginger ale or 1 bottle white wine or ½ bottle of each
  Fruited Ice Mold

Reconstitute frozen beverages as directed on cans. Add 4 cups more cold water and put in punch bowl. Just before serving, add ginger ale and ice mold. Makes about 4 quarts.
Fruited Ice Mold. Cover bottom of ring or other mold with ice cubes. Arrange lemon, orange, lime or apple slices; strawberries or grape clusters around or between ice cubes. Fill with water and freeze. (Ice cubes help hold fruit in place.)

Spiced Mulled Orange Drink

COFFEE EGGNOG

    4   eggs, separated
    ¾   cup sugar
    ¼   teaspoon salt
    3   tablespoons instant-coffee powder
    ⅓   cup water
    4   cups milk
    ½   cup heavy cream
    1½ teaspoons vanilla extract
        Ground nutmeg

Beat egg yolks, gradually add ½ cup sugar and salt, beating until fluffy. Dissolve coffee in water; stir in milk, cream and vanilla; chill. Beat egg whites until stiff; gradually add remaining ¼ cup sugar, beating thoroughly. Fold into egg-yolk mixture. Pour into punch bowl. Mix well before serving. Sprinkle with nutmeg. Makes 2 quarts.

HOLIDAY EGGNOG

    ½   cup sugar
    6   eggs, separated
    4   cups milk, scalded
    ¼   teaspoon salt
    2   cups heavy cream, whipped
    ½   cup brandy
    ¼   cup rum
        Ground nutmeg

In top part of double boiler, beat ¼ cup sugar into egg yolks. Gradually stir in milk and cook, stirring, over hot water until mixture coats a metal spoon. Remove from hot water, cool and chill. Add salt to egg whites and beat until foamy. Gradually add remaining ¼ cup sugar and beat until stiff. Fold egg whites into first mixture, then fold in cream. Add brandy and rum and chill several hours. Pour into chilled punch bowl and sprinkle with nutmeg. Makes about 2½ quarts.

CHILLED FRUITED DRINKS

SANGRIA
[Red-wine Punch]

    1   tablespoon sugar
    1   bottle Spanish red wine, burgundy, rosé or dry red
        wine, chilled
    1   bottle (12 ounces) carbonated water, chilled
        Spirals of lemon peel
        Orange slices

Put sugar in large glass pitcher. Add wine, ice cubes and carbonated water. Drop in lemon peel and decorate with orange slices. Makes about 1½ quarts.

CRANBERRY-ORANGE TWINKLE

    1   bottle (28 ounces) orange-flavored carbonated bev-
        erage, chilled
    1   bottle (28 ounces) carbonated water, chilled
        Cranberry ice cubes (see Note)
        Fresh mint (optional)

Mix beverages just before serving and serve over ice cubes in punch bowl. Top with mint sprigs, if desired. Makes about 2 quarts.
NOTE: To make ice cubes, put a lemon slice in each section of ice-cube tray and fill with cranberry-juice cocktail. Freeze. If desired, 1 can (1 quart 14 ounces) orange drink can be substituted for orange carbonated beverage.

CLARET LEMONADE

Fill chilled glass three fourths full with cold lemonade. Tip glass slightly and slowly pour small amount of chilled claret down side of glass so that it settles on the bottom.

STRAWBERRY-GRAPEFRUIT SPARKLE

    1   can (6 ounces) frozen grapefruit-juice concentrate,
        reconstituted
    1   package (10 ounces) frozen sliced strawberries, par-
        tially thawed
    1   bottle (28 ounces) carbonated water, chilled

Whirl first 2 ingredients in blender. Pour into punch bowl or pitcher and add carbonated water. Makes about 2 quarts.

THREE-FRUIT DRINK

    1   can (6 ounces) frozen grapefruit-juice concentrate,
        reconstituted
    1   can (6 ounces) frozen orange-juice concentrate, re-
        constituted
    1   can (8½ ounces) crushed pineapple
    ¼   cup grenadine
        Maraschino cherries

Combine all ingredients, except cherries, in large pitcher or punch bowl. Chill thoroughly. Serve with ice cubes and top with cherries. Makes about 1¾ quarts.

APPLE-BERRY CHILLER

    1   can (6 ounces) frozen apple juice, reconstituted
    1   package (10 ounces) frozen raspberries, thawed
    1   bottle (28 ounces) carbonated water, chilled

Combine all ingredients just before serving. Serve with ice cubes, if desired. Makes about 2 quarts.

APRICOT-WINE MEDLEY

Mix equal parts of chilled apricot nectar and white wine. Serve in chunky glasses with skewered fruit stirrers. Delicious for a special brunch or an afternoon party.
Skewered Fruit Stirrers. Thread whole grapes, strawberries, mandarin orange sections and pineapple chunks on 6- to 8-inch wooden or metal skewers.

HOLIDAY FOODS—Here's a fascinating assortment of goodies to serve with holiday beverages. Perfect for those times when you're serving more than a drink, but less than a meal.

LEMON PEAR HALVES

    1 can (29 ounces) pear halves, drained and syrup
        reserved
    1 cup sugar
        Grated rind and juice of 1 lemon
        Green food coloring

Put pear halves in sterilized 1-quart glass jar with screw lid. Combine pear syrup, sugar, lemon rind and juice and a few drops green food coloring in saucepan. Bring to boil, stirring, and simmer, stirring occasionally, 15 minutes. Pour over pears and seal. Refrigerate. Serve as a condiment and garnish for meat or, topped with chocolate or custard sauce, as a dessert. Keeps about 1 week. Makes about 10 pear halves.

ORANGE-NUT COFFEE CAKE

    1 package active dry yeast
    ¼ cup warm water
        Butter or margarine
    ¾ cup milk
    ½ teaspoon salt
    ¼ cup sugar
    1 egg
    3½ cups all-purpose flour
    ⅔ cup finely chopped candied orange peel
    ⅓ cup each finely chopped nuts and sugar
        Pecan halves, honey
        Candied pineapple (optional)

In mixing bowl, dissolve yeast in water (105°F. to 115°F.). Melt ⅓ cup butter in small saucepan, add milk and heat to warm (105°F. to 115°F.). Combine with yeast mixture, salt, sugar, egg and 1½ cups flour. Beat with rotary beater until smooth. Cover and let rise in warm place about 40 minutes. Beat in remaining 2 cups flour, ½ cup at a time. Turn dough out on lightly floured board and knead until smooth and elastic. Divide in quarters. Shape each quarter to 1-inch wide roll and cut each in 10 pieces. In center of each piece put about ½ measuring teaspoonful orange peel, seal and shape in an even round bun. Then brush each bun with melted butter (about ¼ cup for all) and roll in mixture of nuts and sugar. Put buns close together in lightly greased 9 x 3-inch springform pan or loose-bottom pan. Let rise in warm place 1 hour, or until doubled in bulk. Bake in preheated moderate oven (350°F.) 40 minutes, or until done (protect oven while baking with piece of foil on bottom to collect any dripping butter). Cool in pan on rack. Remove rim and decorate with pecan halves brushed with honey, and thin slices of candied pineapple, if desired. Serve in thin wedges. Store tightly wrapped in refrigerator. Can be frozen and decorated after thawing. Makes 40 wedges.

SPICED ORANGE WEDGES

    6 medium seedless oranges
    2½ cups sugar
    ¾ cup white vinegar
    1 teaspoon whole cloves
    3 sticks cinnamon, each 3½ inches long
    2 cups water

Wash oranges and cover with water. Bring to boil, reduce heat and simmer 20 minutes, or until quite tender. Drain and cut in eighths. Combine remaining ingredients and heat, stirring, until mixture boils. Add orange wedges and simmer about 20 minutes. Pack into hot sterilized jars and seal. Good as a condiment, especially with poultry or ham. Makes about 3 pints.

HOLIDAY MINCEMEAT PIE

    1¾ cups all-purpose flour
    1 teaspoon salt
    ⅓ cup solid white vegetable shortening
    ⅓ cup margarine
    ⅓ cup ice water
    1 jar (32 ounces) prepared mincemeat
        Grated rind of 1 lemon
    1 egg yolk beaten with 2 teaspoons milk or cream
        (optional)
    2 to 3 tablespoons light rum (optional)
        Chopped pistachio nuts

Combine first 2 ingredients in mixing bowl. Cut in shortening and margarine until mixture resembles small peas. Sprinkle with water and quickly gather into ball. Do not knead. Wrap in waxed paper and chill well. Combine mincemeat and lemon rind and set aside. Roll out two thirds of pastry and line 9-inch piepan. Trim edges and flute in a pretty pattern. Pour in mincemeat. Roll out remaining pastry ⅛-inch thick and cut out ten ¾-inch wide strips; arrange 6 strips crosswise and 4 strips lengthwise, lattice fashion, on pie. Trim ends of strips and press into sides of shell. Brush pastry with egg-yolk and milk mixture if desired. Bake in preheated hot oven (425°F.) 10 minutes; reduce heat to 350°F. and bake 25 to 30 minutes, or until done. Sprinkle with rum and nuts and serve slightly warm.
NOTE: Pie can be made ahead. Bake and cool; cover tightly and refrigerate up to 1 week. At serving time bring pie to room temperature, sprinkle with rum and nuts and reheat in preheated slow oven (325°F.) 15 to 20 minutes.

HOLLANDAISE

HOLLANDAISE—A rich sauce of French origin made with egg yolks and butter. It is served with eggs, fish, vegetables, and, occasionally, meat. The origin of the name is obscure; there is no historical evidence that it originated in Holland. There may be a slight clue in the old French culinary language where we find that fish served with melted butter was called *à la hollandaise,* since the sauce we know today as hollandaise is so rich in butter.

HOW TO COOK SUPERBLY: HOLLANDAISE

by HELEN EVANS BROWN

Hollandaise sauce is not only a classic accompaniment for asparagus, broccoli, and other vegetables, it is the base of other famous sauces: Béarnaise, mousseline, maltaise, and choron. It is also a chef's way of obtaining a beautiful brown glaze on many entrées and a necessary ingredient for many famous dishes including eggs Benedict. It is really no great feat to make hollandaise perfectly for, unlike an omelet, it requires no practice. There is just one simple thing to remember, and that is not to let it cook over too high heat. If you do, it will break or separate. But even that catastrophe can usually be remedied.

There are three ways to make hollandaise. The one usually found in most cook books I will skip, because I consider the other two better, each for a different reason. The first of these, the method used by most European-trained chefs, has the advantage of perfect flavor and consistency and is easy to make. The second, or blender method, is even easier, although the resulting sauce has two small faults, probably recognized only by experts: the egg yolks have a slightly raw taste and the consistency is a bit too fluffy.

First Method

EQUIPMENT
You will need a kitchen bowl, preferably a heavy crockery one (not metal) that will heat slowly and hold the heat. Select a size that will fit over a saucepan or the bottom part of a double boiler without touching the hot water beneath. A 3-cup bowl is usually right as it allows room for beating. You will also need a wire whisk. The French type (called a *fouet* in France) is perfect but there are American whips that do very well. One is a spoon-shape device edged with a coil of wire; the other is also spoon-shape, but crisscrossed with wire. A split or slotted spoon,

Apricot Wine Medley

or a bundle of twigs such as those used in Sweden, can also be used, as can a spoon or plastic scraper if you work fast. A fork doesn't reach the curves of the bowl; therefore some of the mixture may overcook. You will also need a knife for cutting the butter or a small pan for melting it, if you prefer that method.

INGREDIENTS
- 3 egg yolks
- ¼ cup hot water
- 1 tablespoon fresh lemon juice (or to taste)
- White pepper or cayenne to taste
- Ground nutmeg to taste (optional)
- ½ cup (¼ pound) soft butter, cut into slices, or melted butter

HERE'S HOW
1. Put the bowl over the pan of warm water, making sure that the bottom is at least ½ inch from the top of the water. Place pan over low heat.
2. Put egg yolks in the bowl and, while whisking or stirring vigorously, drizzle in the hot water. Add lemon juice and pepper or cayenne, continuing to beat. Add nutmeg if you wish (early French recipes called for it, but it is rarely used today). Don't let the water boil or you'll have scrambled eggs. If it approaches that point, remove from heat. (If it does boil, put bowl in cold water for a minute to cool it slightly.) The egg-and-water mixture will become fluffy and thickened, the whisk coated, and the yolks will lose their raw taste.
3. When the egg mixture reaches that point, add a slice of butter and stir until it melts. The sauce should begin thickening. Add more butter, whisking the while, until all is added and the sauce is so thick that the bottom of the bowl will show for a split second when you stir. If it doesn't thicken properly, give it more heat but not too much. A quicker method is to melt the butter and drizzle it in with one hand while beating with the other. This works very well if you are careful to pour very slowly, at least at first until the mixture starts to thicken. It has an added advantage in that you can leave the milky residue in the melting pan, thus improving the flavor of the sauce.
4. Your sauce is now done and can be held over warm (never hot) water until you're ready to serve (up to 1 hour or more). Remember that hollandaise is a warm, not hot, sauce. Makes about 1½ cups.

Second Method

EQUIPMENT
All you need is an electric blender.

INGREDIENTS
Cut egg yolks to 2 and hot water to 1 tablespoon. All of the other ingredients remain the same. Melt butter until it is very hot, almost boiling.

45

HOLLANDAISE

HERE'S HOW

1. Rinse container of blender with hot water; put in place, add egg yolks, hot water, lemon juice, and seasonings, and whirl at high speed for 3 seconds.

2. Remove top (just the small opening if your blender is so provided, otherwise just lift lid enough to add butter). Pour foaming butter in very slowly, keeping the blender turned on. (You may get splattered if you stand too close, so watch it!) As soon as all the butter (but not the milky residue) is added, your hollandiaise is ready to serve. Makes about ⅔ cup.

HINTS

Separation—If your hollandaise should separate from overheating, try adding a few drops of boiling water or thick cream while beating vigorously.

Thinness—If it is too thin, it means you haven't cooked it enough or have added the butter too fast. If you suspect the first, just return the bowl to water that is under the boil and beat until thickened. If you think you may have added the butter too quickly, warm a bowl in hot water, then put about 1 teaspoon of heavy cream and 1 tablespoon of the sauce in it and whisk vigorously. Gradually add the remaining sauce, 1 spoonful at a time, until all is added and the sauce is thick.

Reheating—Hollandaise can be kept in the refrigerator for 2 or 3 days or frozen for weeks. (Remember that egg yolk is a perfect culture for bacteria, so don't let it stand around in a warm place.) When reheating, put a bowl over warm water, as above, and add 1 spoonful of the sauce at a time, beating after each addition. If it should separate, treat as above. Or put it over warm water all at once and beat hard until smooth and warm.

VARIATIONS

Béarnaise Sauce—Follow Hollandaise recipe but omit lemon juice. Instead soak 1 teaspoon dried tarragon in 2 tablespoons tarragon vinegar and cook with 2 teaspoons chopped shallots or green onions until the vinegar is absorbed. Add to the hot water and continue as above. Omit nutmeg but add a dash of dry mustard, if desired. Strain if you wish. Serve with steaks, lamb, meat loaf, fish, and vegetables.

Choron Sauce—Add 2 tablespoons tomato paste to 1 recipe of Béarnaise Sauce. Serve with fish, eggs, steaks, meatballs, or meat loaf.

Mousseline Sauce—Combine 1 recipe of Hollandaise Sauce with ½ cup heavy cream, whipped. Serve with soufflés, vegetables.

Maltaise Sauce—Follow Hollandaise recipe but substitute ¼ cup fresh orange juice for the hot water, in either method; in the blender method use 3 egg yolks. Also add 1 teaspoon grated orange peel. Serve with boiled vegetables or fish.

SPECIAL USES

For additional richness, add 2 or 3 tablespoons hollandaise to 1 cup Béchamel or cream sauce.

Or add ¼ cup hollandaise to 1 cup whipped cream (or ½ cup each of whipped cream and cream sauce) and use for masking foods that are to be glazed or browned under the broiler.

OTHER VARIATIONS

Curry Hollandaise—Follow basic recipe, adding ¾ teaspoon curry powder with other seasonings. Serve with lamb, chicken or vegetables.

White-Wine Hollandaise—Follow basic recipe, adding 2 tablespoons white wine just before serving.

Creamy Horseradish Hollandaise—Follow basic recipe, adding 3 tablespoons drained prepared horseradish and 2 tablespoons heavy cream, whipped, just before serving. Good with ham or vegetables. Makes about 1⅓ cups.

Cucumber Hollandaise—Follow basic recipe, adding 1 cup finely chopped cucumber, well drained, just before serving. Good with fish or shellfish. Makes 1½ cups.

Creamy Cold Hollandaise—Cool basic hollandaise to room temperature. Whip ⅓ cup heavy cream until stiff and blend in ¼ cup mayonnaise. Fold into hollandaise and serve on fish, poultry or molded vegetable salad. Makes about 1½ cups.

MOCK HOLLANDAISE

3 tablespoons butter
2 tablespoons all-purpose flour
½ teaspoon salt
1 cup hot water
2 egg yolks
1½ tablespoons lemon juice

Melt butter in top part of small double boiler over boiling water. Blend in flour and salt. Gradually add hot water and cook, stirring, 5 minutes, or until smooth and thickened. Beat egg yolks and lemon juice well. Pour slowly into mixture while beating. Cook about 1 minute. Good on any vegetable. Makes about 1 cup.

NOTE: Sauce can stand over hot water 30 minutes or longer. If necessary, beat with rotary beater before serving.

CREAM-CHEESE HOLLANDAISE

Cheese replaces butter in this recipe

    2 packages (3 ounces each) cream cheese
    2 egg yolks
    2 tablespoons lemon juice
       Dash each of salt and white pepper

Beat cheese until light and fluffy. Add egg yolks one at a time, beating thoroughly after each. Add remaining ingredients and put mixture in top part of small double boiler over hot (not boiling) water, not allowing bottom to touch water. Cook, stirring, until smooth and thickened. If sauce seems too thick, add about 1 tablespoon hot water and mix well. Especially good on hot cooked asparagus with a garnish of paprika. Makes about 1 cup.

HOMESTYLE—The word describes a home-kitchen way of cooking food or a home-cooked meal. When food is cooked for hotels, restaurants, institutions, and factories, the dishes taste differently from those prepared at home. The difference in flavor and texture is due to the fact that the food is cooked in large amounts at one time, that many of the ingredients are prepared in advance rather than just at cooking time, and that the food is kept hot on steam tables and other equipment instead of being cooked just before serving.

To cook homestyle is to try to approximate the methods used in home cooking: small quantities, good seasonings, and cooked to order, which means cooked fresh for the meal.

HOMINY—Kernels of hulled dried corn from which the germ has been removed. It is also known as "samp." Ground hominy is called grits. Hominy is apparently a word of Algonquian Indian origin, implying small particles. It is a truly American food, unknown anywhere else.

Hominy is cooked in water or milk, and may then be fried, baked, or served with a sauce. It is a popular staple in the South and Southwest.

Availability and Purchasing Guide—Sold by the pound as pearl, hominy (hull removed mechanically), and lye hominy (hull removed chemically). Hominy grits are available in three grinds: fine, medium, and coarse.

Canned hominy is also available.

Storage
Kitchen shelf: stores indefinitely
Refrigerator shelf, cooked and covered: 4 to 5 days.

Nutritive Food Values—Good source of carbohydrate. Hominy and hominy grits, 2/3 cup, cooked = about 84 calories.

Basic Preparation
To Cook Hominy—Soak overnight in water to cover. Pour hominy into salted boiling water (1 part hominy to 4 parts water). Cook over low heat. Cover and simmer for 4 to 5 hours, or until hominy is tender. Stir often during cooking. Use as is or beat butter into the hominy before serving. Beating whitens hominy. Milk or cream (½ cup for each 1 cup raw hominy) may be beaten into the hominy before serving.
To Cook Hominy Grits—Soak 1 cup grits in water to cover for 1 hour. Drain. Add 3 cups boiling water and 1 teaspoon salt, and cook in double boiler up to 1 hour, or until tender. Length of cooking time will depend on whether grits are fine, medium, or coarse.

SALT PORK, BEANS, AND HOMINY

    ½ pound navy beans
    ½ pound hominy
       Water
    ½ pound salt pork
       Salt and pepper
       Crumbled dried marjoram

Soak beans and hominy overnight. Drain and cover with fresh water. Cut salt pork into strips and mix with beans and hominy. Season to taste with salt, pepper, and marjoram. Simmer, covered, for at least 5 hours, or until beans and hominy are tender. Makes 6 to 8 servings.

HOMINY AU GRATIN

    1 can (1 pound 13 ounces) cooked hominy
    1 cup water
    1 teaspoon salt
    ½ cup grated sharp cheese
    ¼ cup butter or margarine
    1 cup warm milk

In a skillet combine all ingredients except milk. Simmer over low heat for 10 minutes, or until butter and cheese are melted. Stir occasionally. Gradually stir in milk and cook, stirring occasionally, over low heat until thick and bubbly. Put under broiler and cook until top is golden-brown. Makes 8 servings.

MEXICAN HOMINY

    1   medium onion, minced
    1   medium green pepper, chopped
    ¼   cup butter or bacon fat
    3½ cups (one 1-pound 13-ounce can) cooked hominy,
        drained
    1   teaspoon chili powder
    ½   teaspoon salt
    ⅛   teaspoon pepper

Cook onion and green pepper in the butter in top pan of chafing dish over direct heat for about 10 minutes. Add remaining ingredients, and heat. Makes 4 servings.

FRANKFURTER, HOMINY, AND GREEN-PEA CASSEROLE

In a greased 2-quart casserole, arrange in 3 pie-shape portions the following: 1 pound frankfurters, brushed with melted margarine and scored with sharp knife; 1 can (1 pound 13 ounces) cooked hominy, drained; 1 can (1 pound) peas, drained. Pour ¼ cup margarine over hominy and peas. Sprinkle with 4 slices of cooked bacon, chopped. Bake for 25 minutes in preheated moderate oven (350°F.). Makes 4 servings.

BAKED HOMINY GRITS

    2 cups cooked hominy grits
    ⅔ cup milk
    3 tablespoons melted butter or margarine
    2 eggs, beaten

Combine all ingredients and pour mixture into a buttered shallow 1-quart baking dish. Place pan in a pan of hot water. Bake in preheated moderate oven (375°F.) for 1 hour. Makes 6 servings.

FRIED HOMINY GRITS

    2 cups cooked hominy grits
    2 eggs, beaten
    2 tablespoons milk
    ¼ cup fine cracker crumbs
    ½ cup shortening
      Bacon

Press hominy into a small loaf pan, 7⅜ x 5⅜ x 2¼ inches. Chill for several hours. Unmold. Cut into ½-inch slices. Beat eggs with milk and dip slices into mixture. Roll slices in cracker crumbs and coat well. Heat shortening; fry slices to a golden brown on both sides. Serve with slices of crisp bacon. Makes 4 to 6 servings.

HOMINY PUFFS

    2 cups cooked hominy grits
    2 eggs, separated
    ¼ cup all-purpose flour
    1½ teaspoons baking powder
    ½ teaspoon salt
      Fat or lard for deep frying

Mix hominy with egg yolks. Stir in flour sifted with baking powder and salt. Beat egg whites until stiff but not dry, and fold them into the hominy mixture. Drop by tablespoonfuls into hot deep fat (360°F. on a frying thermometer). Fry until deep brown. Makes about 18 puffs.

HOMOGENIZE

HOMOGENIZE—This is a word of Greek origin, composed of *homos,* meaning "the same," and *"genos,"* kin or kind. In culinary language, "to homogenize" is to reduce an emulsion to particles of the same size and to distribute them evenly. The word is most frequently used for milk, but also for salad dressings and mayonnaise.

The homogenized milk we drink is pasteurized milk that has been processed mechanically to break up the fat globules into a tiny size so that they will stay in the liquid part of the milk rather than rise to the top. In other words, the cream is incorporated into the milk so that the milk is uniform rather than consisting of thin milk topped by cream.

The origin of homogenized milk lies in patents granted to two Frenchmen in 1892. They wanted to make margarine and invented machines that were the first homogenizing machines. These machines blended fats and water into a smooth whole. Their use for milk came later, in 1899, when another French inventor, Auguste Gaulin, noticed the fat globules in milk and decided to make a smooth, homogenous milk emulsion, which he did, adapting the principles of the homogenizing machines and taking out his own patents. This new milk appeared for the first time at the World's Fair in Paris in 1900, where it stirred up great curiosity. The milk was called Gaulin's Milk or *lait homogénéisé,* and from this developed our name.

The first time American readers heard about homogenized milk was in April 1904, when it was described to them in *The Scientific American.* The first introduction, in Quebec, Canada, in 1904, was not successful. The new milk was reintroduced in Ottawa in 1927, and by 1932 it could be found in many large Canadian cities.

In the United States, the first homogenized milk was introduced experimentally at the University of Illinois in 1921, but it did not become popular until the early thirties. Studies made at the Children's Hospital in Philadelphia, which proved that homogenized milk was more digestible for babies than ordinary milk, led to its acceptance in American homes. Today, over two thirds of all American milk is homogenized.

HONEY COOKBOOK

HONEY—A sweet sticky liquid made by honeybees from the nectar of plants. The bees suck the nectar from the flowers and store it in their honey sacs where it undergoes certain changes. Later the bees deposit the liquid in honeycombs where, with other changes, it becomes honey.

Honey is the oldest sweetener known to man. It was the only one known to Europeans until 325 B.C. when an admiral of Alexander the Great in India wrote of reeds "that produce honey, although there are no bees." Crusaders more than thirteen centuries later brought home sugar from the Holy Lands, but it was not until the 17th century, when sugar cane grown with slave labor in Brazil and the West Indies made sugar cheaper and more plentiful, that sugar replaced honey in most households.

In the early days, honey was gathered from the hives of wild bees in rocks, crevices, and trees. Later on, tame bees and their hives were part of every monastery, castle, or farm garden. As honey was the principal sweetener until the 18th century, almost every small rural household kept its bees. We read in old English manor account books how the tenants often paid their rent in honey, and in old cookbooks how hams were originally cured in honey, and fruits preserved in honey solutions. The rinsings of the combs were used to make mead, the ancient honey drink that was known to all the people of antiquity, from the Druids in Britain to the Persians.

Throughout the world honey was used not only in cooking, but also for medicinal purposes, in ceremonials, and in worship. The wax from the combs was equally part and parcel of daily life. Strips of clean linen dipped into melted wax were used to bind up wounds. The wax was used to waterproof leather, smooth sewing yarn, and even to make a kind of primitive chewing gum.

Honey is served plain on bread, muffins, biscuits, waffles, or pancakes. It blends well with butter or peanut butter for sandwiches. Honey is used in cooking in cakes, cookies, breads, and sauces. It may be used as a sweetener for milk, fruit drinks, or hot beverages and is popular on hot or cold cereal, ice cream, and fruits. Honey is also used as a glaze for baked ham. It can be used to glaze carrots and sausage links, to drizzle warm over ice cream or on broiled grapefruit, to sweeten lemonade or iced tea, to mix with cream cheese for salad, to sweeten baked apples, and to sweeten raw cranberry relish.

Availability and Purchasing Guide—Honey is available year round in jars, cans, pails, and cardboard containers. The flowers from which bees gather nectar largely determine the color, flavor, and aroma of honey. When there is no designation of the flower source on the container, the honey is a blend of different floral types. Sweet clover, clover, and alfalfa honey constitute well over half of the honey produced in this country.

Color—The color varies from the water-white of sage honey through the golden color of clover honey to the reddish brown of buckwheat honey. Usually the lighter the color of honey, the milder the flavor.

Style—Honey is available in three styles: extracted, comb, and chunk. About three fourths of the yearly crop is sold as extracted honey.

Extracted honey—This is the liquid honey separated from the comb. Some processors filter it to make it clear. It is the type most used in honey cookery.

The crystallized or granulated form of extracted honey with its fine creamy texture makes a smooth spread for breads. This is labeled granulated, creamed, fondant, spread, or spun. Whipped honey is crystallized honey which has been whipped to make it light and fluffy. Also available is honey butter, a blend of honey and butter.

Comb honey—Sections of the waxen comb, filled with honey just as the bees stored it. Section-comb is sold from the hive in wooden frames usually weighing about 1 pound. Cut-comb honey has been taken from the frames and cut into small squares. Both of these are fragile and hard to handle so few stores stock them but they are available at farm markets and roadside stands.

Chunk honey—Consists of parts of the comb in a container with extracted honey filled in around the chunks.

Granulated or Solid—Sometimes called candied, creamed or honey spread.

Storage—Honey should be stored in a tightly covered container at room temperature in a dry place. If container is left open, the honey will absorb moisture and may ferment. If tightly covered, honey may be kept for several months at room temperature (about 70°F.) at a low relative humidity. Do not store in refrigerator for the cold temperature hastens crystallization of the sugar. Crystallization will occur if kept too long but this does not harm the honey. To reliquefy, place the container in a pan of warm water until the crystals disappear. The water should not be hotter than the hand can stand.

Nutritive Food Values—Honey is almost pure carbohydrate and in no way superior to sugar. Much sweeter than sugar, it cannot be used freely by diabetics nor does it have any value in treating arthritis despite occasional claims to that effect.

3½ ounces, extracted = 304 calories
1 tablespoon, strained = 61 calories

Basic Preparation—Use low to moderate oven temperatures for baking, for honey caramelizes at a low temperature and will brown quickly. Honey cakes and cookies will remain moist longer than those made with sugar and are generally leavened with baking soda.

Honey should be measured accurately. Thick honey rounds up over the top of a measuring spoon or cup, so cut off with a spatula. Be sure to scrape all the honey from the measuring container; heated honey will pour more easily than cold honey and heating makes it easier to measure. When baking with honey, measure the shortening first and then measure the honey in the same cup. The honey will slide out easily. Honey becomes darker and thicker with age and is not desirable for baking. It can be used as a spread or syrup.

When honey is substituted for sugar it is necessary to adjust the amount of liquid in the recipe. To substitute honey for sugar: 1 cup honey contains about ¼ cup water,

therefore deduct ¼ cup liquid from the amount in the recipe for each cup of honey used. One cup honey is as sweet as 1 cup sugar so no adjustment is necessary for taste. Honey's tendency to absorb moisture presents problems when it is substituted for sugar in frostings, confections, and crisp cookies. Since the amount of moisture absorbed tends to make baked products temperamental, the amount of flour used in any recipe in which honey is substituted for sugar may have to be changed from what the recipe specifies. This has to be done by experimentation, adding flour a little at a time until the desired consistency of dough is achieved.

WAYS TO SERVE HONEY

Serve as a sweetener on hot or cold cereals.

Use to sweeten lemonade, hot spiced tea, milk drinks and eggnogs.

Sweeten whipped cream with honey for a dessert topping.

Drizzle honey over fresh fruit, fruit salad or ice cream.

Serve on waffles, pancakes, muffins and toast. Or mix with equal parts of butter for a spread. Add grated orange rind or cinnamon for variety.

Add honey to whipped sweet potatoes.

Dip orange sections in honey, then roll in toasted shredded coconut. Serve for breakfast or as a salad.

Add honey, mustard and a little ginger to canned baked beans.

Blend honey with peanut butter for a glaze for baked ham.

Stir ¼ cup honey into ¾ cup dairy sour cream for a fruit-salad dressing.

MAIN DISHES

SWEET-AND-PUNGENT HONEY BEEF AND BEANS

1 pound ground beef
1 teaspoon instant onion
¼ cup fine dry bread crumbs
½ teaspoon salt
Dash of pepper
1 egg, slightly beaten
¼ cup water
1 cup beef broth
2 tablespoons each honey and soy sauce
¼ cup cider vinegar
½ cup catsup
2 cans (1 pound each) large dried limas, partially drained

Mix beef with next 6 ingredients. Shape in 16 to 18 balls. Put beef broth in skillet, bring to boil and add meatballs. Cover and simmer about 20 minutes. Combine remaining ingredients, except beans. Add to meatballs and simmer about 10 minutes. Add beans and simmer a few minutes longer. Makes 4 to 6 servings.

PORK AND VEGETABLES, CHINESE STYLE

   2 tablespoons vegetable oil
  ½ pound pork, thinly sliced
  1 green pepper, cut in strips
  1 can (5 ounces) water chestnuts, drained and sliced
  1 can (8¼ ounces) pineapple chunks
  ½ cup broth
  1 tablespoon cornstarch
  2 tablespoons each soy sauce and honey
  ¼ cup water

Heat oil in skillet. Add pork and brown, stirring. Add green pepper and cook, stirring, a few minutes. Add water chestnuts and pineapple. Add broth and bring to boil. Combine remaining ingredients and stir into mixture. Simmer, stirring, a few minutes, or until thick and clear. Serve at once. Makes 4 servings.

BARBECUED ROAST PORK

     Pork loin roast (about 4 pounds)
  1 can (8 ounces) tomato sauce
  ¼ cup each wine vinegar and honey
  1 garlic clove, halved
  1 teaspoon chili powder
  ¼ teaspoon each pepper and salt

Score fat on roast and put meat on rack in shallow pan. Insert meat thermometer in thickest part of meat. Roast in preheated slow oven (325°F.) 35 to 45 minutes per pound, depending on thickness, or 170°F. on meat thermometer. Meanwhile, combine remaining ingredients and simmer 10 minutes; remove garlic. About ½ hour before roast is done, spoon some of mixture over roast; repeat after 15 minutes. Makes 6 servings.
NOTE: Remaining sauce can be used for beef patties or steak.

BRAISED CURRIED CHICKEN

  1 medium onion, chopped
  2 tablespoons vegetable oil
  1 frying chicken (about 2½ pounds) cut up
  1 tablespoon all-purpose flour
  1 to 2 tablespoons curry powder
  ¼ teaspoon ground ginger
  2 tablespoons each honey and soy sauce
 1½ cups canned chicken broth
  2 or 3 medium raw potatoes, each cut in 6 wedges
     Salt

Sauté onion in oil until lightly browned. Add chicken and brown on both sides. Sprinkle with flour, curry powder and ginger and stir. Then add honey, soy sauce and broth. Simmer, covered, about 35 minutes. Add potatoes and simmer 20 minutes longer, or until all is tender. Season lightly with salt if needed. Makes 4 servings.

HONEY-MARINATED LAMB

     Juice of 2 limes
  ¼ cup honey
     Shoulder of lamb (about 5 pounds)
     Salt
  1 teaspoon dried mint leaves, crushed

Combine lime juice and honey in large flat bowl. Add meat, turning to coat well with mixture. Let stand overnight in refrigerator, turning a few times. Put meat in roasting pan and reserve marinade. Score top of meat, season with salt and roast, uncovered, in preheated slow oven (325°F.) about 40 minutes to the pound, basting several times with marinade. When half done, sprinkle with mint leaves and finish roasting. Makes 6 servings.

VEGETABLES

HONEY VEGETABLES PIQUANT

  2 cups each sliced carrots and celery
     Water
  6 small green onions, cut in 1-inch pieces
  1 package (10 ounces) frozen peas
  ¼ cup each honey and cider vinegar
  2 tablespoons each soy sauce and cornstarch
     Salt

Cook carrots and celery in 1 cup water until crisp-tender, about 10 minutes. Add green onions and peas and cook about 2 minutes; add a little more water if necessary. Combine honey, vinegar and soy sauce. Add to vegetables and bring to boil. Thicken with cornstarch mixed with ¼ cup cold water. Simmer, stirring, a few minutes. Add a little salt if needed. Serve at once. Makes 4 to 6 servings.

HONEY-NUT CARROTS

  1 package (1 pound) carrots
  1 tablespoon butter
  2 teaspoons all-purpose flour
  ½ cup milk
  1 tablespoon honey
     Dash of salt
     Toasted almonds

Cook carrots in small amount of water until tender; drain. Melt butter and stir in flour. Add milk, honey and salt and cook, stirring, until thickened. Pour over carrots and sprinkle with nuts. Makes 4 servings.

SALAD DRESSINGS, SAUCES AND GLAZES

HONEY-MINT FRUIT-SALAD DRESSING

½ cup each honey and water
½ teaspoon ground cardamom
1 teaspoon crushed fresh or dried mint leaves
1 teaspoon grated lemon rind
¼ cup lemon juice
⅛ teaspoon salt
¼ cup salad or vegetable oil

Combine honey, water and cardamom. Bring to boil and simmer about 3 minutes. Add mint, chill and strain. Add remaining ingredients and shake or mix well to blend. Chill. Makes 1 cup.

HONEY FRENCH DRESSING

1 cup vegetable oil
½ cup catsup
⅓ cup each cider vinegar and honey
1 teaspoon each salt, paprika and grated onion
1 clove garlic, halved

Put all ingredients in salad dressing bottle (about 3 cups) and shake well. Let stand 10 minutes, then remove garlic. Chill and use as needed. Makes 2 cups.

HONEY BUTTER

Blend ½ cup each soft butter and honey. Store in refrigerator. If a thinner butter is desired, use ¾ to 1 cup honey to ½ cup butter. Serve with hot biscuits or on hot waffles or pancakes. Good, too, in making cinnamon toast.

Honey-Fruit Butter

To recipe for Honey Butter, add a little grated orange or lemon rind; chopped nuts, dates, or dried apricots. Serve on raisin bread.

HONEY-STRAWBERRY BUTTER

¼ cup butter, softened
½ cup honey
1 package (10 ounces) frozen sliced strawberries
Grated rind of 1 orange

Put all ingredients in blender and whirl until smooth. Serve on waffles or pancakes. Make 2 cups.
NOTE: Sliced fresh strawberries can be added, if desired.

HONEY GLAZES

For Baked Ham—Mix 1 cup honey with ½ cup orange juice, cranberry sauce, or cider. About 45 minutes before ham is baked, remove rind. Score fat and insert whole cloves in center of squares. Cover with glaze and finish baking, basting frequently.
For Carrots or Onions—In saucepan melt ¼ cup butter or margarine. Add ¼ cup honey, and blend. Add hot cooked whole carrots or white onions and cook until glazed, turning frequently.

BREADS AND SANDWICHES

HONEY-OATMEAL BREAD
[Refrigerator Method]

1 cup boiling water
1½ cups quick-cooking (not instant) rolled oats
⅓ cup honey
¼ cup butter or margarine
1 tablespoon salt
1 cup dairy sour cream
2 packages active dry yeast
½ cup warm water
2 eggs
4½ to 5 cups all-purpose flour
Honey butter

Combine first 5 ingredients and stir until butter is melted. Add sour cream and cool to lukewarm. Soften yeast in warm water (105°F. to 115°F.). Add yeast, eggs and 2 cups flour to oat mixture and beat until smooth. Add enough more flour to make a stiff dough. Turn out onto lightly floured board and knead until elastic. Cover dough on board with towel or bowl and let rest 20 minutes. Then divide in 2 equal portions and shape in 2 loaves. Put each in a greased 9 x 5 x 3-inch loaf pan. Cover pans loosely with plastic wrap and refrigerate 12 to 24 hours. When ready to bake, remove from refrigerator and let stand at room temperature 10 minutes while oven is heating. Bake in preheated moderate oven (375°F.) 50 minutes, or until done. Remove from pans at once and cool on rack. Slice when cold and serve with honey butter (equal parts honey and butter).

HONEY-PINEAPPLE BREAD

3 cups all-purpose flour
3 teaspoons baking powder
¾ teaspoon baking soda
1½ teaspoons salt
3 eggs
½ cup vegetable oil
½ cup clover honey
1 can (8¼ ounces) crushed pineapple
½ cup water
¾ cup chopped pecans or walnuts

Sift together dry ingredients. Beat eggs until thick and lemon-colored. Combine oil, honey, undrained crushed pineapple and water; mix with eggs. Add to dry ingredients, mixing only until blended. Fold in nuts and spread in greased 9 x 5 x 3-inch loaf pan. Bake in preheated moderate oven (350°F.) 1 hour. Then reduce heat to 325°F. and bake 15 minutes longer, or until center is done. Cool in pan about 5 minutes, then turn out on rack. Cool completely before slicing. Loaf can be sliced thinner if cut the day after baking. Good with whipped cream cheese.

HONEY-RAISIN QUICK BREAD

  2 tablespoons butter or margarine, softened
  ⅓ cup honey
  3 tablespoons sugar
  2 eggs
  ⅔ cup whole-wheat flour
  1 cup all-purpose flour
  ½ teaspoon each salt and baking soda
  ½ teaspoon each salt and soda
  ½ cup buttermilk
  ½ cup raisins, scalded (see Note)
  ½ cup chopped nuts
  1 teaspoon grated lemon rind

Cream first 3 ingredients thoroughly. Add eggs one at a time, beating after each until blended. Add whole-wheat flour. Then add dry ingredients alternately with buttermilk, beating until blended. Blend in remaining ingredients and pour into greased 8½ x 4½ x 2½-inch glass loaf pan. Bake in preheated slow oven (325°F.) about 50 minutes. Turn out on rack and cool thoroughly before slicing.
NOTE: To scald raisins, cover with boiling water and drain.

HONEY MUFFINS

  2 cups all-purpose flour
  1 teaspoon salt
  3 teaspoons baking powder
  1 cup milk
  ¼ cup honey
  1 egg, beaten
  ¼ cup melted shortening or vegetable oil

Sift flour, salt and baking powder. Mix milk, honey, egg and shortening. Add to flour mixture and stir only enough to dampen dry ingredients. Fill greased medium muffin pans one-half full. Bake in preheated hot oven (400°F.) 25 minutes, or until lightly browned. Makes about 12.

QUICK STICKY ROLLS

  2 tablespoons butter or margarine
  ¼ cup honey
  ½ cup broken pecans or walnuts
  1 tube (8 ounces) buttermilk biscuits

Melt butter in 10-inch piepan. Drizzle in honey, sprinkle with nuts and top with biscuits. Bake as directed on package label. Turn out on large plate and serve warm.

HONEY BLUEBERRY MUFFINS

Prepare Honey Muffins, adding ½ cup blueberries to dry ingredients.

HONEY PEANUT BUTTER MUFFINS

Prepare Honey Muffins, substituting ¼ cup peanut butter for the shortening. Mix peanut butter with honey before adding to milk and egg mixture.

SWEETS

HONEYED PEARS

  7 pounds firm ripe pears
  1 cinnamon stick
  1 teaspoon ground ginger
    Grated rind of 1 lemon
  2 cups cider vinegar
  3 pounds honey

Peel and core pears, but leave whole. Combine all other ingredients and bring to a boil. Cook pears in syrup over medium heat until tender; test with cake tester. Cook only a few pears at one time. Remove pears with slotted spoon and place in sterilized jars. Remove cinnamon stick from syrup. Cook syrup until reduced by half. Pour over pears. Seal jars. Makes about 3 quarts.
NOTE: Use firm pears, such as Seckel pears, and serve as a relish with roast meats and poultry.

HONEY MOUSSE

  3 egg yolks
  ¾ cup strained honey
  1 cup heavy cream, whipped
  2 egg whites, stiffly beaten

Beat together egg yolks and honey until light. Fold in whipped cream first, then beaten egg whites. Pack into 1½-quart mold, and freeze. Makes 6 to 8 servings.
NOTE: A fragrant flower honey, such as orange or rose honey, would be excellent for this French recipe.

PENNIES FROM HEAVEN

  ½ cup water
  1 cup honey

Combine water and honey and bring to a boil. Cook until it reaches the soft-ball stage, or 240°F. on candy thermometer. Drop hot mixture, 1 teaspoon at a time, into a dish filled with firmly packed crushed ice. The ice must be as firm as the ice in snow cones.

BUTTERED HONEY NUTS

6 ounces shelled unsalted nuts
1 tablespoon melted butter
1 tablespoon honey

Spread nuts on a cookie sheet. Bake in preheated slow oven (300°F.) for 15 minutes. Mix butter and honey and pour over nuts. Stir until nuts are completely coated with the honey mixture. Store in airtight container until ready to serve. Makes 1⅓ cups.

HONEY-CREAM DESSERT SAUCE

Mix ½ cup honey, ½ cup light cream, and 2 tablespoons butter; cook over low heat for 10 minutes. Add a little rum flavoring if desired. Makes about 1 cup.

LEMON-HONEY SPREAD

2½ cups honey
Grated rind of 1 lemon
¾ cup strained fresh lemon juice
½ bottle (⅓ cup) liquid pectin

Combine honey, lemon rind, and lemon juice in saucepan. Bring to a rolling boil, stirring constantly. Stir in pectin. Bring again to a full boil. Boil for exactly 1 minute. Remove from heat when jelly sheets from spoon. Skim; pour into hot sterilized jelly glasses. Seal with paraffin. Makes 1 quart.
NOTE: This is delicious on hot toast, pancakes, waffles, or with cold meats.

SPICED HONEY TOPPING

½ cup unsalted butter
¼ cup honey
¼ teaspoon each ground cinnamon, nutmeg, mace, ginger, or any combination of these spices desired
½ cup heavy cream, whipped

Cream butter until soft and fluffy. Beat in honey and spices. Gradually beat in whipped cream, beating until mixture is smooth and fluffy. Chill until serving time. Use as a quick topping for cakes, pancakes, waffles, or French toast. Makes about 1 cup.

HONEYSCOTCH TOPPING

½ cup sugar
¾ cup honey
¼ teaspoon salt
¼ cup butter or margarine
⅔ cup undiluted evaporated milk

In saucepan mix sugar, honey, salt, butter and ⅓ cup milk. Cook over medium heat, stirring occasionally, until a small amount of the mixture forms a soft ball when dropped in cold water (234°F. on a candy thermometer). Stir in remaining ⅓ cup milk and cook, stirring, about 3 minutes longer. Serve warm or cold on ice cream, gin-gerbread or other cake or pudding. Especially good on chocolate ice cream with a sprinkling of toasted almonds. Makes about 1½ cups.

HONEYDEW MELON—These melons belong to the muskmelon family, whose varieties include cantaloupes, honeydews, casaba, and Persian melons. Honeydews have a smooth yellowish-white rind, and their flesh is sweet and green.

Honeydews were enjoyed by the Egyptians as early as 2400 B.C. The Persians knew them before that, since muskmelons had been grown in Persia since antiquity. So fragrant were the melons that they reminded the Persians of a favorite perfume, musk. There is a tale of a jeweled Persian prince who had himself wakened at night to eat a melon that had reached the peak of perfection at that particular moment.

Honeydews were brought to the United States about eighty years ago. At first, they were grown under climatic and soil conditions similar to those of their Asiatic ancestors, in low hot river valleys and deltas, but now they flourish in all the irrigated parts of the Southwest, and in California.

Honeydew, cut into wedges, is served with lemon or lime slices. It is a fine accompaniment for meat, seafood, sliced cheese, and, served as melon balls, combines well with other fruits in salads and desserts. Wedges of honeydew are good garnished with other fruits, especially berries.

Availability—Honeydews are available from May to October, with August and September the most plentiful months. A combination of honeydew and cantaloupe balls is available frozen, in sugar pack.

Purchasing Guide—These oblong melons average 4 to 6 pounds and are 7 to 10 inches long. Select melons with creamy yellow rinds that feel velvety. Ripeness is also indicated by a softening at the blossom end.

Storage—Allow underripe melons to ripen at room temperature. Rinse ripe melons, dry well, and wrap in wax paper, foil, or plastic bag. Chill in refrigerator and use within a short time. The tissues of melons held too long at low temperatures break down rapidly at room temperature. Cut melon should be wrapped well and kept in the refrigerator.

Nutritive Food Values—Honeydew contains vitamin C. Fresh, 3½ ounces = 33 calories
Frozen melon balls, syrup pack, 3½ ounces = 62 calories

HONEYDEW RINGS WITH SHRIMP SALAD

Wash 1 medium-size ripe honeydew melon and cut into 6 rings. Save end pieces to add to fruit cup or fruit salad. Remove seeds from rings, peel, and cut into 1-inch wedges. Shred lettuce and place in each of 6 individual salad plates, over which arrange honeydew wedges in circles. Fill center of each with Shrimp Salad. Garnish with fresh parsley and serve with mayonnaise as a main-dish salad. Makes 6 servings.

Shrimp Salad

  3 cups diced cold cooked shrimps
1½ cups diced celery
  ½ teaspoon finely chopped onion
  ½ teaspoon salt, or to taste
  ⅛ teaspoon pepper
  2 tablespoons fresh lemon juice
  ⅓ cup mayonnaise

Combine all ingredients. Toss lightly, and chill. Makes 4½ cups.

AVOCADO-MELON SALAD

Halve avocados and remove seeds. Scoop out pulp carefully. Reserve shells. Cube avocado pulp. Lightly toss avocado cubes with watermelon and honeydew balls. Pile in scooped-out avocado shells. Sprinkle with lemon juice.

HONEYDEW AND ORANGE DESSERT

Place 3 cups fresh honeydew melon balls and 2 cups fresh orange sections in a bowl. Combine 6 tablespoons fresh lemon juice, 2 tablespoons fresh lime juice, and ¼ cup sugar and pour over fruit. Chill, and serve in sherbet glasses. Makes 6 servings.

HOREHOUND [*Marrubium vulgare*]—

Horehound is a member of the mint family, a large family of plants including herbs such as thyme, marjoram, and basil. It shares an aromatic odor with its better-known

relatives, but is very bitter in taste. Horehound also refers to the extract or candy made from the plant and used for coughs and colds.

Horehound is native to the Old World countries of southern Europe, northern Asia, and the Orient, but it is now found in most parts of the world except the tropics. Although it is used mainly for horehound candy, it was known to the ancient Egyptians, whose priests referred dramatically to it as "Seed of Horus," "Bull's Blood," and "The Eye of the Star." As early as the 1st century Pliny the Elder, the famous Roman scholar and historian, recommended it as a medicinal plant of great value. His contemporary, Columella, added that it had great use in killing flies. A dish of milk with horehound should be put in the place bothered by the pests. The 13th-century German philosopher and theologian, Albertus Magnus, mentions it as a cough medicine and Michael Drayton, the English poet (1563-1631) gives other explicit uses: "For comforting the spleen and liver— get for juice, Pale Horehound."

Now, after a long history as a popular medicine and cough remedy, horehound is most often used to make horehound candy, a brittle sugar candy made with brown sugar and leaves or stems of horehound. But the adventurous cook can also use a leaf to flavor braised beef or beef stew and cakes and cookies.

HORS D'OEUVRE—The literal translation of these French words is "outside of the main work." Hors-d'oeuvre are small appetizers that are not part of the menu, but serve as an introduction to a meal.

In American culinary language the terms hors-d'oeuvre, appetizer, and canapé are often used interchangeably for foods served with drinks or as a first course. To be literal about the matter: while it is true that both hors d'oeuvre and canapés are appetizers, canapés are morsels of food with a base of bread or crackers and are eaten with the fingers; hors d'oeuvre, which can be hot or cold, are often eaten at the table with a knife and fork.

An endless variety of foods lend themselves to hors-d'oeuvre: oysters, shrimps, canned fish, meat, crisp vegetables, cold cuts, and cheeses. All the foods served on a Scandinavian smörgåsbord or an Italian antipasto table are perfect hors d'oeuvre foods. Many hors d'oeuvre can be prepared beforehand, frozen, and reheated at serving time.

WILTED CUCUMBERS AND ONIONS

2 large cucumbers
1 large onion, sliced thin
1 cup cider vinegar
1 teaspoon celery seed
1 teaspoon sugar
½ teaspoon salt
¼ teaspoon pepper

Peel cucumbers; slice thin. Add remaining ingredients. Let stand in refrigerator for at least 2 hours before serving. Makes about 2 pints.

MUSHROOM PASTRIES

1 can (3 ounces) chopped mushrooms
2 tablespoons butter or margarine
2 tablespoons all-purpose flour
⅔ cup heavy cream and mushroom liquid
½ teaspoon instant bouillon
½ teaspoon paprika
¼ teaspoon pepper
  Dash of garlic salt
1 teaspoon instant minced onion
½ teaspoon bottled thick meat sauce
1 egg yolk, slightly beaten
  Potato Pastry Shells

Cook mushrooms a few minutes in butter; blend in flour. Stir in cream and liquid, bouillon, and seasonings. Cook until thickened, stirring. Stir small amount of mixture into egg yolk. Add to remainder of filling and cook for a few minutes longer. Fill Potato Pastry Shells. Bake in preheated very hot oven (450°F.) for 10 to 15 minutes. Serve warm or cool. Make these shortly before serving. Makes 30 tiny pastries.

Potato Pastry Shells

½ cup shortening
1 cup sifted all-purpose flour
½ teaspoon salt
½ cup cold riced potato

Cut shortening into flour and salt. With fork, stir in potato. Put a rounded measuring teaspoon of the mixture into each of 30 tiny tart pans. Press with finger firmly on bottom and sides of pans, leaving center hollow.

CURRY PUFFS

2 garlic cloves, mashed
1 slice of green gingerroot, mashed
1½ tablespoons minced onion
1 tablespoon curry powder (or more to taste)
2 tablespoons butter
½ pound ground beef
1 tablespoon fresh lime juice
½ teaspoon salt
  Pastry (2½ cups flour recipe) made with half butter, half lard, unbaked

Sauté garlic, gingerroot, onion, and curry powder together in butter for 5 minutes. Add meat and stir constantly until meat loses red color. Add lime juice and salt, and mix well. Cool. Roll pastry and cut into 2-inch rounds. Place a bit of meat mixture on one round. Moisten edges of round with water and cover with another pastry round, pinching edges well to hold them together. Bake on ungreased cookie sheet in preheated very hot oven (450°F.) for 15 minutes, or until nicely browned. Makes about 2 dozen.

ANCHOVY EGGS

Shell hard-cooked eggs and cut into halves lengthwise.

Spread each half with mayonnaise and top with a drained rolled anchovy fillet.

DEVILED EGGS

3 hard-cooked eggs
1½ teaspoons mayonnaise
½ teaspoon prepared mustard
½ teaspoon pickled-onion juice
¼ teaspoon celery salt
  Salt, pepper, and paprika
  Pickled onions, halved

Cut eggs into halves lengthwise. Remove yolks and mash with mayonnaise, mustard, onion juice, and celery salt. Add salt and pepper to taste. Fill whites with seasoned yolks. Sprinkle with paprika and top each egg half with half a pickled onion. Makes 3 servings.

CLAM PASTRIES

  Potato Pastry Shells (see recipe for Mushroom Pastries)
1 can (10½ ounces) minced clams, drained
1 tablespoon instant minced onion
¼ cup minced green pepper
1 egg
½ cup heavy cream
2 tablespoons minced celery and leaves
½ cup fine dry bread crumbs
1 tablespoon melted margarine
  Dash of cayenne
¾ teaspoon salt
¼ teaspoon pepper

Prepare Potato Pastry. Put 1 rounded teaspoon of pastry into each of 2 dozen 1¾-inch muffin-pan sections, pressing firmly with finger onto bottom and sides of pans; leave centers hollow. Bake in preheated very hot oven (450°F.) about 12 minutes. Mix remaining ingredients and fill baked shells. Put under broiler until golden-brown. Serve hot. Makes 2 dozen.

FRENCHED HAM AND SWISS

Cut the crusts off thin-sliced bread and spread each slice with a mixture of grated Swiss cheese and cream, mixed to a paste. Place a thin slice of ham between each two slices of bread. Dip into beaten egg; then fry in butter. Cut into bite-size pieces. Serve hot.

CHEESE OLIVE PUFFS

2 cups grated sharp Cheddar cheese
1 cup all-purpose flour
½ teaspoon paprika
¼ pound (½ cup) butter or margarine
3 to 4 dozen small stuffed olives

Combine all ingredients except olives; mix very well; chill. For each puff, use a generous teaspoonful and shape into a ball. Push finger into center to make a deep depression, put olive in and shape dough around to fully cover olive. Bake in preheated hot oven (400°F.) about 15 minutes, or until baked but not browned. Serve hot. Makes 3 to 4 dozen.

CRAB MEAT STUFFED MUSHROOMS

¼ teaspoon dry mustard
Salt and cayenne
1 teaspoon Worcestershire
½ cup hot water
½ cup soft bread crumbs
1 tablespoon cream
1 tablespoon butter
1 cup crab meat
15 to 20 medium-large mushroom caps
Melted butter
Buttered crumbs

Combine all ingredients except last 4 in saucepan and simmer about 5 minutes. Add crabmeat. Meanwhile sauté mushroom caps in melted butter. Fill with crab mixture, top with buttered crumbs, and broil just enough to brown crumbs.

CUCUMBER CUPS

1 medium cucumber, diced
¼ cup catsup
¼ cup chili sauce
2 tablespoons lemon juice
1 teaspoon Worcestershire
1 teaspoon prepared horseradish
Dash of hot pepper sauce
1 head bibb lettuce

Combine all ingredients except lettuce and toss to mix. Serve on lettuce leaves. Makes 8 to 10 servings.

TOMATO-AVOCADO HORS D'OEUVRE

1 avocado
1 teaspoon grated onion
½ teaspoon Worcestershire
Dash of cayenne
½ teaspoon salt
2 tablespoons salad oil
1 tablespoon cider vinegar or lemon juice
½ pound tomatoes
Watercress

Peel avocado and mash with fork; add seasonings, oil, and vinegar, and chill. Peel and cut tomatoes into 6 thick slices; chill. Top each tomato slice with a spoonful of avocado, and garnish with watercress. Makes 6 servings.

HERRING SALAD

2 herring in brine
2 cups diced cooked potato
1½ cups diced pickled beets
¼ cup diced sweet pickles
1 large apple, diced
1 small onion, minced
1 cup diced cooked veal
¼ cup cider vinegar
2 tablespoons water
2 tablespoons sugar
¼ teaspoon pepper
2 hard-cooked eggs, quartered

Clean and soak herring in cold water for 24 hours, changing water several times. Remove head, skin, and bones. Rinse, and drain; cut in cubes. Mix with potato, beets, pickles, apple, onion, and veal. Toss lightly. Combine vinegar, water, sugar, and pepper; pour over salad ingredients; toss lightly until all is well seasoned. Chill. Garnish with eggs. Makes 6 to 7 cups.

AVOCADO HORS D'OEUVRE

Peel avocado, cut in two, and remove seed. Slice and marinate in highly seasoned French dressing for 30 minutes. Sprinkle with chopped stuffed olives.

INDIAN BROILED SHRIMPS

1 pound raw shrimps, shelled and deveined
1 cup boiling water
1 teaspoon salt
1 teaspoon ground coriander
½ small onion, minced
8 peppercorns
¼ cup cooking oil
1 teaspoon salt
½ teaspoon ground cuminseed
1 teaspoon ground turmeric
1 tablespoon lemon juice or lime juice
1 large lemon or lime, cut into wedges

Combine shrimps, boiling water, salt, coriander, onion, and peppercorns in saucepan. Bring to a boil; cook for 2 to 3 minutes, or until shrimps just begin to turn pink; drain. Heat oil in skillet; remove from heat. Stir in salt, cuminseed, turmeric, and lemon juice. Add shrimps and toss to coat shrimps with mixture. Place shrimps in shallow baking pan. Broil under medium heat for about 5 minutes, or until shrimps are pink and slightly browned on the edges. Serve with lemon or lime wedges. Makes 4 to 6 servings.

HEAVENLY HORS D'OEUVRE MADE WITH CREAM-CHEESE PASTRY

by RUTH CONRAD BATEMAN

Delicate cream-cheese pastry is a very special treasure in the world of pastry. It puffs up beautifully when baked, has a subtle flavor and aroma unlike any other, and is amazingly easy to make. The greenest beginner can whiz it up in a few minutes. This elegant butter pastry is rich and flakes apart into the sheerest, airiest layers imaginable—much like puff paste, but it has a fragile, light quality that's unique. European cooks have long appreciated cream cheese in pastry making and have used it for many of the classics of the tea table and coffeehouse. I'm thinking in particular of the famous Viennese coffeehouse specialties. Cream-cheese pastry also has limitless possibilities in making appetizers and hors d'oeuvre. Practically all the little bite-size pastries usually made with puff paste or a rich short dough can be done with this dough, in a fraction of the time it takes for puff paste.

You can rework and reroll the dough as long as there's a scrap left. It seems impossible to overdo or ruin it. I've noticed that the rerolled pieces, when neatly stacked in layers, actually puff up more than the original. I've included suggestions for rerolling and folding the dough in most of the recipes, but this step can be omitted if you are pressed for time.

Appetizers and hors d'oeuvre made with cream-cheese pastry can be made in advance and chilled for later baking. The dough itself must be chilled overnight before it can be rolled and shaped easily. The pastries also freeze beautifully, especially the filled turnovers and rolls. I have managed to keep several of the recipes in my zero-degree freezer for three to four months without impairment of flavor. Preheat oven to specified temperature before removing frozen pastries from the freezer. Bake without defrosting. Add 5 to 10 minutes extra baking time—but watch it carefully. If cream-cheese pastry is overbaked or becomes brown (the color should be a rich, deep gold) it tends to lose some of its delicate qualities.

A variety of appetizers follows. You can always use other interesting fillings. Note that some of the recipes specify the full 2-cup recipe for pastry, others only half of it.

CREAM-CHEESE PASTRY

- 1 cup (8 ounces) butter
- 1 package (8 ounces) cream cheese
- ½ teaspoon salt
- 2 cups all-purpose flour
- 1 egg yolk
- 2 teaspoons cream or milk

Beat butter, cheese and salt together in mixer until completely smooth and blended. Work in flour to a smooth dough. (You can use mixer for this step, too, but results are superior if you work in the flour with your fingertips, a fork or rubber spatula.) Flatten dough in foil to form an 8 x 6-inch rectangle. Chill overnight. (You can chill it several days before using.) Remove from refrigerator 8 to 10 minutes before rolling. (Many recipes suggest a 30-minute wait before rolling dough, but it's easier to handle when rolled as cold as possible.) Divide dough for ease in rolling and to insure cold dough. Keep unrolled portion in refrigerator until ready to use. Roll on floured pastry cloth with floured rolling pin (see Note) or between two sheets of waxed paper. The former is easier, in my opinion, and I find absolutely no sticking when I use a pastry cloth and covered pin. I first rub cloth and pin well with flour, then shake out excess. When using waxed paper, loosen it on both sides of pastry several times as you roll. Shape as directed in specific recipes and chill before baking. Brush tops only of all pastries with egg yolk beaten with cream. Bake in preheated moderate oven (350°F.) unless otherwise specified.

NOTE: A pastry-cloth set consisting of heavy canvas cloth and knitted stockinet cover for rolling pin is available at a nominal price in most housewares departments. It's a wise investment for all your pastry making. A clean heavy dish towel stretched over your board and heavily impregnated with flour will work fine, but the canvas holds more flour without making your pastry floury.

SHRIMP TARTLETS

Minuscule pies you eat in one bite.

- ½ recipe Cream-Cheese Pastry
- ½ cup chopped cooked shrimps
- 2 green onions, chopped
- 1 teaspoon Dijon-type prepared mustard
- ¼ teaspoon dried tarragon, or chopped fresh tarragon to taste
- 1 teaspoon lemon juice
- 3 tablespoons mayonnaise
  Salt to taste

Make pastry and chill overnight. Mix remaining ingredients together for filling. Divide dough in 4 pieces. Roll each into rectangle about ⅛ inch thick, fold over itself in thirds, roll again, fold over itself again and roll ⅛ inch thick. Cut in 2-inch rounds. Stack all trimmings in layers and reroll until all dough is used. Put level measuring-teaspoonful of filling in center of rounds; moisten edges and fold over. Seal edges by crimping with floured tines of fork. Place on ungreased cookie sheet and chill 1 hour. Bake in preheated moderate oven (375°F.) 20 minutes, or until golden. Makes about 2 dozen.

HORS D'OEUVRE PATTY SHELLS

Party miniatures you can fill with anything from cold caviar to spicy hot curry, elegant seafood salads to sautéed chicken livers.

Make 1 recipe Cream-Cheese Pastry and chill overnight. Divide in 4 pieces. Roll each into rectangle ⅛ inch thick, fold over itself in thirds, roll again, fold again and roll ⅛ inch thick. Cut with 1½-inch round cutter. Put half the rounds on ungreased cookie sheet and prick. Cut out centers of remaining rounds with small doughnut cutter or thimble. Moisten edges of bottoms, top with cutout rounds and press lightly. (Centers can be baked or stacked with trimmings and rerolled.) Chill 1 hour. Bake in preheated moderate oven (350°F.) 18 to 20 minutes, or until crisp and golden. Fill just before serving (see suggestions below). Makes about 6 dozen.

CAVIAR BOUCHÉES

Season fresh dairy sour cream with finely grated onion, about 1 to 2 teaspoons per cup. Place rounded teaspoonful of cream in each Hors d'Oeuvres Patty Shell. Top with generous dab of chilled black or red caviar. Serve at once.

LOBSTER BOUCHÉES, RÉMOULADE

    2 dozen Hors d'Oeuvre Patty Shells
    1 cup cooked lobster or crab meat
    ½ cup mayonnaise
    ½ garlic clove, puréed
    ½ teaspoon dried tarragon
    1 teaspoon prepared hot mustard or ½ teaspoon dry
      mustard
    ½ teaspoon anchovy paste
    1 teaspoon capers
    1 tablespoon finely chopped gherkins

Make patty shells ahead and cool. Prepare and chill lobster. Mix remaining ingredients for rémoulade; chill. Just before serving, flake lobster in small pieces; moisten with sauce (you'll have some sauce left over for an elegant seafood salad). Place spoonful in each patty shell; top with a few extra capers.

GUACAMOLE IN SHELLS

Mash until smooth a peeled soft-ripe avocado with ¼ cup dairy sour cream. Season with ½ teaspoon salt, 2 teaspoons finely chopped onion, and ½ small tomato, peeled and chopped. Add hot seasoning to taste, few drops of hot pepper sauce, taco sauce or hot chili sauce, or ½ teaspoon prepared chili powder. Tint pale green with a few drops of food coloring. Just before serving, put a spoonful in each shell. Makes enough for 2 to 3 dozen Hors d'Oeuvres Patty Shells.

OLD-CALIFORNIA EMPANADITAS

Diminutive empanadas, or filled turnovers. The green chilies give these the genuine Spanish-California flavor, but you can substitute mild pimientos if preferred.

    ½ recipe Cream-Cheese Pastry
    1 cup finely shredded sharp Cheddar cheese
    2 tablespoons butter
    ¼ cup chopped canned green chilies, seeded and blotted dry
    2 chopped green onions
    ¼ cup chopped ripe olives
      Dried oregano to taste
      Tip of garlic, crushed (optional)

Chill pastry overnight. Combine and blend smooth remaining ingredients. Divide dough in half and roll each half ⅛ inch thick. Cut in 3-inch rounds. Stack trimmings in layers and reroll until all are used. Put a dab of filling on each round, moisten edges and fold pastry over in half-moon shapes. Pinch edges to seal. Place on ungreased cookie sheet and chill 1 hour. Bake in preheated moderate oven (350°F.) 15 to 20 minutes. Makes about 2 dozen.

ANCHOVY-ONION TRIANGLES

Use half the recipe for Cream-Cheese Pastry. Flavor ¼ cup soft butter with about 1 tablespoon anchovy paste. Mince 2 small green onions and tender tops. Add to anchovy butter and mix well. Divide chilled pastry in 2 pieces. Roll each in rectangle, fold over itself in thirds, reroll, fold again and roll into rectangle about 12 x 9 and ⅛ inch thick. Cut in 2-inch squares. In center of each square, place ¼ measuring-teaspoonful of anchovy butter. Shape in triangles and crimp edges with floured tines of fork. Put on ungreased cookie sheet and chill 1 hour. Bake in preheated moderate oven (350°F.) 20 to 25 minutes. Makes about 4 dozen.

SAUSAGE ROLL-UPS

Make and chill Cream-Cheese Pastry. Simmer 2 dozen small link sausages (or large links cut in half) in few tablespoons cold water 4 to 5 minutes. Drain; brown lightly. (If canned sausages are used, simply brown a few minutes.) Cool and cut in bite-size lengths, about 1½ inches each. Divide chilled pastry in 4 pieces; roll each ⅛ inch thick. Cut in small rectangles just big enough to wrap sausage pieces, about 2 x 2½ inches. Moisten one edge, roll up pastry around sausage, press edge to seal and pinch dough at ends. Place, seam side down, on ungreased cookie sheet. Bake in preheated moderate oven (375°F.) 15 to 20 minutes. Serve warm. Makes about 2 dozen.

BLUE DIAMONDS

Use half the recipe for Cream-Cheese Pastry. Chill overnight. Blend 1 cup crumbled blue or Roquefort cheese, 1 teaspoon Worcestershire, a few drops of hot pepper sauce and 1 egg yolk. Divide dough in 2 pieces. Roll each in rectangle, fold over itself in thirds, reroll, fold again and roll in rectangle about 12 x 9 inches. With scalloped pastry wheel, cut in strips 1½ inches wide. Space scant teaspoonful cheese mixture in small mounds about ¾ inch apart on half the strips; top with rest of strips. Press pastry lightly over filling. With pastry wheel, cut on diagonal between mounds, making diamond shapes. Trim other edges all around with wheel to crimp together and seal. Prick once with fork. Place on ungreased cookie sheet; chill 1 hour. Bake in preheated moderate oven (350°F.) 20 to 25 minutes, or until puffed and golden. Makes about 3 dozen.

FENNEL WAFERS

Add 1 teaspoon crushed fennel seed (or aniseed, if preferred) to flour for ½ recipe Cream-Cheese Pastry. Chill dough overnight. Roll in rectangle, fold over itself in thirds, roll again and fold over itself. Divide in half and roll each half in 9 -inch square. Put on ungreased cookie sheet, and with scalloped pastry wheel, mark in 1½-inch squares. Brush with egg yolk beaten with 2 teaspoons cream or milk. Sprinkle with grated Parmesan cheese. Bake in preheated moderate oven (350°F.) about 25 minutes. Cool on wire racks. Separate in wafers. Makes about 6 dozen.

POPPY-SEED ROLLS

A wonderfully subtle combination—poppy seed and cream-cheese pastry. Make half the recipe for Cream-Cheese Pastry; chill overnight. Divide in 2 pieces. Roll each ⅛ inch thick, fold over itself in thirds, roll again, fold again and roll ⅛ inch thick. With scalloped pastry wheel, cut in 2½-inch squares. Brush lightly with soft butter; sprinkle rather thickly with poppy seed. Press into dough with rolling pin. Beginning at one corner, roll to opposite corner. Moisten point; press to seal. Place, point down, on ungreased cookie sheet. Brush tops with egg yolk beaten with 2 teaspoons cream and sprinkle with more poppy seed, if desired. Chill 1 hour. Bake in preheated moderate oven (350°F.) about 15 minutes, or until puffed and golden. Makes about 2 dozen.

DILL STICKS

Add 1 teaspoon dried dillweed to flour for ½ recipe Cream-Cheese Pastry. Chill dough overnight. Roll out, fold over itself in thirds, roll again, fold again and press layers together with rolling pin. Roll to rectangle ⅛ inch thick. Cut in ½-inch strips, roll in ropes and cut in 4-inch sticks. Brush with egg yolk beaten with 2 teaspoons milk or cream; sprinkle with dillseed, and coarse salt, if desired. Place on ungreased cookie sheet and chill 1 hour. Bake in preheated moderate oven (350°F.) 15 to 18 minutes. Makes about 6½ dozen.

HORSERADISH [*Armoracia lapathifolia*]—This tall, hardy plant with glossy green, toothed leaves and large amounts of small white flowers is grown for its pungent roots. These are large, fleshy, white, and cylindrical. When grated they have a sharp flavor and a pungent odor. The roots are usually dug in the fall. Peeled and grated, served as is or in vinegar, they are used as a condiment for fish, seafood, meats, game, and in sauces.

Horseradish is a native of southeastern Europe. It has been used since antiquity, long before Christian times. It is one of the five bitter herbs of the Jewish Passover festival, when it is served symbolically during the Seder services.

Horseradish is sold fresh as a root or commercially prepared as preserved white or red horseradish, which is the grated root mixed with vinegar or beet juice and bottled. Horseradish is also sold blended into various seafood sauces.

Caloric Values—Prepared, 1 teaspoon = 3 calories
Dehydrated, 1 tablespoon = 25 calories

Basic Preparation—Fresh horseradish should be grated as soon as possible after purchase.

Dried horseradish root is also available. To reconstitute, add 2 tablespoons water to each tablespoon dried horseradish. Do this 30 minutes before serving to develop full flavor. Add ½ cup heavy cream for additional flavor. The flavor of dried horseradish is not as strong as that of fresh-grated horseradish.

HORSERADISH SAUCE

- 1 small onion, minced
- 2 tablespoons butter or margarine
- 1 cup light cream
- 2 egg yolks
- ¼ cup freshly grated or prepared horseradish, well drained
  Salt and cayenne

Brown onion lightly in butter. Add cream and bring to boil. Pour over slightly beaten egg yolks. Add horseradish and return to heat. Cook gently until slightly thickened, stirring. Season with salt and cayenne to taste, and serve hot on boiled beef, fish or tongue. Makes about 1 cup.

HORSERADISH WHIPPED-CREAM SAUCE

- ½ cup heavy cream
- ¼ cup prepared horseradish, well drained
- ¼ teaspoon salt
- 1 teaspoon sugar
  Paprika

Whip cream until thick. Fold in horseradish, salt, and sugar. Pile lightly in serving dish, and sprinkle with paprika. Serve on cold roast beef, fish, or vegetables. Makes about 1 cup.

GREEN BEANS WITH HORSERADISH SAUCE

- 1 tablespoon butter
- 2 tablespoons all-purpose flour
  Salt and pepper to taste
- 1 cup milk
- 3 tablespoons prepared horseradish
- 1 can (1 pound 4 ounces) cut green beans, drained

Melt butter in a saucepan. Stir in flour, salt, and pepper; blend. Gradually stir in milk; cook over low heat, stirring constantly, until thickened. Add horseradish and drained beans. Heat quickly. Serve with beef, lamb, or veal. Makes 4 servings.

HOT CAKE—This is another term for a griddle cake, pancake, flannel cake, or flapjack. It is a thin, golden-brown cake, always served hot and with butter, syrup, corn syrup, jelly, jam, or honey.

HOW TO SERVE HOT FOODS HOT AND COLD FOODS COLD

by GLENNA McGINNIS

Do you panic when the potatoes are done and you haven't put the steaks on to broil yet and the salad is wilting while the dessert quietly melts its heart out? Everyone does—unless she's learned a few tricks about keeping what should be served hot hot and what should be served cold cold. Whether you're trying for a photo finish for all the dishes to be served together or just keeping Junior's dinner in edible condition until his bear-hungry return from the baseball game, you'll find a solution to your problem here.

KEEPING HOT FOODS HOT

"Serve piping hot!" Of course hot dishes should go right from the source of heat to the table or buffet, but everyone knows this isn't always possible. There are ways to keep most hot foods hot for a reasonable period without impairing their flavor, nutritive value and appearance to any great degree. Naturally, soufflés, puffs and some delicate sauces won't bear standing.

Here are some tips for keeping hot dishes satisfactorily hot. This means keeping foods hot *without* letting them continue to cook.

If your oven is a modern controlled one, set it at 140°F. or at "warm" and place hot food in it. Cover with a tent of light foil, or if your casserole, Dutch oven or pan has a cover, set it slightly askew, *not* tight.

Some ranges have a warming shelf or other warming area. (If yours doesn't, consider one that does when replacing it.) In some double-oven ranges one oven is smaller than the other. If the smaller oven has a "warm" setting, it is ideal for keeping plates and food warm.

Pour or turn hot food into an ice bucket and cover. (Fill ice bucket with very hot water, let stand 5 minutes, drain and dry before placing food in it.) Serve from ice bucket. *Do not use the lightweight, unlined, Styrofoam type.*

To keep food warm for up to an hour, wrap container in two thicknesses of heavy foil or seventeen thicknesses of newspaper (a good way to transport covered dishes, etc.). To keep food warm for a short while, put container into a heavy or double brown paper bag and close it tightly.

Invest in an electric hot tray and/or trivet. They range in size from a small square or round one for one item to one that will keep many dishes warm. The better ones have "low," "medium" and "hot" settings. Also available are rolling carts with hot-tray tops. Some hot trays have clear plastic bubble covers. However, dishes may be covered as directed for keeping hot in the oven. Always preheat the hot tray.

HOT AND COLD

A controlled electric griddle, skillet, sandwich grill or buffet server set at "warm" or "low" can be used as a hot tray. Just stand the heat-proof container of food on or in it.

If food is cooked in an electric wok, buffet server, skillet, Dutch oven or hot pot, keep it hot by turning setting to "warm" and covering. A deep fryer (without fat) may also be used if it has a low enough setting.

Heat plates and containers to be used for serving. This can be done in a warm oven, on a hot tray, in an electric plate-warmer, in hot water or in some dishwashers (see use and care book).

Keep smaller amounts of food warm in the top of a double boiler over barely simmering water. Cover tightly.

Set a plate, baking dish, serving dish or platter of food on top of a pot or pan of simmering water. Cover with foil.

A chafing dish will keep foods hot if the water pan is kept properly filled and just *barely simmering.* Fondue pots can be used for gravies, soups and creamed or similar-type dishes.

If food must wait indefinitely or for a lengthy period, consider letting it cool and reheating it in a slow oven, over boiling water or on a low direct heat. (Even a rare roast of beef can be reheated in a 200°F. oven for an hour and remain rare.) If in a controlled appliance, reheat foods on "low" to "medium" setting.

Roasted meats and poultry are juicier and easier to carve if allowed to stand about 20 minutes out of the oven when done. They do not cool off noticeably if covered with a heavy foil tent. After standing, they can be kept in an oven set at 140°F. to 200°F. up to an hour.

Insulated jugs and bottles do an excellent job of keeping foods and beverages hot. Pour boiling water into container, let stand a few minutes, drain and fill with food immediately. Some insulated covered holders have a removable cookware container for oven use.

Stash hot covered casseroles, baking dishes and Dutch ovens in an insulated picnic carrier usually used to keep foods cold or hot in transit. The size and quality of insulation will determine how long food stays hot.

Wrap a common brick or tile in foil, heat in a hot oven 20 minutes, then place in a bread basket to keep bread, rolls, etc., warm. Use tongs or heavy mits when handling brick.

When food cooked out of doors must be kept warm, remove some of the coals or push three quarters of them to the back of the brazier to reduce the heat in the rest of the area, cover rack with heavy foil and put food on top. Cover lightly with foil. If food has been cooked in a container, set it on the rack.

Of course, if you have a microwave range, you can let food cool, then reheat it in a matter of minutes or seconds (check manufacturer's directions first).

A preheated electric bun warmer will of course keep rolls, biscuits, coffee cake, buns and muffins warm indefinitely. It will also keep waffles, fritters, French-fried potatoes, pancakes, crêpes, blintzes, croquettes, sausages, frankfurters, bacon and many other dry foods warm. *Be sure* to line warmer with foil shaped into a boat. For extra heat and protection, line cover of warmer with foil too. Any dish or pan that will fit into a warmer may be filled with food and kept hot.

KEEPING COLD FOODS COLD

Naturally the easiest way to keep the chill on food is to keep the food in a refrigerator, but sometimes lack of space makes this impossible, especially after the food has been arranged for serving. Chilled foods that must be transported or kept cold during service also require special care. Quite often the same device that keeps hot foods hot keeps cold foods cold when serving is delayed. Some foods usually served icy cold actually are at their best, so far as flavor, consistency and texture are concerned, when not too cold. This is true of berries, fruit, cheese, puddings, custards, cold meats, butter, margarine and salad dressings. Any leftovers must, of course, be returned to the refrigerator at once for safekeeping. Here are some ways to keep cold foods cold when serving, when holding for delayed or prolonged service and when on the go.

If possible, chill serving plates and serving dishes in the refrigerator or freezer. (Twenty minutes in the freezer is the maximum ever necessary.)

Many foods can be chilled by placing in a freezer for a few minutes. *(Do not do this to salad greens.)* To chill most efficiently, spread food out on a waxed-paper-lined cookie sheet, then cover with waxed paper. Check after 5 minutes, for it should take no longer to chill food without the outer edge freezing.

Use your ice bucket. Let ice cubes stand in it 15 minutes, empty, fill with chilled food at once and cover.

Set a carafe or a bowl of dressing, sauce or dip in slightly crushed ice in an ice bucket to serve.

Use ice buckets as wine coolers.

Fill a large bowl with slightly crushed ice to keep a smaller bowl or other container of food chilled. To hasten chilling, mix ice with a little salt. Use kosher, cooking or ice cream salt if possible.

Buy or make your own "canned" ice. Fill an appropriate plastic container with ice cubes and seal. Fill non-leaking containers that close tightly seven eighths full of water and freeze. Coffee or other cans with plastic covers,

62

plastic containers, tin boxes, some types of closable milk cartons, glass jars, etc., can be used. They can be kept in the freezer until ready for use. Containers with one or more flat surfaces work best. They may be used in many ways to keep foods cold:

Place one or more under a platter or tray of cold food. (Be sure the surface beneath is protected with foil or plastic if not moistureproof.)

Submerge a plastic container in a tureen or a salad or dessert bowl filled with chilled food. Frozen plastic bowls work well for this.

Wrap one or more, depending on size, in foil and put in a container with cans or bottles of beer or soda. Use enough containers to do the job, with some beneath and others on top.

Use to keep food cold in transit. Often the melted ice is appreciated for drinking when you're traveling or picnicking on a hot day.

Freeze water in a shallow pan or glass baking dish and place it underneath a platter or serving dish large enough to keep it from showing. (Be sure to protect surface if not moisture-proof.)

Set a serving bowl or dish in which you plan to place food in a larger bowl and fill the smaller bowl with a weight (use a plastic bag of dried beans, a foil-wrapped brick or any clean, heavy thing that fits and won't be harmed by freezing). Pour water around the smaller bowl and freeze. Remove small bowl and weight. (To loosen, pour a little hot water into bowl.) Keep big bowl frozen until serving time, then put chilled food-filled bowl in the center. For a nice touch, decorate ice with green leaves or fresh flowers.

Freeze water in a ring or other fancy mold. Unmold and use in punch bowl. You can pretty up the ice by freezing fruit slices, berries, flowers, parsley or mint sprigs in it. Fill container half full with crushed ice, arrange decorations and fill with more crushed ice. Add just enough water to fill crevices. Freeze. If you need the mold, you can unmold the ice when frozen and store it in a plastic bag. Ice rings will also decorate and keep some foods chilled during service. Fill the center with food such as shrimps, raw vegetable relishes, melon cubes or balls. A dip served in a glass bowl or fluted grapefruit shell can be placed in the center of an ice ring.

Many inexpensive, colorful, covered, pitcherlike insulated plastic containers are available for keeping liquids chilled. They're excellent for serving reconstituted frozen juices or other chilled beverages, soups, etc.

Slush mugs and other insulated mugs, tumblers and pitchers do a good job of keeping their contents icy to the last drop. Insulated containers for keeping casseroles and other serving dishes hot will also keep cold foods cold.

Cover chilled foods with a heavy foil cap when standing.

A double wrapping of foil or seventeen thicknesses of newspaper will keep containers of cold foods cold up to an hour.

Partially freeze freezable foods before traveling with them or serving them when they must stand. Take solidly frozen packages of fruit on a picnic; they will thaw but still be cold for serving.

When the refrigerator is full, put food arranged for serving in an insulated picnic carrier to keep chilled. Put a plastic bag of ice cubes or some canned ice in carrier. The cubes can be used for beverages after keeping the food cold.

HUBBARD SQUASH—A large winter squash, with a thick, hard, and warty skin. The plant is a long running vine with compound tendrils and large round leaves. There are several varieties, such as the Green, Blue, or Golden Hubbard. Some of them, like the Blue Hubbard, grow so large that they are sold in pieces or sections.

Squash, and its first cousin the pumpkin, are vegetables of American origin.

Availability and Purchasing Guide—Fresh squash is available from late August to March. It is also available canned and frozen.

Look for fresh squash with hard warted rind free from blemishes. Avoid squash with watery spots.

Storage—Will keep well for months in a dry cool place at temperature of about 50°F. For long storage, select squash which are unbruised and have stem attached.
Refrigerator shelf, uncut: 4 to 6 months
Refrigerator shelf, cooked: 4 to 5 days
Refrigerator frozen-food compartment, cooked and prepared for freezing: 2 to 3 months
Freezer, cooked and prepared for freezing: 1 year

Nutritive Food Values—Excellent source of vitamin A, ½ cup providing more than a day's quota. Contains a fair amount of iron and riboflavin.
Baked, mashed, 1 cup = 100 calories

Basic Preparation—Wash thoroughly. Cut into serving pieces or pieces small enough to handle. A large knife and a mallet are useful. Remove seeds and stringy portion. Peel if desired.

To Cook—Use 1 inch of boiling salted water and cook, covered, for 25 to 30 minutes. Remove from rind with a spoon and mash, adding seasonings and butter, or serve in individual pieces with rind.

To Bake—Season with salt and pepper. Put a small piece of butter in each piece of squash; add a little honey, if desired. Bake, covered, in preheated moderate oven (375°F.) for 45 to 60 minutes.

To Freeze—Use firm squash. Wash, cut into pieces, and remove seeds. Cover with water and cook until tender. Remove rind and press pulp through a sieve. Cool. Pack in containers, leaving ½-inch headspace. Seal.

COMPANY SQUASH PIE

    1 cup strained cooked Hubbard squash
    1 cup heavy cream
    1 cup sugar
    3 eggs, slightly beaten
    2 tablespoons brandy
    1 teaspoon each ground cinnamon and nutmeg
    ½ teaspoon ginger
    ½ teaspoon salt
       Pastry for 1-crust 9-inch pie, unbaked

Mix all ingredients, except pie shell. Pour into shell and bake in preheated moderate oven (375°F.) about 45 minutes, or until firm. Cool before serving.

HUBBARD SQUASH BAKED IN SHELLS

    3 pounds Hubbard squash
       Butter or margarine
    2 tablespoons minced onion
    2 slices of bread
    1 egg
    1 teaspoon salt
    ⅛ teaspoon pepper
       Fine cracker crumbs

Remove seeds and stringy portion, and cut squash in 2- to 3-inch pieces. Put in baking pan, and top each piece with a little butter. Bake in preheated moderate oven (350°F.) for 1 hour, or until tender. Scoop out squash, keeping shells intact. Mash squash. Cook onion lightly in 2 tablespoons butter. Add squash. Dip bread in water, squeeze dry, and add to squash. Cook over low heat, stirring frequently, for 15 minutes. Stir in egg and seasonings. Pile lightly in reserved shells and sprinkle with crumbs. Dot with butter and bake in preheated moderate oven (350°F.) for 15 minutes, or until golden-brown. Makes 6 servings.

HUBBARD SQUASH MUFFINS

    2 cups sifted all-purpose flour
    2 teaspoons baking powder
    2 tablespoons sugar
    ¾ teaspoon salt
    1 egg, beaten
    ⅔ cup milk
    1 tablespoon cooking oil
    1 cup strained cooked Hubbard squash

Sift dry ingredients into bowl. Mix egg and remaining ingredients, and add all at once to first mixture. Stir only enough to dampen dry ingredients. Fill greased muffin cups half full with the mixture, and bake in preheated very hot oven (450°F.) for 15 to 20 minutes. Makes 16 medium-size muffins.

WINTER SQUASH CASSEROLE

    2 cups mashed cooked Hubbard squash
    4 tablespoons butter or margarine
    3 tablespoons brown sugar
    1 tablespoon prepared mustard
    1 egg, slightly beaten
       Salt and pepper to taste
    ½ cup crushed corn flakes or corn-flake crumbs

Mix squash with 2 tablespoons each butter and brown sugar, mustard, egg, and salt and pepper. Put in greased shallow 1-quart baking dish or 9-inch pie pan. Mix corn flakes with remaining butter and brown sugar and sprinkle on top. Bake in preheated moderate oven (350°F.) for 20 minutes, or until thoroughly heated. Makes 4 to 6 servings.

HUCKLEBERRY—An edible berry of the species *Gaylussacia*, and the shrub of the same name. The huckleberry is dark blue to black in color and is found growing from the tropics to the arctic. There are a number of varieties, growing on low or high bushes and in an acid soil. The bushes are very prolific, and they can take over a neglected field.

In many parts of the United States the term huckleberry is also applied indiscriminately to blueberries, which belong to the genus Vaccinium, but a huckleberry is more acid than a blueberry, and each huckleberry contains ten hard little seeds, whereas a blueberry has a larger number of seeds so minute they are hardly noticeable.

Availability—June, July, and August, usually sold locally since they do not ship well.

Purchasing Guide—Select clean, plump, and dry berries with a deep-black or dark-blue color. Berries may have a light bloom; this varies with the species.
1 pint = about 2 cups berries

Storage—Sort first if necessary, but do not wash until ready to use.
Kitchen shelf: 1 to 2 days
Refrigerator shelf: 1 to 2 weeks
Refrigerator frozen-food compartment, prepared for freezing: 2 to 3 months
Freezer, prepared for freezing: 1 year

Caloric Values
3½ ounces = 62 calories

Basic Preparation—Wash berries gently just before using. Do not allow berries to soak in water. Remove any stems. Serve huckleberries with cream or milk. Use to make jam, in tarts, puddings, and pies, and in any recipe calling for blueberries.
To Freeze—Wash berries in cold water. Drain. Dip berries into boiling water for 20 to 30 seconds. Chill quickly in cold water.
To Freeze, Loose Pack—Spread berries in a single layer on a shallow pan with sides or tray. Freeze until firm. Pour into freezer container, leaving no headspace.
To Freeze, Sugar Pack—Mix 4 cups berries with ½ cup sugar. Stir gently until sugar dissolves. Pack in containers, leaving ½-inch headspace. Seal.

HUCKLEBERRY GRIDDLE CAKES

2 cups all-purpose flour
2 teaspoons baking powder
½ teaspoon salt
3 tablespoons sugar
1 egg, well beaten
2 cups milk
2 cups well-drained huckleberries, coated lightly with flour

Sift flour with baking powder, salt, and sugar. Beat egg with milk and add all at once to flour. Beat until smooth. Fold in huckleberries. Bake pancakes on a lightly greased hot griddle. Serve with whipped butter and honey, if desired. Makes 4 to 6 servings.

HUCKLEBERRY SHORTCAKE

4 cups sifted all-purpose flour
4 teaspoons baking powder
1 teaspoon salt
½ cup butter or margarine
2 eggs
1¼ cups milk
4 cups well-drained huckleberries
Sugar
Grated orange rind

Sift flour with baking powder and salt. Cut in butter until mixture resembles coarse cornmeal. Beat egg with milk

and add all at once to flour mixture. Stir only until just blended. Place dough on a lightly floured board and knead a few times to form dough into a smooth ball. Cut dough into halves and roll each half into a rectangle 12 x 8 inches. Place one oblong on a well-greased cookie sheet. Mix huckleberries with sugar and orange rind and spread on dough, making a layer of berries about ¾ inch thick. Moisten outside edges of rectangle with water. Top with second rectangle and pinch edges to seal. Bake in preheated moderate oven (350°F.) for 30 to 40 minutes, or until top is deeply browned. Cut into squares and serve with thick cream. Makes 10 to 12 servings.

HUCKLEBERRY COTTAGE PUDDING

¼ cup butter or margarine
⅔ cup sugar
1 egg, slightly beaten
2 cups all-purpose flour
3 teaspoons baking powder
¼ teaspoon salt
1 cup huckleberries
1 cup milk
Lemon Hard Sauce

Cream butter until light and fluffy. Add sugar and beat until light. Add egg and beat well. Sift dry ingredients; sprinkle ¼ cup of mixture on berries. Add remainder alternately with milk to first mixture, beating until smooth. Fold in berries. Bake in greased pan, 8 x 8 x 2 inches, in preheated moderate oven (350°F.) about 35 minutes. Serve hot with Lemon Hard Sauce. Makes 6 large or 9 small servings.

HUCKLEBERRY CREAM-CHEESE PIE

1½ cups huckleberries
12 ounces cream cheese
1 tablespoon all-purpose flour
3 egg yolks
2 egg whites
3 tablespoons sugar
½ teaspoon salt
¾ cup dairy sour cream
Pastry for 1-crust 8-inch pie, unbaked

Rinse huckleberries in colander and let drain thoroughly, or dry on paper towels. With fork stir softened cream cheese until smooth. Add flour and mix thoroughly. Lightly beat egg yolks with 1 egg white; add sugar, salt, and sour cream. Combine egg mixture with cream-cheese mixture, stirring well. Line 8-inch pie pan with pastry and brush lightly with remaining egg white. Dust huckleberries lightly with flour and place in thick layer in pastry-lined pan. Smooth cream-cheese mixture evenly over huckleberries and bake in preheated moderate oven (350°F.) for 30 minutes, or until set. Makes 6 servings.

HUNGARIAN COOKERY

by Nika Hazelton

Hungary is a country blessed with an original and delicious cookery of her own, developed and refined by a people who care greatly for excellent food.

Hungary lies at the crossroads of West and East. Through the centuries, many people crossed, fought, and settled in the lands of the Magyars, which is the name the Hungárians use for themselves. The Magyars came from the distant slopes of the eastern part of the Ural Mountains, in what is now Russia, as long ago as 896 A.D., and founded their state on the banks of the Danube. Turks, Slovaks, Serbs, Croats, Poles, Slovenes, Russians, Germans, and Austrians mingled in Hungary in the centuries that followed and contributed to the Hungarian kitchen and to the country's food habits and traditions.

The Turkish conquest of Hungary in the 16th and 17th centuries left a lasting influence, for the Turks introduced coffee, melons, spices, nuts, and, above all, the use of paprika.

But strains from even farther away can be found in Hungarian cooking. Through the centuries, the cooks brought by the princes and princesses who married Hungary's royalty introduced new ways of cooking and seasoning. The influence of the courts of France and Austria was especially marked since the Hungarians adopted their ways with enthusiasm, as we see in the old Hungarian cookbooks which are full of French cooking terms. In their turn, these foreign recipes were translated into dishes that are still part and parcel of present-day Hungarian cooking, such as the meats and fish dishes cooked with wine, the use of fruit, etc. To Austrian influences goes some of the credit for Hungary's excellent dumplings and superlative cakes, to which the Hungarians added their own twist, such as filling strudel dough with ground poppy seed.

Another factor that contributed to the excellence of Hungarian food was the resources of the country. In the warm yet temperate climate, fruits and vegetables grow to rare lusciousness. The plains yielded tender beef and lamb, the farmyards fattened pigs into famous hams and pork products, and fattened geese and ducks as well. Hungarian goose liver is comparable to the renowned goose liver of Alsace. The deep forests abounded in game, including wild boar, and hunting was a favorite sport. Hungary has no access to the sea, but the trout of her mountain streams and, above all, the unrivaled *fogas,* a very white and extremely delicate kind of perch-pike found in beautiful Lake Balaton, is famous throughout Europe. And finally, the wheat of the great Hungarian plains was considered the finest for baking. In the old days, European cookbooks specified that fine baking required Hungarian flour.

The most typical ingredients of Hungarian cooking are paprika powder, onions, green peppers, tomatoes, sour cream, lard or goose fat, instead of other shortenings, noodles and other pastas.

The Hungarian housewife does not use paprika as a garnish the way we do, but by teaspoonfuls or tablespoonfuls as an integral part of a meat, soup, or vegetable dish, to give it flavor and a rosy color.

The color of paprika is a fiery-red, but the spice itself need not be any hotter than pepper, if as hot. This spice with the exquisite aroma and mildly pungent taste is made from the capsicum pepper, which grows especially well on Hungarian soil. The ground spice is produced from special pepper varieties which are grown for the prupose and widely exported. There are many degrees of pungency in the spice, ranging from the hottest to the mildest, and they are graded according to government specifications. It is important that paprika, whatever its degree of pungency, be used as freshly ground as possible, when fragrance is most enticing. In fact, Hungarian paprika, called "noble and sweet" by the people, has a fragrance unmatched by the paprika of any other country. In cooking, it should not be added to the sizzling fat, but rather to the dish, one school of cooks says. And of course, hot or mild paprika, and the grades in between, are a matter of individual preference, in Hungary as well as anywhere else.

Other Hungarian food specialties whose fame has spread are the sausages, Herz salami, quite possibly the best dry salami ever made, and *tarhonya,* a kneaded dough of flour and eggs which is broken into pieces the size of small peas. The paste is then dried quite hard, so that it will keep for a long time. *Tarhonya* can be cooked in water or broth like noodles and served like them as an accompaniment with gravy dishes, or browned first in lard with minced onions and paprika and then simmered in as much liquid as it will absorb.

When it comes to noodles, the Hungarians use them often in an original manner combined with cottage cheese, nuts, or poppy seeds. Some noodle dishes are sugared and used as desserts.

The most famous Hungarian desserts are dumplings filled with fresh fruit, pancakes, and strudels. Every kind of fruit and nuts is used for strudel fillings, and there are also nonsweet ones, such as cabbage and cheese.

Among the many delicious fruits grown in Hungary which are liberally used by all of the population fresh, as compotes, or in jams, special mention must be made of the apricots. They are exquisite in flavor and either as fruit or distilled into brandy, they are delicious.

SOUPS

SÓSKA LEVES
[Sorrel Soup]

- ½ pound sorrel
- 4 cups chicken consommé
- 2 egg yolks
- 2 tablespoons heavy cream
- Salt and white pepper
- 1 cup dairy sour cream

Clean sorrel and chop into fine pieces. Cook for 10 minutes in consommé. Mix egg yolks and cream and add slowly to soup, beating constantly with wire whisk. Season to taste. Cool, then chill in refrigerator. Just before serving, beat in sour cream, and top with a spoonful of the sour cream. Makes 4 servings.

NOTE: To serve hot, beat in sour cream and heat gently.

GULYÁSLEVES
[Goulash Soup]

3 medium onions, chopped
2 tablespoons butter or margarine
1½ pounds beef chuck, cut into ½-inch cubes
2 tablespoons paprika
½ teaspoon caraway seeds
1 garlic clove, crushed
½ teaspoon grated lemon rind
4 cups beef bouillon
   Salt to taste
2 medium raw potatoes, peeled and cut into ½-inch cubes

Cook onions in butter until golden. Add beef and paprika and cook, stirring constantly, until slightly browned. Add caraway, garlic, lemon rind, and bouillon. Season to taste. Simmer, covered, for 1½ hours. Add potato and cook for 30 minutes longer. Makes 4 to 6 servings.

MEAT, FISH, AND POULTRY

MAGYAR GULYÁS
[Hungarian Goulash]

2 pounds lean beef chuck, cut into 1½-inch squares
   Salt and pepper to taste
¼ pound lard or unsalted butter
1 to 1½ pounds onions, sliced
2 tablespoons sweet paprika or 1 tablespoon hot paprika
1 tablespoon all-purpose flour
   Hot water or dry white wine
2 cups dairy sour cream

Season meat with salt and pepper. Heat lard almost to smoking point in heavy saucepan; add meat and brown on all sides; add onions. Stir in paprika; there should be enough paprika to color meat and onions a reddish brown. Over low heat cook, stirring, until all the pan juices have been absorbed. Sprinkle with flour and cook for 1 minute. Add hot water or wine to cover meat. Simmer, covered, over low heat for 1 to 1½ hours, until meat is tender and the onions have cooked down to a pulp. Check occasionally for liquid; if necessary, add a little more. Stir

in sour cream and heat through but do not boil. Serve with buttered noodles sprinkled with caraway seeds. Makes 4 to 6 servings.

MAJORANNÁS TOKÁNY
[Beef Stew with Marjoram]

2 pounds beef chuck or round, in one piece
2 tablespoons lard
1 pound (3 medium) onions, coarsely chopped
2 teaspoons dried marjoram
   Salt
   Pepper (there should be quite a lot of pepper)
2 cups water
1½ cups dry white wine
½ pound lean bacon
1 cup dairy sour cream

Cut beef into strips 1 x 3 inches. Heat lard in Dutch oven to smoking point. Cook onion in hot lard until soft and golden; add meat. Sprinkle with marjoram and season to taste with salt and pepper. Add water and wine. Simmer, covered, over lowest possible heat for 45 minutes, or until half done. While meat is cooking, cut bacon into strips the same size as the meat. Cook bacon partially until limp and until most of the grease has cooked out. Drain bacon and add to meat. Continue to simmer, covered, for 45 minutes longer, or until meat is tender. Remove from heat and stir in sour cream. Return to heat; heat through but do not boil again. Serve with rice or noodles. Makes 4 to 6 servings.

BÁRÁNY PÖRKÖLT ÁRPAKÁSÁVAL
[Lamb and Barley Stew]

2 pounds lamb shoulder, cut up and trimmed of excess fat
   Flour
   Salt and pepper to taste
2 tablespoons cooking oil
1 cup chopped onions
4 medium tomatoes, quartered
2 bay leaves
2 tablespoons pearl barley
6 dried prunes, pitted
1 garlic clove, minced
1 teaspoon paprika
1 cup water or bouillon
2 tablespoons sweet or dairy sour cream (optional)

Coat lamb pieces evenly with flour mixed with salt and pepper. Brown on all sides in oil in heavy skillet or Dutch oven. Add onions and cook until onions are soft but not brown. Add all other ingredients except cream. Cover and simmer over low heat for 1½ to 2 hours; or bake in preheated very slow oven (250°F.) for 3 to 4 hours. (This stew should cook as slowly as possible.) Check for moisture; if too dry, add a little more water or bouillon, 1 tablespoon at a time. Remove from heat and stir in cream. Do not cook again. Makes 4 to 6 servings.

SAVANYU ÖKÖRFAROK
[Sour Oxtail Ragout]

2 oxtails, disjointed
½ cup cider vinegar
1 onion
1 carrot
1 garlic clove
Grated rind of 1 lemon
2 bay leaves
2 whole cloves
6 peppercorns
½ teaspoon salt
Boiling water
2 tablespoons fat
2 tablespoons all-purpose flour
¼ cup dairy sour cream
Paprika

In a large saucepan combine oxtails with vinegar, onion, carrot, and seasonings. Cover with boiling water and cook, covered, over low heat until meat is tender. Drain, and reserve 1 cup liquid. Melt fat and stir in flour. Gradually stir in reserved liquid. Cook over low heat, stirring constantly, until smooth and thickened. Add oxtail pieces. Just before serving, stir in sour cream and sprinkle with paprika. Makes 6 servings.

Savanyu Ökörfarok

HÉT VEZÉR TOKÁNY
[Seven Chieftains' Tokany]

2 tablespoons lard
4 slices of bacon
½ pound onions, sliced
1 tablespoon paprika
1 pound lean boneless pork, cut into strips 3 x 1 inch
1 pound beef chuck or round, cut into strips 3 x 1 inch
1 pound boneless veal, cut into strips 3 x 1 inch
1 cup hot water
2 green peppers cut into strips
2 small tomatoes, peeled, seeded, and chopped
Salt and pepper
½ cup dairy sour cream
1 tablespoon all-purpose flour

Heat lard in Dutch oven. Cook bacon until limp. Remove bacon and cut into strips; reserve. Cook onions in hot fat until soft and golden-brown. Stir in paprika. Cook for 2 minutes. Add pork. Simmer, covered, over low heat for 30 minutes. Add beef and veal and simmer for 45 minutes. Add water to prevent sticking. Add green peppers, tomatoes, salt and pepper to taste, and bacon. Simmer, covered, for 20 minutes, or until peppers are tender, stirring occasionally. Combine sour cream and flour to a smooth paste. Stir into stew. Simmer over low heat

Diós Tészta

for 4 minutes, stirring constantly. Serve with steamed rice or noodles. Makes 6 to 8 servings.
NOTE: Hungarians often combine different meats in their stews for a tastier effect. The seven chieftains are national heroes who led the Magyars to the present country in the 9th century.

SZÉKELY GULYÁS
[Szekely Sauerkraut Goulash]

- 1 pound boneless beef chuck
- 1 pound boneless veal shoulder
- ½ pound lean pork
- 2 small onions, sliced
- 2 teaspoons butter
- 1 pound sauerkraut
  A few peppercorns
- 2 teaspoons paprika
- 1 teaspoon caraway seeds
- 1 cup bouillon
- 2 cups dairy sour cream

Cut meat into cubes as you would for any stew. Cook onions in butter to golden-yellow. Add meat, sauerkraut, peppercorns, paprika, caraway seeds, and bouillon. Cook, covered, about 1 hour. Very slowly pour juice from the cooking pan into sour cream, stirring all the while so it will not curdle. Thicken with a little flour and water paste if necessary. Pour the mixture back into the pan and let it stand on an asbestos pad over low heat until used. It improves with waiting and can be reheated. The use of salt depends on taste and on the saltiness of the sauerkraut. If the kraut is too salty, wash it. Makes 5 to 6 servings.

BORJÚ PÖRKÖLT
[Veal Paprika]

- 2 pounds veal cutlet, sliced thin
- 2 tablespoons butter or margarine
- 1 garlic clove, minced
- 1 tablespoon paprika
- 1 cup water
- 1 cup heavy cream
- ½ teaspoon salt

Pound veal well. Pat dry with absorbent paper. Melt butter. Brown veal quickly with garlic and paprika. Add water, cover, and simmer for 1 hour. Add cream and salt. Heat through, and serve. Makes 4 to 6 servings.

DISZNÓKARAJ MAGYAROSAN
[Hungarian Pork Chops]

- 6 pork chops, about ½ inch thick
  Salt and pepper
- 1 medium onion, chopped
- 1 garlic clove, minced
- 3 tablespoons lard or butter
- 1 bay leaf
- ¾ cup chicken bouillon
- 1 cup dairy sour cream
- 2 teaspoons paprika

Trim excess fat from pork chops and sprinkle with salt and pepper. Sauté onion and garlic in lard until soft and golden. Push aside or remove from skillet. Add pork chops and brown on all sides. Pour off fat. Lower heat and add bay leaf and bouillon. Cook, covered, over low heat about 1 hour. Transfer chops to hot serving plate and keep hot. Reduce pan juices to half by cooking over high heat. Add sour cream and paprika and blend thoroughly with pan juices. Heat through, but do not boil. Pour sauce over chops. Makes 4 to 6 servings.

CSIRKE PAPRIKÁS
[Chicken Paprika with Sour Cream]

- 1 frying chicken (about 3 pounds), cut into pieces
- 2 medium onions, chopped fine
- 2 tablespoons paprika
- 3 tablespoons butter or margarine
- ½ cup chicken bouillon
- 1 cup dairy sour cream
  Salt and pepper

Brown chicken, onions, and paprika in butter. Add bouillon. Simmer, covered, over low heat for 30 minutes, or until tender. Stir in sour cream and heat through. Season to taste. Makes 4 servings.

SONKÁS PALACSINTA
[Pancakes Layered with Minced Ham]

- 1 cup cold milk
- 1 cup cold water
- 4 eggs
- 1 teaspoon salt
- 2 cups sifted all-purpose flour
- ¼ cup melted butter or margarine
  Ham Filling
- ¼ cup buttered bread crumbs

Beat together milk, water, eggs, and salt. Add flour gradually, beating constantly until smooth. Add melted butter. The consistency should be that of heavy cream. Refrigerate at least 1 hour before baking pancakes. Lightly grease a 7-inch crêpe pan or skillet, heat to smoking, and pour in just enough of the batter to coat the bottom lightly. Tilt pan to be sure that all is covered. Brown lightly on one side. Turn and brown on the other. Put one pancake in a baking dish, spread some of the Ham Filling on it, then top with another pancake. Keep warm in preheated slow oven (300°F.). Continue layering in this manner until all pancakes (about 12) and Ham Filling are used. Sprinkle top with buttered bread crumbs. Bake in preheated moderate oven (350°F.) for 20 minutes, until filling is set. Cut into wedges to serve. Makes 8 servings.

Ham Filling

- 1 pound cooked ham, minced
- 4 eggs, separated
- 1 cup dairy sour cream
  Salt

Mix ham, egg yolks, and sour cream. Beat egg whites until stiff. Fold into mixture. Season to taste.

SZEGEDI CSIRKE PAPRIKÁS
[Chicken Stew]

3 tablespoons lard
4 large onions, sliced
1 tablespoon paprika
1 teaspoon caraway seeds, crushed
2 frying chickens (about 3 pounds each), cut into
  pieces
  Salt
3 cups water
1 pound raw potatoes, peeled and quartered
3 medium carrots, thickly sliced
3 cups canned tomatoes
  Pepper

Heat lard in Dutch oven. When smoking hot, add onions.
Cook until soft and golden-brown. Add paprika, caraway
seeds, and chicken pieces. Toss and cook over medium
heat for 5 to 10 minutes, or until chickens are golden-
brown. Sprinkle with salt; add water. Simmer, covered,
over lowest possible heat for 30 minutes, or until chicken
is half done. Add potatoes, carrots, and canned tomatoes.
Season to taste with salt and pepper. Continue to simmer,
covered, for 30 minutes longer, or until chicken and
vegetables are tender. Serve with buttered *tarhonya* or
buttered noodles and a green salad. Makes 6 servings.

TEJFELES SÜLT PONTY
[Pike Baked in Cream]

2 pounds pike fillets
1 teaspoon caraway seeds
½ teaspoon salt
½ cup fine dried bread crumbs
1 cup dairy sour cream

Place ⅓ of fish in greased baking dish. Sprinkle with ⅓
of caraway seeds, salt, bread crumbs, and sour cream.
Repeat until all ingredients are used. Bake in preheated
slow oven (325°F.) for 20 to 30 minutes, or until fish is
flaky. Makes 4 servings.

VEGETABLES, PASTAS, AND SALADS

RAKOTT KRUMPLI
[Potato and Egg Casserole]

6 slices of bacon, chopped
1 tablespoon butter
6 medium raw potatoes, boiled and sliced
6 hard-cooked eggs, sliced
  Salt and pepper
2 tablespoons chopped parsley
½ to ⅔ cup dairy sour cream

Cook bacon in hot butter until crisp. Drain; reserve fat.
Place alternate layers of potatoes, hard-cooked eggs, and
bacon in greased 2-quart baking dish. Season each layer
with salt and pepper to taste, but remember that bacon
may be very salty. Sprinkle with parsley. Stir reserved
bacon fat into sour cream. Pour over potato mixture.
Bake, covered, in preheated moderate oven (350°F.) for
15 to 20 minutes, or until golden. Makes 4 servings.

TEJFELES BAFFÖZELÉK
[Dried Beans in Sour Cream]

½ pound dried white beans, washed
  Salt
1 medium onion, chopped fine
2 tablespoons butter or margarine
2 tablespoons all-purpose flour
1 tablespoon cider vinegar
1 cup water
½ cup dairy sour cream

Soak beans in water overnight. Drain. Cover with fresh
water, add 1 teaspoon salt, and simmer for 2 to 3 hours,
or until tender. Brown onion in butter; blend in flour. Add
vinegar and water, and stir until thickened. Drain beans
when done and mix into sauce. Stir in sour cream and
allow to heat through but do not boil. Season to taste.
Makes 4 to 6 servings.

ZELLER SALÁTA
[Celery-Root Salad]

3 celery roots
  Salt, pepper, and mayonnaise

Peel celery root and cut into julienne strips. Drop into
boiling salted water and cook for 15 minutes, until tender.
Drain and cool. Season with salt, pepper, and mayonnaise to taste. Chill for 2 hours. Makes 6 servings.

ZÖLD PAPRIKA SALÁTA
[Green-Pepper Salad]

4 large green peppers
½ cup olive oil
2 to 4 tablespoons cider vinegar, depending on
  strength (dressing should be mild)
  Salt and pepper to taste
½ teaspoon sugar

Remove seeds and inside ribs of peppers. Cut into ½-
inch slices. Drop for 1 minute into boiling water. Drain.
Place in glass serving dish. Make a French dressing with
remaining ingredients. Pour over peppers. Marinate at
room temperature for 1 hour. Serve as is or chilled. Makes
4 servings.

TARHONYA
[Egg Barley]

4 cups all-purpose flour
5 eggs
1 teaspoon salt

Sift flour. Make a well in the center. Break eggs into well and mix together with flour; add salt. Knead dough until it is perfectly smooth. Allow to dry a little. Chop with a knife until pieces resemble barley in size. Or press through a special sieve which will make pieces of the same size. Spread pieces out and allow to dry for 24 hours. Store in jars with tight lids. To cook, brown *tarhonya* lightly in butter; then add water to cover and simmer for 15 minutes. Or, if it is to be served in a soup, it can be cooked in that without browning.

DIÓS TÉSZTA
[Boiled Noodles with Walnuts]

8 ounces fine noodles
½ cup chopped walnuts
2 tablespoons butter or margarine

Cook noodles in salted water according to package directions. Drain. Meantime, sauté walnuts in butter until lightly browned. Add to drained noodles. Place in top part of double boiler over hot water for 30 minutes before serving to meld the flavors. Makes 4 servings.

MAKOS TÉSZTA
[Boiled Noodles with Poppy Seeds]

Cook noodles as above. Drain. Toss with ¼ cup butter and 2 tablespoons ground poppy seeds. Omit nuts. Or substitute 1 tablespoon caraway seeds for the poppy seeds. Omit nuts.

DESSERTS

HUSZÁRCSÓK
[Hussar's Kisses]

⅔ cup unsalted butter (must be butter)
⅓ cup sugar
1 egg yolk
2 eggs
1⅓ cups sifted all-purpose flour
⅓ cup finely chopped nuts
⅓ cup raspberry jam

Cream butter with sugar. Add egg yolk and 1 egg. Blend in flour. Chill. Pinch off walnut-size pieces of dough and shape into balls with floured hands. Put on ungreased cookie sheet. With pencil or finger make a deep depression in center of each ball. Beat remaining egg and brush cookies with it. Sprinkle with nuts. Bake in preheated moderate oven (350°F.) for 15 minutes, or until golden. Cool. Fill depressions with jam. Makes about 32.

ALMÁSRÉTES
[Apple Strudel]

Strudel Dough:

1 egg, slightly beaten
½ teaspoon salt
Cooking oil
1 cup all-purpose flour
1 tablespoon warm water
Butter
Sugar

Apple Filling:

¼ cup seedless raisins
2 tablespoons water
6 to 8 medium apples
Sugar
¾ cup fine soft bread crumbs
⅓ cup butter
½ cup chopped blanched almonds
1 tablespoon ground cinnamon

Mix egg, salt, 2 tablespoons oil, and flour. Add warm water and mix to form soft dough. On lightly floured board knead for 10 to 15 minutes., or until dough is very smooth and very elastic. Brush top with oil and cover with a warm bowl. Let stand for 30 minutes. Soak raisins in water. Peel apples, slice thin, and sprinkle with ½ cup sugar. Brown crumbs in ⅓ cup butter.

Roll strudel dough as thin as possible on a large lightly floured cloth about 36 inches square. Melt ½ cup butter and brush some on top of dough. With palms up, slip hands underneath dough and stretch dough carefully to paper thinness, working from the center out. If edges remain thick, cut them off. Dough should almost cover the cloth. Brush with more melted butter to keep pliable. Pile apples in a row about 2 inches from one end of dough. Combine undrained raisins, bread crumbs, almonds, cinnamon, and ½ cup sugar; spread over remaining dough. Fold over the dough about 1 inch along the edges of dough at the top and bottom of the row of apples. Lift edges of cloth nearest the apples so that the dough falls over apples; continue to roll dough over and over with the help of cloth. Put roll on cookie sheet in a U shape. Bake in preheated hot oven (400°F.) for 30 minutes. Brush 2 or 3 times with melted butter. Five minutes before strudel is done, sprinkle thickly with more sugar. Makes 1 dozen 3-inch pieces.

CHEESE STRUDEL

1 recipe Strudel Dough
1 tablespoon butter
¼ cup sugar
4 eggs
1 pound cottage cheese, sieved
3 tablespoons dairy sour cream
⅓ cup seedless raisins
2 tablespoons melted butter

Prepare dough as for Apple Strudel. Cream butter with sugar. Beat in eggs. Mix in cottage cheese, sour cream, and raisins. Spread mixture evenly over the dough which has been brushed with melted butter. Bake as for Apple Strudel.

NUT STRUDEL

1 recipe Strudel Dough
1 cup ground nuts
1 cup sugar
½ cup milk
Grated rind of 1 lemon
½ cup golden raisins
2 tablespoons melted butter

Prepare dough as for Apple Strudel. Mix nuts with sugar and milk. Cook over low heat until mixture is slightly thickened. Add lemon rind and raisins. Spread filling on strudel dough which has been brushed with melted butter. Bake as for Apple Strudel.

POPPY-SEED STRUDEL

1 recipe Strudel Dough
1 pound freshly ground poppy seeds
½ cup sugar
Grated rind of 1 lemon
½ cup milk
⅓ cup raisins
2 tablespoons melted butter

Prepare dough as for Apple Strudel. Mix poppy seeds with sugar, lemon rind, and milk. Cook over low heat until thickened. Add raisins and blend well. Cool, and then spread on strudel dough which has been brushed with melted butter. Bake as for Apple Strudel.

Sóska Leves   Sonkás Palacsinta   Cseresznye Kisütve

CHERRY STRUDEL

1 recipe Strudel Dough
2 tablespoons melted butter
½ cup dry bread crumbs
½ cup ground blanched almonds
1½ cups dark sweet cherries, pitted
1 cup sugar
¼ cup dairy sour cream

Prepare dough as for Apple Strudel. Brush with melted butter and sprinkle with bread crumbs and almonds. Scatter cherries over the dough and sprinkle with sugar. Roll up and brush with sour cream. Bake as for Apple Strudel.

CABBAGE STRUDEL

3½ cups grated cabbage
1 tablespoon salt
1½ tablespoons sugar
2 tablespoons fat
½ teaspoon white pepper
1 recipe Strudel Dough
2 tablespoons melted butter

Mix cabbage with salt. Let stand for 30 minutes. Squeeze out liquid. Add sugar and cabbage to hot fat and cook until lightly browned and tender. Stir in pepper. Prepare dough as for Apple Strudel. Spread cooled cabbage mixture over the dough which has been brushed with melted butter. Bake as for Apple Strudel.

SZILVÁS GOMBÓC
[Plum Dumplings]

12 plums
   Almond extract
12 small lumps of sugar
⅓ cup butter
2 cups sifted all-purpose flour
2 cups cooked potatoes, riced and chilled
1 teaspoon salt
2 eggs
2 tablespoons butter
¾ cup fine dry bread crumbs

Cut plums just enough to remove pits. Keep fruit as intact as possible. Sprinkle a drop of almond extract on each lump of sugar. Push 1 sugar lump into cavity of each fruit. With pastry cutter or two knives, cut butter into flour until it resembles coarse meal. Stir in potatoes and salt. Add eggs and mix thoroughly. With hands work dough until smooth. On slightly floured board roll out dough ¼ inch thick. Cut into 3- or 4-inch squares, depending on size of fruit. Place a plum on each square. Moisten edges of dough and fold dough over fruit. Pinch edges together. With floured hands roll dumplings into round balls. Cook a few at a time in kettle of gently boiling water. The water must continue to boil. Cook for 10 to 15 minutes,

depending on size. Carefully lift out with slotted spoon and keep warm. Heat butter and brown crumbs in it. Roll dumplings in buttered crumbs. Serve hot. Makes 6 servings.
Variation—Use apricots instead of plums.

CSERESZNYE KISÜTVE
[Deep-Fried Cherries]

1 cup sifted all-purpose flour
¼ cup sugar
½ teaspoon ground cinnamon
⅓ cup milk
½ cup dry white wine
3 eggs, lightly beaten
1 pound ripe firm sweet cherries, with stems
   Shortening for deep frying
   Confectioners' sugar

Combine flour, sugar, and cinnamon. Stir in milk and wine to make a smooth paste. Beat in eggs. Let batter rest for 30 minutes. Tie 4 or 5 cherries into clusters with thread. Dip each cluster into batter, making sure cherries are well coated. Carefully lower clusters into hot deep fat (370°F. on frying thermometer). When browned, remove with slotted spoon. Cook only a few clusters at one time. Drain on absorbent paper and sprinkle with sifted confectioners' sugar. Serve immediately. Serve 1 or 2 clusters for each individual helping.

HYDROGENATE—Hydrogenation is a
process which converts liquid oils into semisolid, malleable fats. Further processing incorporates air or an inert gas, resulting in a solid bland fat (hydrogenated fat) which is soft and creamy in consistency and creamy-white in color. When melted, it has the same keeping quality for successive fryings and the same high smoking point as the original oil. It will not readily acquire food flavors if foods are properly cooked in it. This hydrogenated fat is sold under many trade names and is excellent both for frying and baking. Corn, cottonseed, and soybean are the oils most frequently used to make hydrogenated vegetable fats. The process of hydrogenation is also employed to better the consistency of animal fats such as lard, in the manufacture of some margarine, and for industrial purposes such as soapmaking.

The importance of the hydrogenation of fats cannot be overemphasized. It is done on an enormous scale, and has made possible the use of vegetable-seed oils as substitutes for the more expensive animal (hog and beef) fats and for butter in cooking and baking.

The first research in hydrogenation was done by French chemists between 1897 and 1905. It was carried on in England, where a process was patented by W. Norman in 1903. An English firm is said to have hydrogenated whale oil in 1906 or earlier.

Today, practically every American producer of shortening oils and margarine uses the hydrogenation process and so do comparable manufacturers throughout the world. Processors of nonedible oils and fats use it, too.

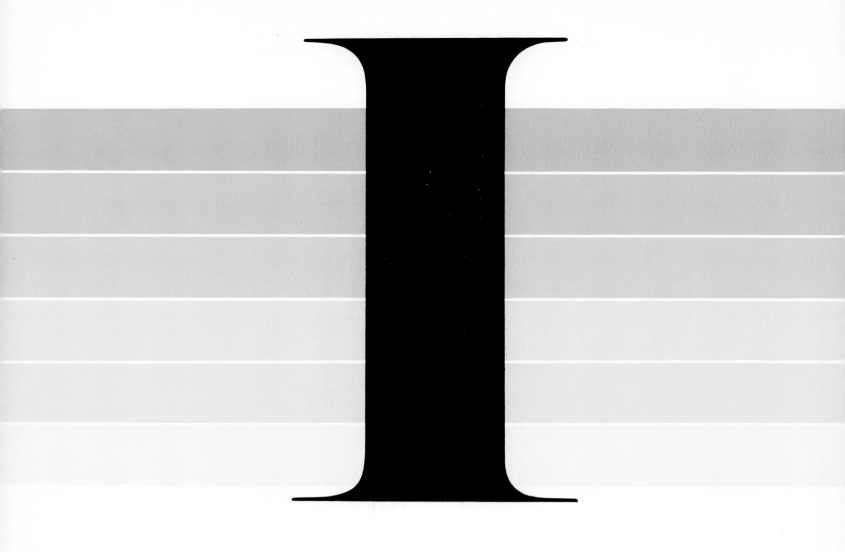

ICE—When water solidifies, it is called ice. Water, like all liquids, when sufficiently cooled becomes solid. The freezing point of water is 32°F. or 0°C. Ice is transparent in color and also lighter than water, which accounts for the familiar sight of ice floating on water. Ice is greater in bulk than the corresponding amount of water. Its mass increases almost ten percent upon freezing.

The verb "to ice" means to cover or to chill or cool with ice. It is also applied to coating, as, a cake, with an icing.

For most household purposes, ice is frozen in the refrigerator frozen-food compartment or as ice cubes generally. Ice can also be bought commercially in blocks varying from twelve and a half to 300 pounds, or as snow, marbles, cubes, etc.

Although today, anyone with a refrigerator can cool drinks with ice, this was not always so. Ice has a history as a luxury product. Cooled wines, drunk by Solomon, are mentioned in the Bible. Hippocrates, the early Greek physician, thought cold drinks to be unhealthy. He wrote that "it is dangerous to heat, cool, or make a commotion all of a sudden in the body—let it be done which way it may—because anything that is excessive is an enemy to nature. But for all this, people will not take warning, and most men would rather run the

hazard of their lives or health than be deprived the pleasure of drinking out of ice."

In the 1st century A.D., the Roman Emperor Nero sent slaves to the nearby mountains to gather ice for chilling. Pliny the Elder, the famous Roman naturalist, shared Hippocrates' distrust of iced drinks, but for sanitary reasons. He put his drinks in jars in the ice and snow, to prevent contamination.

Another disapproving statement on the practice of chilling by ice was made by Seneca, a Roman philosopher of the same time. His objection was not only on sanitary grounds, but also because of the great trouble and expense. He tells how the snow carried from the mountains was used to pack perishable foods. Snow, packed in chaff or straw pits, solidified into ice and was used to ice drinks. So many slaves had to be sent out to the mountains to gather snow, that it was an expensive practice that only the rich could afford.

A refinement on the packing of snow into pits to turn it to ice was the discovery that boiled water in a container packed in the middle of the snow would turn to ice. In mid-16th century, the Italians, who were the primary drinkers of iced drinks, discovered that saltpeter added to the packing around the container hastened the cooling process.

Experiments in ice-making were common during the 17th century. Francis Bacon, one of the first great English experimental scientists, died in 1626 as a direct result of a cold caught while stuffing a fowl with snow to try to preserve it.

Colonial Americans used and stored ice where it could be gathered from frozen ponds and streams. The ice business in America began in 1799 when a shipload was sent from New York to South Carolina. Five years later a Boston entrepreneur shipped ice to the West Indies, and shortly afterward another Boston firm introduced ice to the English.

In the 19th century every southern plantation had its own icehouse, and all industrial centers built ice storage houses. The supply of natural ice was limited, however, and it seemed as if ice would end its history as it had begun it, by being a luxury item.

However, since 1755, when the first experiments to create ice by mechanical means were attempted by Dr. William Cullen of Scotland, many other inventors were working on the problem.

By 1870 there were four commercial ice-making plants in the United States. At the end of the century, pressed by the need for ice. the industry expanded rapidly. In 1944, 6,800 plants were producing almost fifty million tons. Today the great growth in mechanical refrigerators and freezers, electric or gas, has turned almost every American home into its own ice-making plant, and coin-operated ice-cube dispensers are found in convenient public locations.

THE USES OF ICE IN COOKERY

Ice Cubes—The most popular ice form used is the ice cube which can be frozen in special ice-cube trays at home. Ice cubes may be plain water, water mixed with fruit juices or punches, and double-strength coffee or tea. They can be frozen plain or for decorative use by placing cherries, mint leaves, gumdrops, small pieces of lemon and lime, strawberries and pineapple into the water before freezing.

Ice Rings and Blocks—Water, plain, or colored with vegetable coloring, may be frozen in ring molds or pans and used to chill large bowls of punch. Flowers, leaves, fruits may be placed on top of the ice or may be frozen into the ice.

To keep ice clear, use boiled cooled water or distilled water for freezing. Freeze ice quickly; when ready to unmold, keep ice mold in the refrigerator for thirty minutes and then remove to room temperature until ice melts slightly. Unmold and place into chilled punch. If ice is subjected to too rapid temperature changes, it will crack.

Ice Bowls—An ice bowl may be made by filling a large bowl with water and pressing a smaller bowl into the water. Hold in place with a weight. Tape the bowls together so they will not move during freezing. Freeze until firm. Dip bowls into lukewarm water for a few seconds to loosen ice bowl. Leave the ice bowl in the freezer until ready to fill. Fill with ice cream or chilled fruits or chilled seafood or sherbet. Be sure to use a serving dish under it which can hold the water from melting ice.

Shaved Ice—The ice is shaved or crushed finely and used in preparing mint juleps and daiquiris; to chill melon, grapefruit, relishes, shrimp cocktail, vichyssoise, jellied consommé, oysters, clams on the half shell, and other dishes which must be served and eaten icy cold.

Shaved ice is also shaped into cones. Sweet flavored syrup is spooned over it and it is eaten much as one would eat ices.

Ice Sculpture—Many restaurants and hotel chefs specialize in ice sculpture of great beauty. However, this is an art in itself which requires years of skill and a cold room in which to work. Simple ice molds can be made using the various metal molds usually used for molding gelatin desserts. Handle and unmold as directed in Ice Rings and Blocks above. Dry ice underneath the mold can prevent its melting during the meal.

DRY ICE

Dry Ice is the trademarked name of a product made of solidified carbon dioxide. It can burn if touched, and dissipates when it melts. Any room in which Dry Ice is being used should be ventilated. It serves as a refrigerant and is usually available at ice supply houses or from distributors who supply it to manufacturers. Any home owner who stores an appreciable amount of food in a freezer should know who the local suppliers are. In the event of a power shutdown lasting more than a day or two, dry ice put into the freezer can help prevent the deterioration or spoilage of frozen food.

Ices

The word ice is also used to describe a frozen mixture of a fruit juice or purée, a sweetener, and water. Occasionally ices are made with coffee or wine instead of fruit juice. Such mixtures are often called "water ices" to distinguish them from the sherbets, ice creams, and other frozen desserts to which eggs, milk, cream, etc., are added.

Most ices are stirred often during the freezing process so that the finished product has a smooth texture, and they are frozen firm. Frappés are ices frozen only to a mushy consistency and granités are ices which, although frozen firm, are stirred very little so that their texture is rough and icy.

Ices are usually one part sugar to four parts liquid. Ices may be frozen in a refrigerator or freezer, or, for best results, churned in a crank freezer. When ices are not frozen in a crank freezer, they must be stirred every thirty minutes to break up ice crystals and make them as small as possible. They may also be frozen halfway, then whipped with a beater, and frozen until firm. Ices can be frozen in any kind of container or mold or even in individual molds.

Ices are sold commercially in a variety of flavors, both in bulk and prepackaged containers.

The bright fresh flavor of ices allows them to be served

very simply or in elegant style. Place scoops into fruit juices or punches, in fruit cups, on melon wedges, any fresh or canned fruit; ices can be used to fill hollowed-out apples, oranges, grapefruit, drizzled with liqueurs, or topped with candied fruits and nuts.

Flavored ices have been a delicacy from the earliest days. It is thought that the Chinese were the first to perfect this art and that they taught it to the Indians, Persians, and Arabs. It might also be a development of the early Greek and Roman practice of putting ice and snow in their beverages.

Marco Polo, the famous 13th-century Italian voyager to China, brought back reports, if not recipes, of the oriental custom of eating water ices. They became popular, first in Venice and then throughout Italy, from the 14th century on. It is said that Bernard Buontalenti, a 16th-century Italian architect, was the first to manufacture frozen drinks and desserts.

Catherine de Medici helped spread the custom of eating ices. When she came to France in 1533 as a fourteen-year-old bride to marry the future Henry II, she brought with her Italian cooks who knew the secret of ices. The frozen desserts became so popular that Catherine's son, Henry III, is said to have eaten ices every day.

Until 1660, when an Italian cook who was to Gallicize his name into Procope arrived in Paris from Italy, ices were the province solely of the court. When the Café Procope was founded as a place serving ices, the eager Parisians ate the ices to such an extent that soon other restaurateurs were following the lead of the clever Italian. By 1676 there were so many shops that they had to incorporate and the members of the corporation had to be officially authorized to sell their popular products.

In the 18th century the development of ices was rapid. Ices, frozen into fantastic shapes and equally fabulously decorated, were popular desserts at elegant banquets. The late 18th century and the first French Empire set up ices as the height of fashionable elegance.

Some modern versions of ices provide a striking contrast to their royal history. It was in America in 1926 that a California fair concessionaire named Epperson came to New Jersey to visit friends. He left his glass of lemonade, with a spoon in it, on his windowsill one cold day. When he returned he found the lemonade frozen, with the spoon rigid in the middle. Carrying the glass to the bathroom he ran water on it, and the ice came out in a single piece with the spoon frozen in, acting as a handle. He was quick to see the possibilities of his discovery and christened it the "epsicle." Later this was changed to the now famous "popsicle."

APRICOT ICE

   1 cup sugar
   2 cups water
   2 cups apricot or other fruit nectar
  ¼ cup fresh lemon juice

Combine sugar and water, and cook for 5 minutes; cool. Stir in apricot nectar and lemon juice. Pour into freezer trays and freeze until almost firm. Remove to bowl, and

beat until smooth. Return to trays and freeze until firm. Makes 4 to 6 servings.

WATERMELON GRANITÉ

   4 cups ripe watermelon meat, seeds removed
   2 tablespoons fresh lemon juice
  ½ cup sugar

Purée watermelon in blender or food mill; add lemon juice and sugar and stir until dissolved. Pour into refrigerator tray and freeze for 30 minutes to 1 hour. Do not let it get too solid. Makes 4 to 6 servings.

FRESH COCONUT ICE

   2 large coconuts to yield 6 cups grated coconut and 4¼ cups extracted coconut "milk"
  3½ cups boiling water
  ½ teaspoon vanilla extract
   1 cup coconut water
   1 cup sugar
    Grated coconut

Crack coconuts and reserve coconut water. Grate; there should be 6 cups grated coconut meat. Pour boiling water over grated coconut. Let stand for 15 minutes. Strain through a triple layer of cheesecloth, squeezing out as much of the "milk" as possible. Combine coconut milk, coconut water, vanilla, and sugar, and stir until sugar is dissolved. Freeze in refrigerator trays or in ice-cream freezer as usual. Serve with additional grated coconut sprinkled on top. Makes 6 to 8 servings.

COFFEE ICE WITH WHIPPED CREAM

  1½ cups ground Italian-style coffee
  ⅓ cup sugar
   5 cups boiling water
    Whipped cream, sweetened to taste

Combine coffee, sugar, and water in top part of double boiler. Steep over simmering water for 30 minutes. Cool. Filter through a strainer lined with a triple thickness of cheesecloth or coffee filter paper. Freeze in ice-cube tray until almost firm. Remove to bowl and beat until smooth. Return to trays and freeze until almost firm; the ice should be a little on the mushy side. Spoon into glasses and top with whipped cream. Makes 6 servings.

CURRANT-JELLY AND RASPBERRY ICE

  12 sprigs of fresh mint
   1 cup currant jelly
  1¼ cups boiling water
   1 cup fresh raspberries

Cut mint fine, using scissors. Combine with jelly and boiling water; simmer for 5 minutes. Cover and let stand until cold. Strain. Add raspberries. Pour into chilled freezing can of ice-cream freezer. Cover; surround with mixture of 4 parts crushed ice and 1 part rock salt. Turn crank slowly and steadily until turning becomes difficult. Remove dasher; repack in ice and salt. Let stand at least 1 hour before serving. Makes 5 to 6 servings.

APPLE AND GRAPE-JUICE ICE

2 cups apple juice
1 cup grape juice
½ cup light corn syrup
Few grains of salt

Combine ingredients and pour into chilled freezing can of ice-cream freezer; cover. Surround with mixture of 4 parts crushed ice and 1 part rock salt. Turn crank slowly and steadily until turning becomes difficult. Remove dasher; repack in ice and salt. Let stand at least 1 hour. Makes 1½ quarts.

FRUIT-JUICE ICE

4 cups water
1½ cups sugar
2 cups orange, pineapple, apple, cranberry, etc., juice, or ¾ cup fresh lemon juice plus 1¼ cups fruit juice

Cook water with sugar until it boils, and boil for 5 minutes. Cool, and add fruit juice. (Use one fruit juice or a blending of many fruit juices.) Pour mixture into freezer container and freeze until very firm, stirring mixture every 30 minutes if frozen in a freezer tray. Makes 8 to 10 servings.

LEMON FRAPPÉ

1 cup fresh lemon juice, or more, depending on tartness desired
Grated rind of 1 large lemon
3 cups water
1 cup sugar

Combine lemon juice and lemon rind. Boil water and sugar together for 5 minutes. Cool; stir in juice and rind. Freeze in refrigerator trays at coldest temperature. Stir twice during freezing, the second time stirring to a firm mush just before serving. Makes 4 servings.

MUSCATEL ICE

1 can (29 ounces) canned apricot halves
1½ cups sugar
2 cups boiling water
1 cup cold water
Juice of 2 lemons
1 cup Muscatel wine (or Tokay or Malaga)
¼ teaspoon salt

Drain apricots and reserve syrup. Purée apricots in a blender or food mill. Combine fruit and syrup. Dissolve sugar in boiling water; cool. Add apricot purée and remaining ingredients. Pour into container of ice-cream freezer. Pack ice around with rock salt, and churn. Makes about 2 quarts.

INSTANT BLENDER LEMON ICE

6 or 8 ice cubes
⅓ to ½ cup sugar
1 lemon, cut into small pieces, peel and pulp

Put all ingredients into a blender. Whirl until well combined. Serve at once. Makes about 4 servings.

ORANGE ICE

4 cups fresh orange juice
1 can (6 ounces) frozen orange-juice concentrate
1 tablespoon grated lemon rind
Juice of 1 lemon
¼ cup light corn syrup or honey

Combine all ingredients. Freeze in refrigerator trays until mushy. Beat and freeze again. Serve with a dash of orange liqueur or on fruit salad, if desired. Makes 6 to 8 servings.
NOTE: This may be frozen in cubes to flavor drinks.

PEACH ICE

1 package (12 ounces) sweetened frozen peaches
⅛ teaspoon almond extract
1 egg white
Few grains of salt

Thaw peaches and put through ricer or coarse sieve; add almond extract. Pour into freezing tray and freeze until thick and mushy. Remove to well-chilled bowl; beat with rotary beater until mixture is fluffy. Fold in stiffly beaten egg white and salt. Beat again with rotary beater; return to freezing tray until ready to serve. Makes 4 to 6 servings.

STRAWBERRY, APRICOT, RASPBERRY, OR PEACH FRAPPÉ

2 cups fruit purée made from fresh or canned fruit
Fresh lemon juice
4 cups water
1½ cups sugar

If fruits are fresh and firm, cook them before puréeing. If fruits are soft, purée them as they are and do not cook. Add lemon juice to taste. Boil water with sugar for 5 minutes. Cool, and add to puréed fruit. Pour mixture into freezer tray or into an ice-cream freezer. If using a freezer tray, stir ice every 30 minutes to keep ice crystals small, or freeze until half frozen and beat with a rotary beater until smooth. Freeze again to a thick mush just before serving. Makes 8 to 10 servings.

ICE CREAM

COOKBOOK

ICE CREAM—America's favorite dessert is a frozen food made from milk products, sweetening, flavoring, and other ingredients, depending on whether it is homemade or made commercially. By far the largest amount of ice cream consumed in the United States is commercial ice cream. Homemade ice cream has become a delicacy, made only for special occasions.

Ice cream may contain cream, fresh or evaporated milk, a sweetener such as sugar or honey or an artificial sweetener and sometimes eggs. Fruits, nuts, and flavorings are added to suit the fancy. The choice of flavorings is varied: from vanilla to liqueurs.

Commercially made ice cream also contains milk fat (also called butterfat), stabilizers added to improve the body of the ice cream, to make the ice cream smooth by keeping the ice crystals small, and to give it more resistance to melting. It may contain some nonfat milk solids.

It is impossible to say who invented ice cream. Marco Polo, who traveled extensively through China in the late 13th century, reported the oriental practice of making water and milk ices. Water ices were popular in Venice and Italy from the 14th century on. In 1660 an Italian confectioner set up in Paris a café serving ices, which was soon copied throughout Paris. It is possible that some of these early water ices may have contained milk and cream.

The first recorded occasion of the appearance of ice cream was at an elaborate banquet given by the English king, Charles I, around 1640. The frozen "cream ice" was such a surprise and such a success that Charles called in the cook and ordered him to keep the recipe a secret forever. To prove that he was serious, the king pensioned off this cook for a generous sum. But the cook did not keep his word and ice cream became a popular, if at first strictly luxurious, specialty.

Later in the century, across the channel in France, Louis XIV's guests at a state dinner were surprised to see, as one of them has reported, "in silver gilt cups, what apparently was a freshly laid egg colored like those of Easter, but before the company had time to recover from their surprise at such a novelty for dessert, they discovered that the supposed eggs were delicious sweet-meats, cold and compact as marble."

The American colonists were not far behind their European neighbors. A guest of Governor Bladen of Maryland describes a dinner of 1744: "We had a dessert no less curious; among the rarities of which it was compos'd was some fine Ice Cream which, with the Strawberries and Milk, eat Most Deliciously."

In 1774 there was a public announcement of the delicacy. Philip Lenzi of London would prepare special orders of ice cream, declared an advertisement in a New York paper. Three years later an ice-cream advertisement read: "Ice cream of what sort they will please to order."

Many leaders in American government were connected with the rise in popularity of ice cream in this country. The first President, George Washington, had two "pewter ice cream pots," presumably for making ice cream at Mount Vernon. He was introduced to ice cream by Mrs. Alexander Hamilton, the wife of the Secretary of the Treasury, in 1789. Thomas Jefferson, the third president, was an enthusiastic gastronome and had learned recipes for ice-cream dishes while in France. Guests at his state dinners were sometimes served such luxuries as meringue glacée and baked Alaska.

Ice cream's rich flavor and taste was so soothing and popular that Emerson, the famous Concord writer, complained about the lack of conversation in homes in 1841: "We dare not trust our wit for making our house pleasant to our friends and so we buy ice cream."

As early as 1893, only forty-two years after the making of the first American commercial ice cream in 1851 by Jacob Fussel, an American magazine called ice-cream sodas "the national beverage." Ice-cream cones first appeared at the St. Louis Fair in 1904. Credit for their discovery goes to Mr. E. Hamwi, a Syrian waffle vendor. Ice cream was sold in little dishes at the Fair. One day, an ice cream vendor located next to Mr. Hamwi's stand ran out of dishes. Mr. Hamwi, observing the predicament, helped out by rolling one of his thin, wafer-like waffles into the shape of a cone. This hardened as it cooled. The ice cream was put into it to the customer's delight, and a great new American institution was born.

MAKING ICE CREAM AT HOME

Homemade ice cream is made by either the stirred or the still-frozen method. The *stirred method* uses a crank freezer surrounded by ice and salt and turned by hand or by an electric motor. It is important to be sure that the lid, can, and dasher (scraper) are sterilized in boiling water, that the lid fits properly, and that melted ice does not seep into the can. For freezing ice cream, a mixture of one part salt to six parts ice by weight, or one part salt to twelve parts ice by measure, is frequently used. Coarse ice-cream salt must be used, because table salt dissolves too rapidly. The dasher is turned slowly until it begins to be difficult to turn so that the warm mixture will not be churned, then the dasher is turned more quickly to whip air into the ice cream. A hardening period of about 1 hour is necessary to complete freezing. There are also small electric ice-cream freezers that may be filled and placed in the freezing compartment of a refrigerator for the freezing process.

The *still-frozen method* (refrigerator ice cream) requires some means other than continuous stirring to keep the ice crystals small and to incorporate air. Rapid freezing and the use of a variety of materials that interfere with crystal formation are relied on to keep the crystals small. Rapid freezing is aided by setting the controls of the refrigerator at the lowest setting. The mixture can also be removed from the refrigerator occasionally and stirred to remove it from the sides of the container. Air can be incorporated by folding in a fluffy beaten product such as whipped cream, or by taking the ice cream from the refrigerator and beating before freezing is completed.

Even when a good recipe is skillfully used, the texture of refrigerator ice cream is usually less smooth than that of ice cream made in a crank freezer and becomes coarser on storage because the ice crystals grow. Refrigerator ice cream is best eaten soon after freezing.

COMMERCIAL ICE CREAM

Commercial ice-cream mixtures are pasteurized, homogenized, aged, frozen, and hardened. By federal or state standards ice cream must contain per gallon a minimum of 10 per cent milk fat, minimum 20 per cent total milk solids, stabilizer maximum .5 per cent (not more than .2 per cent emulsifier permitted), as well as a weight of minimum 4.5 pounds per gallon and minimum 1.6 pounds food solids per gallon.

There are some diet ice creams available in which noncaloric sweeteners are used.

Milk sherbet or fruit sherbet is a frozen dessert made of a milk product such as milk, or milk and cream, fruit or fruit juice, and sweetening. Water, flavorings, and stabilizers may be added. The number of calories supplied are slightly less than those from plain ice cream.

Frozen custard, French ice cream, or *French custard ice cream* are all frozen products in which eggs or egg yolks are added to the usual ice cream ingredients.

Ice milk is a frozen dessert similar to ice cream but contains less milk fat and total milk solids. Ice milk is often served from the freezer in the soft state at refreshment stands, under various trade names.

Imitation ice cream or *mellorine* is a frozen dessert in which fats other than butterfat are used. It may resemble ice cream or ice milk depending on its fat content, as the other ingredients are similar. The fat most commonly used is a blend of hydrogenated vegetable oils. Its sale is regulated by state laws and is permitted in fourteen states.

Storage—Refrigerate in refrigerator frozen-food compartment with temperature control at coldest setting.
Refrigerator frozen-food compartment, in ice-cream carton: 2 to 3 days
Freezer, in ice-cream carton: 8 months

Nutritive Food Values—Small amounts of protein and calcium, depending on the amount of milk solids used in making the ice cream. High in fat content, especially when made with cream.

The caloric value of 3½ ounces of ice cream product varies with the ingredients used and the amount of fat content, from about 193 to 222 calories. One cup weighs about 5 ounces. The diet ice creams contain about 150 calories in 3½ ounces. For 3½ ounces of ice milk the caloric value is 152.

STILL-FROZEN ICE CREAMS

VANILLA ICE CREAM

4 cups milk
1 box (3 ounces) vanilla pudding mix
1 cup light corn syrup
1 teaspoon vanilla extract
1 teaspoon almond extract
1 cup heavy cream or chilled undiluted evaporated milk

Add milk gradually to pudding mix, add corn syrup; mix until smooth. Cook over low heat until thickened, stirring constantly. When cool, freeze in refrigerator trays. When frozen around the edges, remove to chilled bowl and beat well with rotary beater. Add vanilla and almond extracts. Whip cream; fold into partially frozen pudding mixture. Freeze until firm. Makes about 1½ quarts.

CHOCOLATE ICE CREAM

4 cups milk
3 squares (3 ounces) unsweetened chocolate
1 cup sugar
1 tablespoon all-purpose flour
¼ teaspoon salt
2 eggs
1 envelope unflavored gelatin
¼ cup cold water
2 teaspoons vanilla extract
1 cup heavy cream or chilled undiluted evaporated milk

Pour 2 cups milk into top part of a double boiler; add chocolate; heat until melted. Combine ½ cup sugar with flour and salt; add hot milk slowly, stirring well. Return to double boiler; cook for 10 minutes, stirring frequently. Combine remaining ½ cup sugar and remaining 2 cups milk with beaten eggs; add to hot mixture; add gelatin soaked in water. Cook until custard coats a silver spoon. When cool, freeze in refrigerator trays. When partially frozen, beat well; add vanilla. Whip cream until stiff; fold into mixture; freeze. Makes about 1½ quarts.

PINEAPPLE ICE CREAM

½ cup sugar
1 cup water
Dash of salt
1 can (9 ounces) crushed pineapple
1 cup heavy cream, whipped

Bring first 3 ingredients to boil and boil for 5 minutes; cool. Add pineapple; pour into tray. Freeze in freezing compartment of refrigerator or in freezer until mushy. Fold in cream; freeze until firm. Makes 1 quart.

Beat eggs and sugar until light in top part of double boiler; stir in water and fresh milk. Cook, stirring constantly, over hot, not boiling, water until thick enough to coat a metal spoon. Chill. Whip partially frozen cream until stiff. Fold in egg mixture and almond extract. Freeze in refrigerator tray at coldest temperature until frozen 1 inch in from edge of tray. Turn into chilled bowl and beat with a rotary beater until creamy. Return to tray and chill until firm. Makes 6 servings.

ICE 'N CREAM

    1 cup grape juice
    1 cup apple juice
    ¼ cup lime juice
    ¾ cup superfine sugar
    1½ cups heavy cream
    1 teaspoon vanilla extract
    ⅔ cup chopped nuts

Combine fruit juices and ½ cup sugar. Pour into refrigerator tray, and freeze. Whip cream with remaining ¼ cup sugar; add vanilla and half of nuts. Pour over frozen fruit juices, and freeze. Serve garnished with remaining nuts. Makes 8 servings.

STIRRED ICE CREAMS

RUM-RAISIN ICE CREAM

    2 egg yolks
    ½ cup sugar
    Few grains of salt
    1 cup light cream
    1 cup heavy cream
    1½ teaspoons vanilla extract
    ½ cup seeded raisins, slivered or ground, soaked for
        several hours in 2 to 3 tablespoons Jamaica rum

Beat yolks until light, add sugar, then salt and light cream; blend well. Fold in whipped heavy cream and vanilla. Partially freeze. Stir once, and when it is of frappé consistency add the raisins. Continue freezing. Makes 6 servings.

ALMOND ICE CREAM

    3 eggs
    ¾ cup sugar
    ¼ cup water
    ¼ cup fresh milk
    1¾ cups heavy cream or 1 can (14½ ounces) undiluted
        evaporated milk, partially frozen
    ¾ teaspoon almond extract

FRENCH VANILLA ICE CREAM

    6 egg yolks
    2 cups milk
    1 cup sugar
    ¼ teaspoon salt
    2 cups heavy cream
    1 tablespoon vanilla extract

In top part of double boiler beat egg yolks and milk with rotary beater. Add sugar and salt; cook, stirring constantly, over hot, not boiling, water until thick enough to coat a metal spoon. Let cool, then add cream and vanilla. Freeze in a crank-type freezer, using 8 parts cracked ice to 1 part rock salt. Makes about 1½ quarts.

Banana Ice Cream

Use recipe above, reducing vanilla to 1 teaspoon. Force 3 large ripe bananas through sieve and add pulp to ice-cream mixture. Freeze.

Peach Ice Cream

Use recipe for French Vanilla Ice Cream, substituting 1 teaspoon almond extract for vanilla. Partially freeze. Add 2 cups sweetened crushed fresh peaches, or use thawed frozen peaches. Finish freezing. Makes 8 to 10 servings.

Strawberry Ice Cream

Use recipe for French Vanilla Ice Cream, omitting vanilla. Partially freeze. Add 2 cups sweetened crushed fresh strawberries, or use thawed frozen strawberries. Finish freezing. Makes 8 to 10 servings.

Raspberry Ice Cream

Use recipe for French Vanilla Ice Cream, omitting vanilla. Partially freeze. Add 2 cups sweetened strained fresh raspberries, or use thawed frozen raspberries. Finish freezing. Makes 8 to 10 servings.

OLD-FASHIONED CHOCOLATE ICE CREAM

    4 cups milk
    2 squares (2 ounces) unsweetened chocolate
    1 cup sugar
    1 tablespoon all-purpose flour
    ¼ teaspoon salt
    2 eggs
    2 cups light cream
    1 tablespoon vanilla extract

Pour 2 cups milk into top part of a double boiler; add chocolate; heat until chocolate melts. Combine ½ cup sugar with flour and salt, add hot milk slowly and stir until well mixed. Return to double boiler; cook for 10 minutes, stirring frequently. Combine remaining ½ cup sugar with eggs; add to hot-milk mixture; cook until custard coats a silver spoon. Add remaining milk, cool, and strain into freezer can of ice-cream freezer. Add unbeaten cream and vanilla. Pack in ice and salt, using 8 parts chopped ice to 1 part rock salt. Freeze as usual. Makes about 1½ quarts.

BLUEBERRY ICE CREAM

    4 cups fresh blueberries
    ¼ cup water
    1 cup sugar
    ¼ teaspoon salt
      Juice of 1 lemon
    2 cups light cream

Put berries in saucepan with water. Cover and simmer for 10 minutes, or until berries are soft. Mash; put through a sieve. Add sugar, salt, and lemon juice; cool. Mix with cream and freeze in a crank freezer. Makes 1½ quarts.

FRESH STRAWBERRY ICE CREAM

    2 quarts strawberries
    2 cups sugar
    3 quarts heavy cream
      Pinch of salt

Clean and hull berries and sprinkle them with sugar. Cover and let stand for 1½ to 2 hours. Mash them lightly. Mix cream with salt and pour into freezer; freeze until mushy. Remove cover of freezer and stir in strawberries. Re-cover and continue freezing until solid. Makes about 1½ gallons.

ICE CREAM PARFAITS

TWO-TONE CHERRY PARFAIT

Flavor softened vanilla ice cream with a little maraschino-cherry juice and some chopped cherries. Fill parfait or other tall glass (fruit-juice glass can be used) alternately with the cherry-ice cream mixture and pistachio ice cream. Top with whipped cream and a whole maraschino cherry or chopped pistachio nuts. Put in freezer for a short time before serving.

Two-Tone Cherry Parfait

CINNAMON CHOCOLATE PARFAIT

To softened chocolate ice cream add ground cinnamon to taste. Pour some Chocolate Fudge Sauce or canned chocolate syrup into parfait or other tall glass (fruit-juice glass can be used). Fill with alternating layers of cinnamon-chocolate ice cream and Chocolate Fudge Sauce. Top with whipped topping. Sprinkle with ground cinnamon.

BLUEBERRY PARFAIT

Spoon a little Blueberry Sauce (below) into bottom of a parfait or other tall glass (fruit-juice glass can be used). Alternate layers of vanilla ice cream and Blueberry Sauce. Top with whipped cream or whipped topping and whole blueberries.

STRAWBERRY PARFAIT

Alternate layers of thawed frozen strawberries and vanilla ice cream in a parfait glass. Top with whipped ice cream and a maraschino cherry.

SAUCES FOR ICE CREAM

Apricot Cherry Sauce—Combine 1 jar (1 pound) apricot jam and ½ cup coarsely chopped red maraschino cherries. Makes about 2 cups.

Blueberry Sauce—In saucepan blend 2 teaspoons cornstarch and 1 tablespoon water. Add ¼ cup sugar, ⅓ cup water (or syrup from canned blueberries), and ⅛ teaspoon salt. Cook until clear and slightly thickened, stirring. Add 2 cups fresh blueberries, or drained canned or frozen. Boil for 2 or 3 minutes. Makes 2 cups.

Butterscotch Sauce—Combine in saucepan 2 cups firmly packed brown sugar, ½ cup undiluted evaporated milk, ¼ teaspoon salt, ⅓ cup light corn syrup, and ⅓ cup butter. Bring to boil and cook rapidly for 3 minutes (200°F. on a candy thermometer). Makes 2 cups.

Chocolate-Covered Coffee Beans—Melt semisweet chocolate over hot water. Put each bean on tip of teaspoon and dip into chocolate until coated. Place on wax paper. Allow to harden in refrigerator.

Chocolate Fudge Sauce—Melt 3 squares (3 ounces) unsweetened chocolate in ¾ cup milk over low heat, stirring constantly. Beat until smooth. Add ¼ teaspoon salt, 1½ cups sugar, and 3 tablespoons light corn syrup; cook, stirring, for 5 minutes. Add 1 tablespoon butter or margarine and ¾ teaspoon vanilla extract. Serve warm or cold. Makes about 2 cups.

Pineapple Mint Topping—Drain well 1 can (8 ounces) crushed pineapple. Combine pineapple with 2 tablespoons crème de menthe or melted mint jelly. Makes 1 cup.

Raspberry Sauce—Thaw 1 package (12 ounces) frozen raspberries. Press through fine sieve or whirl in blender; strain. Add 3 tablespoons sugar; dissolve in saucepan over medium heat. Cook rapidly for 3 minutes. Cool. Makes about 1 cup.

Flavored Whipped Cream—Before whipping, try adding one of the following to flavor heavy cream:
1. Instant coffee powder
2. Instant cocoa mix
3. Quick strawberry-flavored beverage mix
4. Brown sugar instead of granulated sugar
5. Your favorite flavoring extract

Or, fold one of these into the whipped cream:
1. Chopped nuts
2. Macaroon crumbs
3. Chocolate sprinkles
4. Chopped raisins
5. Grenadine instead of sugar

TOPPINGS FOR ICE CREAM SUNDAES

ORANGE AND BLUE SUNDAE

Top peach ice cream with equal parts of orange segments, sliced bananas, blueberries.

STOP-AND-GO SUNDAE

Mix chopped green and red maraschino cherries; add a little light corn syrup.

HOT CARAMEL SUNDAE

Melt ½ pound caramels with 2 tablespoons water over hot water.

ORIENTAL SUNDAE

Cut up undrained preserved kumquats. Good on chocolate ice cream.

MARSHMALLOW SUNDAE

Top ice cream with bought marshmallow cream. Best on peach, pineapple, chocolate.

GINGER SUNDAE

Top ice cream with ginger marmalade or chopped preserved gingerroot in syrup.

Orange and Blue Sundae

NUTMEG SUNDAE

Grate fresh nutmeg generously over vanilla or peach ice cream.

PEACH SUNDAE

Top vanilla ice cream with frozen or sweetened sliced fresh peaches.

MAPLE-RUM SUNDAE

Top coffee ice cream with hot maple syrup flavored with rum or rum extract.

BRITTLE SUNDAE

Sprinkle crushed nut brittle over coffee, vanilla, chocolate, or caramel ice cream.

CHOCOLATE-MINT SUNDAE

Melt thin chocolate mints over hot water; serve on vanilla, chocolate, pistachio.

BRANDIED FRUIT SUNDAE

Serve cut-up brandied fruit on coffee, pineapple, coconut, banana, or vanilla.

MOLASSES CHIP SUNDAE

Top vanilla, banana, or chocolate ice cream with crushed molasses chips.

PINEAPPLE SUNDAE

Serve canned pineapple pie filling on vanilla or banana ice cream.

CRANBERRY-ORANGE SUNDAE

Add orange segments to cranberry sauce. Or use raw-cranberry relish to top vanilla ice cream.

ARABIAN SUNDAE

Moisten chopped dates with honey. Serve on butter-pecan or burnt-almond ice cream.

CANDIED FRUIT SUNDAE

Serve moist mixed candied fruits on vanilla or pistachio ice cream.

TROPICAL SUNDAE

Add chopped coconut, golden raisins, and nuts to Butterscotch Sauce.

JUNIOR SUNDAE

Pour junior apricot-and-applesauce over vanilla ice cream. Top with raisins.

CEREAL SUNDAE

Top vanilla, coffee, chocolate, or banana ice cream with sugar-coated cereal.

CHOCOLATE-RUM SUNDAE

Melt chocolate rum wafers over hot water; serve on vanilla or chocolate ice cream.

JAM OR PRESERVES SUNDAE

Serve cherry, plum, apricot, or berry jam or preserves on choice of ice cream.

COOKIE SUNDAE

Top choice of ice cream with crushed fig cookies, coconut bars, or macaroons.

ZIPPY SUNDAE

Top choice of ice cream with Cointreau, crème de menthe, or any cordial.

MOCHA SUNDAE

Add powdered coffee to chocolate syrup on chocolate ice cream.

MINCEMEAT SUNDAE

Spike warm mincemeat with rum or brandy, best on vanilla ice cream.

COCONUT SUNDAE

Roll balls of strawberry or other ice cream in coconut. Serve with any sauce.

ORANGE SUNDAE

Top chocolate or vanilla ice cream with frozen orange juice concentrate.

PINEAPPLE-GINGER SUNDAE

Add a small amount chopped candied gingerroot to pineapple jam; serve on vanilla.

PARTY PINK SUNDAE

Top vanilla ice cream with 1 or 2 tablespoons grenadine.

ICE CREAMS MONEY CAN'T BUY

by SYLVIA VAUGHN THOMPSON

Making ice cream all begins with one basic recipe, Philadelphia Ice Cream: a quart of cream, a heaping ½ cup of sugar, and flavoring. It's beautiful ice cream—delicate, crystally and quick-melting. From this model of simplicity, we move along, breaking in egg yolks for silky smoothness, spooning in sugar for added richness, to classic French Custard Ice Cream: a quart of cream, 6 egg yolks, a heaping cup of sugar, and flavoring to match.

Devastatingly rich, divinely creamy—for memorable occasions, this is absolutely it.

Any tasteful combination of cream, sugar, egg yolks if you wish, and flavoring, properly churned and frozen in an ice cream freezer, will freeze deliciously. But don't expect the ice cream you make to have the texture of the commercial ice cream you're accustomed to. As the chief chemist of one of the country's finest ice creameries explained, commercial ice cream plants can adjust the amount of what they call "over-run" in their product. Over-run is the incorporation of air—it's what makes store-bought ice cream so fluffy. Also, the commercial rate of freezing and type of agitation, not to mention the use of emulsifiers and stabilizers, result in a very fine ice crystal, which is what makes store-bought ice cream so smooth and slow to melt.

But these are like the differences between the white bread you buy at the market and the loaf you bake at home. Once you've become accustomed to the old-fashioned texture of the homemade, you're absolutely bound to prefer it.

Apart from nostalgia for a taste of the past, half the reason I make ice cream is flavor. How else get Essence-of-Rose Ice Cream? Or Peach Ice Cream with Grand Marnier? Or a true Mexican Chocolate Ice Cream? Even the fanciest ice cream parlor in town is not going to have that enchanting reminiscence of eighteenth-century England, Mrs. Glasse's Apricot Ice Cream.

The other half of the reason I made ice cream is to get the extra-creamy creaminess of *cream*. There isn't any standard recipe that recommends using more than light cream in making ice cream, especially in this day of low cholesterol. We are 100 percent low-cholesterol in our house—on all days but those on which I make ice cream, because I like the cream in the ice cream I make to be *heavy*.

Simply decide whether the flavor you want for your ice cream goes best with a delectable Philadelphia base (incomparable for fruits) or a luxurious French custard base (most rich non-fruit flavors). Then adjust the basic recipe for sweetness—remembering that, when frozen, the cream will be a trifle less sweet—and brighten up the flavor with lemon juice, almond or vanilla extract or a suitable liqueur.

Equipment. You'll need a crank-type or electric ice cream freezer, preferably with a lightweight plastic tub, and perhaps a mechanical ice crusher. If you intend to make ice cream only rarely, a hammer or rolling pin will crush the ice nicely in a burlap bag. But this can be tedious and keep you from making ice cream often, so a mechanical ice crusher is a smart (and inexpensive) investment.

Here's our system for using a hand-turned crusher. The box is mounted on the kitchen wall at waist height, catching cup removed. Underneath is a tall stool with a large flat pan on it filled with the cubes to be crushed. A large plastic bag is attached by rubber band to the ice crusher. I take the cubes from the pan and grind them up with the fine blade. As each bag fills, I put it straight back into the freezing compartment. I can do 3 bags of ice—about 24 cups, which is what is needed for a 4-quart freezer—in less than 10 minutes, without a speck of a puddle on the floor.

Churning. First, fit the dasher into the chilled can. Then, pour in the aged and chilled cream preparation (more of that in a moment), never filling the can more than two thirds full (it expands). On goes the chilled cover. The can then goes into the *empty* tub, the power unit is fitted on and twisted into lock position. After that, plug in the machine (electric models) and let the can revolve around the dasher 2 minutes.

Now, without pulling the plug, distribute 3 inches of ice—about 6 cups—evenly around the bottom of the tub. Next, sprinkle around ⅓ cup coarse salt (ice cream or water-softening salt). Then 2 cups ice. Alternate these last two proportions until the ice reaches the top of the can. Altogether, this requires some 12 cups ice and 1⅓ cups salt for a 4-quart tub.

Do not be tempted, no matter what a recipe may say, to use more salt. If you do, the cream will freeze too rapidly and form a crust on the wall of the can. Then the can won't be able to turn about the dasher and the motor will stall. So use just 1⅓ cups salt to 12 cups ice, and in 15 minutes or less the motor will sound labored, which means the cream has reached the texture of heavy whipped cream.

For hand-cranked freezers, use the same proportion of ice to salt and distribute it precisely as described. However, the method of churning differs. The ice and salt must go around the can before cranking begins, and the chilled cream mixture must rest in the ice and salt 3 minutes before cranking begins. Turn the crank, 40 turns a minute, until you feel resistance from the mixture. Then crank at the rate of 2 turns a second the next 5 to 6 minutes. Add whatever bits and pieces of fruits or nuts you want at this point, then replace cover and churn at 80 turns a minute about 3 minutes longer.

Freezing. Remove the dasher, scraping back what you can into the ice cream, and if there are any fruits or bits of this or that you want to add to the electric churned ice cream, now's the time to fold them in. Cover can with foil (both hand and electric models), plug up the lid, replace it on can and seal by winding some adhesive tape twice around the edge. Drain off the melted ice and salt, then mix in about 2 cups more salt with 6 cups more ice—you want it to freeze quickly now. Cover with some insulating material (a clean rug or blanket or heaps of newspapers) and let firm up for a couple of hours.

Molding. Or you may have a fancy ice cream mold you wish to use (ice cream molds are made with tight-fitting lids, but you may use any mold you like, as long as you cover it with buttered brown paper, waxed paper or several thicknesses of heavy aluminum foil). Chill mold, pour in whipped-cream-textured cream, cover with foil, seal with adhesive tape and freeze.

Unmolding. Just like a gelatin mold: dip the whole sealed mold briefly in cool water, remove cover and foil, run a knife around edge, turn onto serving dish, and if the cream doesn't slip out easily at this point, lay a hot damp cloth on top for a moment and it will.

Serving. There are all sorts of pretty ways to serve your homemade ice cream. The French like to scoop it out with dessert spoons, thus shaping ice cream eggs. Americans are partial to the ball scoop, and one famous hostess we know likes to pass an enormous bowl of ice cream balls, three or four flavors and colors heaped together. If you have a freezer, what could be more delightful than serving homemade ice cream this way? In summer, you might mingle whole unstemmed strawberries among the balls; in winter, candied violets strewn about are a lovely touch.

Making. When you make ice cream, prepare the cream well in advance. That is, scald it and add sugar, egg yolks if a custard recipe, and flavoring, then cover and refrigerate it. In 12 to 24 hours the cream mixture will have aged and become thoroughly chilled. The Philadelphia cream preparation will keep 3 to 4 days this way, and the custard preparation may be refrigerated as much as 2 days in advance of freezing. Why do this? Because thoroughly chilled cream churns up to a greater volume and finer consistency, and aged cream preparations tend to produce a mellower flavor. Too, making the ice cream in two steps is a labor-saving device.

PHILADELPHIA ICE CREAM
[Basic Recipe]

4 cups cream, heavy preferred
½ cup sugar (about)
Flavoring to taste

Bring cream to boil, add sugar and stir until dissolved. Cool, add flavoring, cover and chill 12 to 24 hours. Churn and freeze as directed. Makes 1 quart.
NOTE: Add any bits and pieces—nuts, fruits other than purées, etc.—just before freezing. More sugar may be required for the bitterer flavors, such as chocolate or lemon.

MRS. GLASSE'S APRICOT ICE CREAM
[Updated]

From *The Art of Cookery, Made Plain and Easy,* published in London, 1788. I find it possibly the purest, most delicate ice cream I've ever made.

2 cups cream, heavy preferred
¾ cup sugar
2 cans (17 ounces each) apricots, pitted and drained
2 tablespoons lemon juice
Few drops of almond extract
1 tablespoon frozen orange-juice concentrate

Bring cream to boil, add sugar and stir until dissolved. Purée apricots in blender or force through food mill. Add to cream, cool and add remaining ingredients. Chill, covered, 12 to 24 hours. Then churn and freeze as directed. Makes 1 quart.

RED-CURRANT AND RED-RASPBERRY
ICE CREAM

4 cups heavy cream
¾ cup red-currant jelly
¾ cup seedless red-raspberry jam
⅛ teaspoon almond extract
½ teaspoon red food coloring
3 tablespoons kirsch

Scald cream. Melt jelly and jam together, stirring until absolutely smooth. Stir cream into jellies and cool. Add almond extract and coloring, strain into bowl, cover and chill 12 to 24 hours. Add kirsch, churn and freeze as directed. Makes 1½ quarts.
NOTE: Try these other combinations of preserves and liqueur:
Strawberry jelly and orange marmalade with kirsch
Cherry jam and red-currant jelly with kirsch
Apricot preserves and orange marmalade with apricot brandy
Mint jelly with green crème de menthe
Apricot preserves and apple jelly with apple brandy
Peach preserves with Cointreau or Grand Marnier
Add color as needed and liqueur to taste—it gives a beautiful edge to the flavor and keeps the ice cream from being too sweet.

FRENCH CUSTARD ICE CREAM
[Basic Recipe]

4 cups cream, heavy preferred
6 egg yolks
1⅓ to 1½ cups sugar
Flavoring to taste

As you bring cream to boil, whisk yolks and sugar in bowl until thick. Carefully whisk in boiling cream. Return to heat and stir over low heat until mixture is slightly thickened and custard coats spoon. If mixture overcooks and curdles slightly, pass through fine sieve. Flavor as desired, then cover and chill 12 to 24 hours. Churn and freeze as directed. Makes 1 quart.

VANILLA-BEAN ICE CREAM

1 vanilla bean
1 recipe French Custard Ice Cream

Add bean to cream, bring to boil, then let steep ½ hour. Split bean lengthwise and scrape out all the tiny seeds into cream; discard bean. Make custard base with this cream as directed, using 1½ cups sugar. Chill, churn and freeze. Makes 1 quart.

ESSENCE-OF-ROSE ICE CREAM

Purchase rose water at the pharmacy. This is the ice cream great-grandmother knew best.

1 recipe French Custard Ice Cream
Rose water to taste (it varies in strength; begin with 1 teaspoonful)
4 to 6 drops red food coloring

Prepare and cool custard, add rose water and coloring. Chill, churn and freeze as directed. Makes 1 quart.

HONEY-ALMOND ICE CREAM

4 cups cream, heavy preferred
6 egg yolks
⅔ cup honey (Greek Hymettian or California eucalyptus honey gives an exotic flavor)
⅛ teaspoon almond extract
½ cup sliced almonds

Make a custard base with the cream, yolks and honey (in place of sugar) as directed in basic recipe. Cool and add almond extract. Chill as directed. Roast almonds in preheated slow oven (300°F.) 15 minutes, then chill at the same time as custard. Add almonds to cream when churning is finished, then freeze as directed. Makes 1 generous quart.

MEXICAN CHOCOLATE ICE CREAM

This is a bit of a variation from the basic recipe. The condensed milk gives the desired caramel overtaste so typically Mexican and makes a very smooth, concentrated ice cream.

2 squares (2 ounces) unsweetened chocolate
2 cups sweetened condensed milk (not evaporated)
1 cinnamon stick
½ teaspoon ground ginger
2 egg yolks
2 cups heavy cream, chilled
1 teaspoon vanilla extract
⅛ teaspoon almond extract
1 teaspoon grated orange rind
Dash of salt

Melt chocolate in top part of double boiler over low heat and slowly stir in milk. Add cinnamon and ginger. Then put over boiling water and stir constantly until mixture thickens, about 10 minutes. It will hold its shape from the spoon and be thick and glossy like pudding. Add yolks, whisking rapidly, and cook another minute or two. Remove cinnamon stick. Then beat with mixer at medium speed 5 minutes, or until cool. Whip cream until stiff but still soft. Fold in flavorings, orange rind and salt. Then fold this into chocolate mixture. Churn and freeze as directed. Makes 1 generous quart.

NOTE: Many recipes call for folding in whipped cream at the end. This is the only recipe I feel warrants the extra step.

DOUBLE-FLAVOR ICE CREAMS

Reprinted by permission of Harold Ober, Assoc. Inc. c/r 1969 by Fawcett Publications, Inc.

by CAROL TRUAX

You can double the fun of ice cream by doubling the flavor. Buy any of the very satisfactory ice creams, sherbets and water ices and take it from there. You don't need to improve on the consistency; but you can improve, change and augment the flavor at will.

It's so easy. You soften the hard frozen ice cream in the package enough to spoon it out into a chilled bowl. Then, working rapidly, stir in the flavoring of your choice and quickly return the ice cream to the freezing compartment. If you haven't allowed it to melt, it will harden again with the same mellow texture, or even mellower. Your double-good re-created ice cream is ready to serve after refreezing about three hours. It keeps for weeks. You can make it up well in advance in quantities as large as you have space for in the freezer.

The mixture can go into the freezer in the bowl you mixed it in, or you can spoon it into freezer trays, a plastic freezer box or, if you haven't added too much bulk, into the carton it came in. At serving time you can dish some or all into a cold serving bowl or directly into chilled dessert plates.

If you enjoy the elegance of serving ice cream in molded form, swathe the bowl momentarily with a hot towel and turn it out. A smooth-surfaced cabochon or melon mold will work the same way. It's even easier to use the same container you will carry to the table. This may be a handsome fairly heavy serving bowl, parfait glasses or sherbet cups.

IRISH-COFFEE ICE CREAM

1 quart coffee or vanilla ice cream
2 to 5 tablespoons instant-coffee powder
¼ cup (2 ounces) Irish whiskey

Soften ice cream and put in chilled bowl. (It should be softened only enough to stir in instant coffee.) If coffee ice cream is used, add 2 tablespoons coffee only; add 4 tablespoons to vanilla. Taste for flavor, and perhaps add a little more coffee. Quickly stir in whiskey and spoon mixture at once into serving bowl or parfait glasses. Stand in freezing compartment at least 3 hours. Top with a sprinkling of instant coffee if you wish. Makes 6 servings.

DOUBLE-STRAWBERRY ICE CREAM

2 packages (10 ounces each) frozen sliced strawberries
Few drops of lemon juice
1 quart strawberry ice cream

Thaw berries and whirl in blender or mash through coarse strainer. Sprinkle with lemon juice. Meanwhile soften ice cream. Stir in purée and blend well. Work quickly so that ice cream won't melt. Spoon into glass bowl or parfait glasses and refreeze at least 3 hours. Makes 6 to 8 servings.

Double-Raspberry Ice Cream. Thaw 1 package (10 ounces) frozen raspberries and force through sieve or food mill to remove seeds. Blend with 1 quart vanilla or raspberry ice cream and proceed as for Double-Strawberry Ice Cream. Makes 6 to 8 servings.

MOCHA ICE CREAM

1 quart chocolate ice cream
2 to 3 tablespoons instant-coffee powder

Soften ice cream slightly in cold bowl. Stir in coffee. Taste to see if you need more. Put bowl in freezer or put mixture into serving bowl or glasses and refreeze several hours. Makes 6 servings.

Spanish Chocolate Ice Cream. To 1 quart chocolate ice cream, add ½ teaspoon (or to taste) cinnamon. Proceed as for Mocha Ice Cream. Makes 6 servings.

Viennese Chocolate Ice Cream. To 1 quart chocolate ice cream, add ½ teaspoon almond extract and proceed as for Mocha Ice Cream. Makes 6 servings.

MAPLE ICE CREAM

1 cup maple syrup
3 egg yolks, slightly beaten
1 quart vanilla ice cream

Heat syrup and pour slowly, stirring, onto egg yolks. Cook in double boiler over simmering water, stirring until thickened. Chill. Soften ice cream and stir in syrup mixture. Spoon into serving bowl or individual glasses and refreeze. Makes 6 to 8 servings.

CRÈME DE MENTHE ICE CREAM

1 quart vanilla or mint ice cream
6 tablespoons (3 ounces) green or white crème de menthe
Few drops of green food coloring (optional)

Soften ice cream and stir in crème de menthe. If vanilla ice cream is used, use green crème de menthe. (If white crème de menthe is used, add a few drops of green coloring.) If mint ice cream is used, add only 1½ ounces crème de menthe to start with, adding more to taste. Refreeze at once in serving bowl. Makes 6 servings.

APRICOT-BRANDY ICE CREAM

1 package (10 ounces) frozen or 1 pound fresh peaches
2 tablespoons sugar (optional)
1 pint peach ice cream
6 tablespoons (3 ounces) apricot brandy

Whirl thawed peaches in blender or force through coarse sieve. If fresh peaches are used, peel, slice and add sugar; whirl in blender. Combine peach purée with softened ice cream and stir in brandy. Work quickly, especially if fruit is not cold. Refreeze in bowl or parfait glasses. Makes 4 servings.

COINTREAU-ORANGE SHERBET

1 quart orange sherbet
3 tablespoons frozen orange-juice concentrate
3 tablespoons Cointreau

Soften sherbet slightly in very cold bowl. Add orange concentrate and Cointreau. Stir and refreeze, working quickly since sherbet melts very fast. Sherbet looks prettier in glass than in pottery or silver. Makes 6 servings.

DATE-NUT ICE CREAM

½ cup dates, cut in small pieces
½ cup chopped nuts
1 quart vanilla ice cream
2 tablespoons brandy (optional)

Stir dates and nuts into softened ice cream, blending well. Add brandy, if desired. Refreeze at once in bowl or parfait glasses. Makes 6 to 8 servings.

PARFAIT LAFAYETTE

1 quart coffee ice cream
1 cup heavy cream, whipped (optional)
2 tablespoons instant-coffee powder
3 ounces (6 tablespoons) brandy

To enrich ice cream, soften slightly and stir in most of whipped cream. Add instant coffee and blend well. Fill 6 parfait glasses. Put into freezer several hours. Make a hole about the size of a lead pencil down center almost to bottom. Fill with brandy and top with remaining cream. Leave in freezer until ready to serve. Makes 6 servings.

ICE CREAM COMBOS— THE ULTIMATE IN DESSERTS

by SHIRLEY SARVIS

I have long established that, for me, dessert is the best part of the menu. And though I love nearly all desserts, I have also quite long ago established that good-ice-cream desserts are about the best. I do not mean just good ice cream alone; I mean good ice cream linked with a sumptuous foil. Because, as a cook and as an eater, I am intrigued with all the possible lovely linkages with ice cream: I think it was a wonderful genius who first thought up ice cream with cake; the combination may now be simple and obvious, but it is fully fascinating. And some pies just have to have ice cream with them; together they have greatness beyond their single beings. Tart rich-flavored fruits with creamy ice creams also often combine beneficently.

PEACH MELBA MERINGUE

½ cup egg whites (about 4)
½ teaspoon cream of tartar
1 cup sugar
1 teaspoon vanilla extract
2 pints (about) peach or vanilla ice cream
  Sliced fresh, frozen or canned peaches, well drained
  Raspberry Sauce

To make meringue, put egg whites and cream of tartar in large bowl of electric mixer. Beat at high speed until frothy. Beat in sugar, adding about 1 tablespoon a minute. Add vanilla and beat 1 minute longer. Grease a piece of heavy brown paper and put on baking sheet. Trace an 8-inch circle onto center of paper, using bottom of 8-inch layer-cake pan as a guide. Spread a portion of the meringue mixture inside the circle. Put remaining meringue in pastry tube. Build edge of circle by forcing

meringue from tube in zigzag pattern, forming a shell. Bake in preheated very slow oven (250° F.) about 30 minutes. Turn off heat and allow meringue to dry out in oven 3 to 4 hours. When ready to serve, put meringue on serving plate and fill with scoops of ice cream. Top with peaches and sauce. Cut in wedges. Makes 6 servings.
Raspberry Sauce. Partially thaw 1 package (10 ounces) frozen raspberries. Whirl in blender until just liquid.

WARM DEEP-DISH RAISIN PIE. MOCHA-FUDGE ICE CREAM

2 cups seedless raisins
2 cups water
⅔ cup granulated sugar
3 tablespoons cornstarch
¼ teaspoon each salt and ground cloves
2 tablespoons mild red-wine vinegar
  Butter
  Pastry for 1-crust 8-inch pie, unbaked
2 tablespoons firmly packed brown sugar
½ cup chopped walnuts
  Mocha-fudge, mocha-chip or coffee ice cream (about 1 to 1½ pints handpacked)

In saucepan, bring raisins and water to boil. Stir together granulated sugar, cornstarch, salt and cloves; stir into raisin mixture. Cook over medium heat, stirring, until mixture boils and becomes clear and slightly thickened. Remove from heat and stir in vinegar and 2 tablespoons butter. Turn into buttered 1½-quart baking dish. Roll out pastry to fit top of baking dish and cut decorative vents. Arrange over top of fruit, turning under and fluting edges. Bake pie in preheated hot oven (425° F.) 25 minutes, or until pastry is browned. Stir together ¼ cup melted butter, brown sugar and walnuts and spoon evenly over pastry. Bake 5 minutes longer, or until nuts are lightly toasted. Cool until warm. Spoon into bowls and top with ice cream. Makes 6 servings.

ICE CREAM WITH FLAMED BRANDY ORANGES

¾ cup orange marmalade
4 oranges, peeled and cut in sections (remove membrane)
1 tablespoon grated orange rind
1 tablespoon grated lemon rind
½ cup brandy
4 scoops hard-frozen coffee and/or vanilla ice cream (about 1 pint hand-packed)
¼ cup lightly toasted slivered almonds

Heat marmalade over low heat in chafing dish until melted. Add oranges and rinds and heat just to bubbling. Add brandy at edge of dish, heat just to warm and light. Gently spoon flaming juices over oranges, lifting high to allow oxygen to reach them, until flames die. Put ice cream in individual serving dishes and top with oranges and juices. Sprinkle with almonds and serve at once. Makes 6 servings.

Cherry Ice Cream Soda

Peach or Apricot—Put ⅓ cup mashed frozen, canned, or sweetened ripe fresh peaches or apricots in a large glass. Add ¼ cup milk, a large scoop of peach or vanilla ice cream, and almost fill with chilled soda water; stir.

Pineapple—Put ⅓ cup drained, canned crushed, or fresh shredded pineapple in large glass. Add ¼ cup milk and a large scoop of vanilla or pineapple ice cream. Almost fill with chilled soda water; stir.

Strawberry or Raspberry—Put ⅓ cup frozen or crushed, sweetened, fresh berries in a large glass. Add 3 tablespoons milk and a large scoop of vanilla ice cream. Almost fill with chilled soda water; stir.

ICE-CREAM CAKES AND DESSERTS

HARLEQUIN CRINKLE CUPS

Melt separately 6 ounces each of semisweet chocolate and butterscotch pieces in top part of double boiler over hot water. Place 10 to 12 paper baking cups (3 to 4 inches in diameter) in muffin-pan sections. With spatula, line half the inside and bottom with melted chocolate and the other half with melted butterscotch. Put muffin pan in refrigerator until ready to use. Then quickly peel off paper cups. Fill crinkle cups with butter-pecan ice cream. Decorate with pecan half.

ICE-CREAM SODAS

Each recipe makes one serving.

Black-and-White—Follow the directions for Chocolate Soda (below), substituting vanilla for chocolate ice cream.

Chocolate—Put 2 to 3 tablespoons chocolate syrup in a large glass. Add ¼ cup milk and a large scoop of chocolate ice cream. Almost fill with chilled soda water; stir.

Cherry—Put 2 tablespoons bought cherry-sundae topping in tall glass. Add ¼ cup milk and vanilla ice cream. Fill with chilled soda water; stir; top with cherries.

Coffee—Several hours before making sodas, bring to a boil ½ cup sugar, ½ cup light corn syrup, ¾ cup water, and dash of salt, stir constantly. Remove from heat and stir in 2 tablespoons instant coffee powder; cool. Add ½ teaspoon vanilla extract. Refrigerate. For each soda, put 2 to 3 tablespoons syrup in large glass; add ¼ cup milk and large scoop of vanilla or coffee ice cream; almost fill with chilled soda water; stir.

Cola, Root-Beer, Sarsaparilla, or Ginger-Ale—Put a scoop of vanilla ice cream in a large glass. Almost fill with chilled beverage desired; stir.

Lemon—Put 2 tablespoons frozen, concentrated lemonade in tall glass. Add a scoop of vanilla ice cream. Almost fill with chilled soda water; stir.

Harlequin Crinkle Cups

LADYFINGER ICE-CREAM CAKE

Line a 2-quart mold or mixing bowl with about 2 dozen ladyfingers, split. Pack with 3 pints peppermint-stick ice cream. Cover with foil; freeze for several hours or overnight. Unmold and garnish with a wreath of whipped cream; sprinkle with multicolored "shot" candies; arrange candy fruit slices around the cake base. Makes about 8 to 10 servings.

ICE-CREAM SHADOW CAKE

  1 large angel-food cake ring
  2 pints chocolate ice cream, softened
  2 cups heavy cream, whipped and sweetened
    Chocolate sauce

Cut angel cake into three layers. Spread 1 pint ice cream between each two layers. Spread whipped cream on top and sides of cake; freeze. When ready to serve, remove from freezer and dribble chocolate sauce over top and sides of cake. Cut into wedges to serve. Makes 12 servings.
NOTE: If freezer isn't available, chill cake and have cream whipped before filling cake. Fill with ice cream; spread with cream. Dribble sauce over top and sides and serve at once.

ICE-CREAM CAKE

Cover bottom and sides of three 8-inch layer-cake pans with one piece of wax paper or foil; spread 1 pint softened ice cream in each. Strawberry, coffee, or any desired flavor or combination of flavors may be used. Put in freezer until firm. Split two 8-inch sponge layers into halves, making 4 layers. Cover with foil a circle of cardboard cut to fit the cake. On it assemble cake by placing ice-cream layers between sponge layers; remove wax paper or foil from ice cream. Press slightly so layers will stay together. Put in freezer until ice cream is hard. Whip 1½ cups heavy cream, ¼ cup sifted confectioners' sugar, and 1 teaspoon vanilla extract until stiff; spread on top and sides of cake. Reserve some of cream and use in pastry tube to decorate cake. Return cake to freezer; let stand until cream is frozen. Package, and keep in freezer until ready to serve. Cut and serve while it is frozen. Makes 12 to 16 slices.

CHOCOLATE ICE-CREAM ROLL

  4 eggs
    Sugar
  ½ cup sifted cake flour
  ½ teaspoon baking powder
  ¼ teaspoon salt
  1 teaspoon ground cinnamon
  ¼ teaspoon baking soda
  3 tablespoons cold water
 2½ squares (2½ ounces) unsweetened chocolate, melted
    Ice cream (French Vanilla or Banana)

Beat eggs slightly. Gradually add ⅔ cup sugar and beat until thick and lemon-colored. Sift flour, baking powder, salt, and cinnamon. Add to egg mixture and blend well. Add 3 tablespoons sugar, soda, and water to chocolate; mix. Fold into batter. Grease a jelly-roll pan, 15½ x 10½ x 1 inch, line with wax paper, and grease again. Pour in batter. Bake in preheated moderate oven (375° F.) for about 15 minutes. Turn out on damp towel; remove paper carefully. Roll lengthwise with towel; cool. Unroll, and spread with softened ice cream; re-roll. Freeze until firm. Cut into slices to serve. Makes 8 servings.

JELLY-ROLL SANDWICHES

For each serving use two ½-inch slices of jelly roll or poundcake; put together with a slice of ice cream. Serve at once, or package airtight in foil and freeze. Top with sundae topping or strawberry jam, if desired.

COFFEE-CHOCOLATE PIE

  ½ cup fine chocolate-cookie crumbs
  1 quart coffee ice cream
  ¼ cup chocolate syrup

Butter a 9-inch pie pan and sprinkle with cookie crumbs, reserving 2 tablespoons for top of pie. Carefully spread softened ice cream over crumbs. Sprinkle remaining crumbs on top around edge of pie. Place in freezer until hard. Run tines of fork deeply over pie; pour chocolate syrup into hollows thus formed. Freeze uncovered; then cover with foil; keep in freezer until ready to serve. Cut into 6 or 8 pieces.

APRICOT ICE-CREAM PIE

  1 baked 9-inch pastry shell
  ¼ pound marshmallows
    Apricot preserves
  2 egg whites
  ⅛ teaspoon salt
  ¼ cup sugar
  1 quart vanilla ice cream

Chill pastry shell. Heat marshmallows and 2 tablespoons preserves in top part of double boiler over boiling water until marshmallows are half melted. Remove from heat and beat until smooth. Beat egg whites with salt until foamy; gradually add sugar and beat until stiff. Fold in marshmallow mixture. Press ice cream quickly into chilled shell. Spread with ½ cup preserves. Cover with marshmallow meringue, spreading to cover ice cream completely. Put under preheated broiler for 1 or 2 minutes, or until lightly browned. (This meringue browns very quickly.) Cut into wedges and garnish each with spoonful of preserves. Makes 6 to 8 servings.

SUMMER SNOWBALLS

Scoop vanilla ice cream onto cookie sheets; cover with transparent plastic wrap; freeze firm, package in plastic bags, and store in freezer until ready to use.

If preferred, cut bulk ice cream into cubes. Roll in one of the following coatings and serve with sauce:

Plain or toasted coconut coating with butterscotch or chocolate sauce.

Chocolate "shot" candy or chopped candied-fruit coating with soft custard or Nesselrode sauce.

Crushed peppermint candy or chopped nut coating with chocolate or marshmallow sauce.

Crushed peanut-brittle coating with chopped peaches or soft custard sauce.

MERINGUES GLACÉES

⅛ teaspoon salt
½ teaspoon cream of tartar
2 egg whites
½ cup sugar
½ teaspoon vanilla extract
1 pint strawberry ice cream
1 package (10 ounces) frozen strawberries, thawed

Add salt and cream of tartar to egg whites and beat with rotary beater until foamy; gradually add sugar and continue beating until very stiff. Add vanilla. Spoon some onto lightly buttered brown paper on cookie sheet and flatten to make 4 thin bases about 1½ inches in diameter. With a pastry tube or spoon, surround bases with remaining meringue to height of 2 inches, leaving center unfilled. Bake in preheated very slow oven (250° F.) for 1¼ hours. Transfer paper to a damp board and remove meringues with a spatula. When cold, fill with ice cream and top with strawberries. Makes 4 servings.

ICE-CREAM BONBONS

1 quart ice cream
2 cups chopped pecans or other nuts
1 large package (12 ounces) semisweet chocolate pieces.
½ cup margarine
1 tablespoon instant coffee powder

Make ice-cream balls with large melonball scoop. Immediately roll each ball in nuts. Put in freezer until thoroughly frozen, at least 1 hour. Melt chocolate and margarine in top part of double boiler. Add coffee, and mix. Remove from heat, but keep warm over hot water. Use a fork to dip ice-cream balls into chocolate, working as quickly as possible. When you've dipped 10 or 12, place them in freezer and continue. When chocolate is thoroughly firm, set bonbons in paper cups, 3 or 4 to each individual serving. Cover or wrap with foil or plastic wrap; store in freezer. Makes 30 to 36.

FROZEN CRÊPES

To make crêpes: Beat until smooth 2 egg yolks, ¾ teaspoon salt, 2 teaspoons each of melted butter and sugar, ½ cup all-purpose flour, and 1 cup milk. Beat 2 egg whites until they form soft peaks. Fold into batter and let mixture stand about 1 hour. Brush a 5- or 6-inch skillet with oil. Heat until very hot. Pour on batter by scant ¼ cupfuls. Tilt until pan is completely covered. Turn crêpe after about 15 seconds. Makes 16.

To fill—Place narrow roll of ice cream in center of each crêpe. Bring edges to center. Store in freezer as each is made. Serve with hot Chocolate Fudge Sauce or chocolate syrup. Top with chopped nuts.

BANANA SPLIT

1 ripe banana
1 scoop each of vanilla, chocolate, and strawberry ice cream
2 tablespoons strawberry preserves
2 tablespoons pineapple preserves
2 tablespoons chocolate sauce
　Whipped cream
2 tablespoons chopped nuts
1 maraschino cherry

Cut banana into halves lengthwise. Put on plate, cut side up. Arrange ice cream scoops in row between banana halves. Spoon strawberry preserves over one scoop, pineapple over another, and chocolate sauce over the last. Top with cream and garnish with nuts and cherry. Makes 1 serving.

ICE CREAM AS A DESSERT SAUCE

Serve softened vanilla ice cream over:

Fresh strawberries with Cointreau

Toasted angel-food cake wedges

Chocolate cake or gingerbread

Brownies with chocolate sauce

Sliced bananas and oranges

Peach or apple crisp, oven-warm

Strawberry or peach shortcake

Fruited or plain gelatin dessert

Waffles with fruit or berry sauce

INDIA'S COOKERY

by William Clifford

India is a world apart, a land unto itself. From the Vale of Kashmir to Cape Comorin, from Gujarat to Assam, it spans nearly as much of the globe as all of western Europe from Scandinavia to Greece. The sacred earth of Mother India nurtures even more human beings (not to mention cows, buffaloes, monkeys, insects, and cobras) than there are Europeans. So many people, living in such a vast expanse of land, tropical and temperate, lush and arid, mountainous and flat, naturally enough, enjoy all sorts of foods.

The foods of India and the Indian ways of serving them have evolved over thousands of years. By contrast, classical French cooking dates only from the 18th century. Age alone is no proof of greatness, but anything that survives so long a test of time is certainly worth close scrutiny. What one finds, on looking closely at India, is a national cuisine of such variety and subtlety that it is rivaled only by the Chinese and the French. This will come as a great surprise to most westerners, who tend to think of Indian cooking as beginning and ending with curry. While it is true that a simple curry does not exemplify all the treasures stored away in the many chambers of the house of Indian cuisine, it is also true that an understanding of curry opens the door to that house.

One sometimes hears that curry is not really Indian or that Indians do not use ready-mixed curry powders. The first claim is not true. The word curry appears in languages of both north and south India, and to Indians it means a dish of vegetables or meat with a spicy sauce, not a dry dish. The claim that Indians never use prepared curry powder has more truth, but an Indian wife who grinds and mixes fresh spices every day ends up with powders and pastes much like the ones you can buy prepackaged. She changes the quantities and combinations according to the food she is cooking, family preferences and traditions, or her mood. You can do the same by adding individual spices to commercial curry powders.

Curry powders vary greatly in strength and taste, and you might like to make a taste test of several of them. Include both American and Indian-made ones, together with curry pastes, which are made of the same spices as the powders, mixed with oil and vinegar. Generally the Indian powders and pastes are hotter. All of them, domestic and foreign, contain the same basic six ingredients: coriander, turmeric, cuminseed, fenugreek, black pepper, and cayenne or chili pepper. The proportions vary from brand to brand, or from home to home in India. Although more coriander than anything else is generally used, I have seen formulas where it was used in equal measure with turmeric and cuminseed.

After these basic six there are at least twenty other ingredients that turn up in curry powders in smaller amounts. These include mustard, anise, poppy, celery, and caraway seeds; various dried green leaves including bay; dried peas, onion, and garlic; ginger, dill, nutmeg, mace, cardamom, cloves, cinnamon, orange peel, sugar, and salt. The sweeter spices such as cardamom, cloves, and cinnamon are less often found in Indian curry mixtures than in American ones. Indians tend to reserve them for puddings and other sweets, elaborate rice dishes, and other special preparations.

The reason Indians began to prepare food with all these spices and seasonings is not positively known. One theory holds that curry was invented to cover up the taste of food that was of inferior quality or that had gone bad in the tropical climate. The trouble with this idea is that a good blend of curry brings out the fundamental flavor rather than kills it. Spices will help to preserve good food, but they do not make bad food palatable.

Another possibility is that the eating of highly spiced, hot foods is done instinctively in tropical lands because this causes perspiration, opening the pores and offering relief from the heat. A third and most reasonable explanation holds that the spices came to be used because they were there. If you live in a land where cloves stud the trees and tempt you with their aroma as you walk by, you are likely to use more of them than if they must be shipped thousands of miles and sold by the ounce in a store.

To taste and compare curry powders, I recommend first frying the powder in a couple of tablespoons of oil or butter, then adding chopped onions and more butter, and finally whatever principal ingredient you want to flavor with the sauce. This can be meat or chicken, or for a shorter cooking time something precooked like hard-cooked eggs or fish balls. Add water if necessary, simmer for a few minutes to blend flavors, add salt, and taste. This gives you a much more authentically Indian sauce than the cream sauce into which curry powder is so often blended in western cooking.

While properly blended spices enhance the flavor of the food you put them with, too much hot pepper can scorch your tongue and kill your taste temporarily. If you get accidentally burned in your curry experiments, be reassured that the fire will die away in half an hour or less and leave no scars, and the knowledge you gain is worth the risk. Until you taste eggplant in curry, you do not know the full taste of eggplant. A delicate fish that gives up the ghost when deep fried with tartare sauce will reveal hidden depths of taste in the right spices.

After tasting your curry powders, try out the basic six ingredients individually in the same way. Black and cayenne peppers you already know. Coriander, the plant that dominates curry powder, is a member of the parsley family. It grows in every Indian garden, and its fresh green leaves look something like our big-leaved Italian parsley, which is another carrot cousin. It has a strong pungent flavor, one you may have encountered in both Mexican and Chinese cooking, where fresh coriander leaves are used extensively. The ground seeds of the coriander that go into curry powder are much milder than the leaf, and a dish seasoned with ground coriander alone may remind you faintly of a mild chili con carne or a curry. It has no hot peppery quality.

Cuminseed used alone has a pleasant taste, one that might again call to mind a mild chili con carne. Turmeric has a bright yellow color; a pinch of it will color a whole dish, like saffron. Indians use saffron too, but it is very expensive and its assertive flavor is considered most suitable for sweets and fancy rice dishes. The yellow color in most meat and vegetable dishes comes from turmeric. Turmeric alone has a somewhat bitter taste, but it can be combined very effectively with mustard seed and hot pepper in seasoning a fish. Fenugreek alone is generally too rank, although it serves brilliantly to season a dish of creamed spinach, the way the French do it with mace. This illustrates the exciting principle of combining spices, that an ingredient which fails to please on its own may make an invaluable contribution in a mixture.

My own introduction to food in India, twenty years ago, was not so scientific as this.

Ashore in Bombay after a three-week voyage from Liverpool in 1945, I tasted my first food on Indian soil at the venerable Taj Mahal Hotel. A table-d'hôte lunch at the Taj in those days began with hors-d'oeuvre that was basically European but included an Indian taste or two. It is instinctive with an Indian cook to put a bit of coriander leaf into the ravigote, minced hot green chili to pep up anything calling for chopped onion, and a pinch of curry powder in the mayonnaise. There followed an important main dish, a choice of something European or a curry. And finally a macédoine of tropical fruits or ice cream of an indigenous flavor such as mango, coconut, pomegranate, or pistachio.

By a stroke of luck my first curry at the Taj was the most unusual: a curry of quail. I have since been told that in the refined Moghul cooking of Lucknow chicken is served only in the winter and quail only in the summer. It was August, the monsoon season in Bombay, and the tiny birds had been brought in from the nearby marshes. The quail curry of the Taj was rich with butter, coconut, and poppy seeds, included tomatoes and yogurt, and was finished in the Moghul style, with cream, saffron, lime juice, and cashew nuts. Cashews are the chief nuts of southern India. Almonds and pistachios predominate in the North, and peanuts are found everywhere. Any nut, ground, helps to enrich and thicken a curry, as do yogurt and cream, and such minced vegetables as onions, tomatoes, squashes, and cucumbers. Indians do not thicken sauces with flour or cornstarch or meat gelatin.

The Taj curry was positively paraded to the table by a trio of bearers. Number One filled oversize dinner plates with mountains of rice, not ordinary boiled rice, but extra-quality (India is said to have 200 varieties) rice pilaf, rich with onions and spices, butter and stock, saffron and edible silver leaf. Number Two heaped on the curry. Number Three offered an enormous silver tray of condiments. These included thin crisp wafers made of split-pea flour, usually seasoned with crushed black pepper and cuminseeds in north India but plain in the South, called *popadam* or *papar;* deep-fried bits of dried fish with the saltiness of bacon, called Bombay duck; a mango chutney (sweet) and a mango pickle (sour); coconut scrapings with minced hot chilies and coriander leaves; and a mixture of sliced onions, tomatoes, and fresh lime with minced chilies and coriander. There were no raisins or sieved hard-cooked eggs.

This service was what certain colonials would have called a three-boy curry. A six-boy or ten-boy curry meant that many bearers and more dishes to sample and combine. Actually even the third bearer, the one with the condiments, was superfluous with two such nobly seasoned dishes as a Moghul curry and rich pilaf.

When I had gone through the Taj repertory of curries I began to look around Bombay for other types of food. There were several places popular with the British army, but they seemed to serve everything fried: fried mutton or fish cutlets with Indian seasonings, fried steak with fried eggs, fried tomatoes and onions, fried chips, even fried bread. About the only thing not fried was the Sergeant Major's tea, made with condensed milk, strong and sweet. Then I found the India Coffee House, where snacks were available, including small meat or vegetable fritters, together with fine strong south India coffee.

NOTE

Estimated servings are based on using a single meat or fish dish as a main course. If many dishes are offered on a buffet table, more servings are possible from each dish.

BHUNE KAJU
[Cashews]

    2 cups unsalted cashew nuts
 1½ tablespoons butter or margarine
    1 teaspoon salt
  ¼ teaspoon cayenne
  ½ teaspoon ground cumin seed

Sauté nuts in butter in skillet 3 minutes, or until golden brown. Drain. Mix remaining ingredients and toss with nuts.

BOTI KABOBS
[Barbecued Beef on Skewers]

    2 pounds sirloin steak, cut in 1½-inch pieces
    6 tablespoons plain yogurt
    1 teaspoon ground ginger
  ¼ cup instant minced onion
    4 teaspoons ground coriander
    2 teaspoons ground turmeric
    2 teaspoons poppy seed
  ¼ teaspoon cayenne
    2 teaspoons salt
  ¼ cup melted margarine, or vegetable oil

Put meat in bowl and cover with boiling water. Let stand 5 minutes, then drain. Mix remaining ingredients, except margarine, and add to meat. Mix well and let stand at least 1 hour. String on skewers. Baste with margarine and put under preheated broiler or on grill. Cook 7 to 10 minutes, turning once and basting with margarine. Serve on skewers. Makes 6 servings.
NOTE: If desired, pieces of green pepper, tomato wedges or small whole mushrooms can be broiled with the meat.

MULLIGATAWNY SHORBA
[Mulligatawney Soup]

2 tablespoons butter or margarine
1 tablespoon curry powder
4 teaspoons all-purpose flour
1⅓ cup water
2 cans (10½ ounces each) condensed chicken broth
½ cup heavy cream
Hot cooked rice

Melt butter in 2-quart saucepan, add curry powder and heat until sizzling. Blend in flour. Stir water and broth into curry mixture. Bring to boil, stirring. Add cream and heat. Put a few tablespoonfuls rice in each bowl and add soup. Makes 4½ cups.

NOTE—If preferred, broth can be prepared from chicken backs and necks. Season water for cooking chicken with celery, onion, carrot and parsley. Strain before using in soup. Bits of chicken can be added to soup.

PACHADI
[Yogurt Salad]

Here is a thin soupy salad in the style of Madras, cool and nourishing, delicious on a hot day. You can drink it or eat it with a spoon, have it as a first course, or serve it with a hot curry.

1 pint plain yogurt
1 medium tomato, peeled and diced
1 teaspoon minced hot green chili pepper
1 small onion, minced
¼ cup chopped fresh coriander leaves or parsley
1 teaspoon mustard seed
½ teaspoon cuminseed
Salt to taste

Stir all ingredients together until well mixed. (Juice from the tomato will thin out the yogurt.) If fresh hot green peppers are unavailable, use canned Mexican or Italian ones, adjusting the quantity to taste. Makes 4 servings.

MURGHA KARI
[Chicken Curry with Tomatoes]

This dish from the Punjab takes only 30 minutes to prepare. In India, fresh tomatoes would be used in this dish.

4 medium onions, chopped
2 tablespoons curry powder
½ cup butter or cooking oil
1 cup or 1 can (8 ounces) tomato sauce
2 teaspoons salt
1 frying chicken (2 to 3 pounds)
¾ cup hot water

Use a casserole or large skillet with lid. Cook onions and curry powder in butter for 10 to 15 minutes. Add tomato sauce and salt. Disjoint and skin chicken, and place in sauce. Cook, uncovered, over medium heat, turning fre-

quently until sauce becomes quite dry and chicken tests done with fork, about 30 to 45 minutes. Add hot water, cover pot, and cook over low heat for 5 minutes. Makes 4 servings.

KEEMA MATAR
[Chopped Meat with Peas]

A simple north Indian dish, this is one of the best ways to dress up chopped meat.

1½ pounds ground lamb or beef
1 tablespoon minced garlic
2 tablespoons curry powder
1 cinnamon stick
1 teaspoon minced fresh gingerroot, or ½ teaspoon ground ginger
1 teaspoon salt
1 package (10 ounces) frozen peas

Sauté meat in skillet, chopping and turning to break it up. As soon as pan becomes moist, add all other ingredients except peas. Stir and cook until meat is done, keeping it crumbly, not caked. Add peas and cook and stir until just thawed and heated through. Makes 4 servings.

CHAPATI
[Whole-Wheat Pancakes]

1¾ cups whole-wheat flour
½ teaspoon salt
1 cup water (about)

Mix flour and salt. Gradually stir in water, mixing to form a firm dough. Knead lightly 2 to 3 minutes. Break off pieces the size of a small walnut, and roll paper thin on floured board. Cook quickly on both sides on ungreased griddle. Put on baking sheet, and put under broiler until puffed and lightly browned and crisp, turning once. Serve hot with butter. Makes about 2½ dozen.

PALAK GOSHT
[Lamb with Spinach]

This Punjab dish is relatively dry.

1½ pounds lamb, cut into 1-inch cubes
1 cup plain yogurt
1 medium onion, chopped
1 tablespoon ground coriander
1 teaspoon each of ground turmeric and cuminseed
⅛ teaspoon cayenne
2 teaspoons salt
¼ cup butter or margarine
1 pound spinach, washed and chopped

Place lamb in yogurt to marinate at least 2 hours, preferably overnight. Sauté onion and all spices in butter. Add lamb with yogurt, and mix together. Sauté for another 5 minutes. Place spinach on top of meat, cover, and cook over low heat for 40 minutes, or until meat is done. Stir as necessary to prevent sticking; in the end, meat and spinach will be mixed together. Makes 6 servings.

SARSON BHARA KEKDA
[Shrimps with Mustard]

Here is the Bengali specialty that features the taste of turmeric, without the other curry-powder spices.

    2 tablespoons mustard seed, ground
    1 teaspoon ground turmeric
      Water
    ¼ cup mustard oil, or any cooking oil
    1 large onion, ground
    1½ pounds raw shrimps, peeled and deveined
    1 tablespoon minced hot green chili peppers
    1 teaspoon salt

Make a paste of ground mustard seed and turmeric with a little water. Add all other ingredients, cover, and simmer over very low heat until shrimps are fully pink, 5 to 10 minutes, depending on size of shrimps. Makes 4 servings.

KEKDA BENGALI
[Bengali Crab]

This recipe may also be made with fresh lobster meat, scallops, or shrimps. As a matter of fact, the word *kekda* means either crab or shrimp.

    2 packages (6 ounces each) frozen King crabmeat
    2 medium onions, chopped
    6 tablespoons mustard oil or cooking oil
    1 tablespoon minced gingerroot, or 1 teaspoon pow-
      dered ginger
    1 cup plain yogurt
    1 teaspoon each of ground coriander, turmeric, cumin-
      seed, and salt
    1 teaspoon minced hot green chili pepper

Allow crabmeat to thaw partially. Cook onions in oil until brown, add all other ingredients except crabmeat, and simmer for 5 minutes. Add crabmeat and simmer until thoroughly thawed, then simmer for another 5 minutes. Makes 4 servings.

BHAJI MALIDA MACHLI
[Stuffed Fish with Greens]

    1 whole striped bass or haddock (3 to 4 pounds)
    ½ cup chopped fresh coriander or parsley
    ½ cup chopped green onions, including tops
    2 tablespoons hot green chili pepper
    2 tablespoons minced gingerroot, or 1 teaspoon pow-
      dered ginger
    2 teaspoons salt
    ¼ cup cooking oil
    2 tablespoons fresh lime juice

Wash fish and wipe dry. Combine all other ingredients

and place as much in cavity of fish as it will hold. Brush remainder over outside of fish and place on rack in fish steamer or boiler. Steam with small amount of water until flesh tests done with fork. If no steamer is available, fish may be wrapped in foil and baked in preheated moderate oven (350°F.) for 45 to 50 minutes. Makes 4 servings.

SOOWAR KA GOSHT VINDALOO
[Sour Pork Curry]

This is the sour curry popular in Bombay. In this recipe it is made with pork, but it can be made with any meat, with poultry, or even with shrimps.

    2 pounds lean pork, cut into ¾-inch cubes
    ½ cup cider vinegar
    4 medium onions, chopped
    1 teaspoon minced garlic
    1 tablespoon minced gingerroot or 1½ teaspoons
      powdered ginger
    1 tablespoon mustard seed
    1 teaspoon ground turmeric
    ½ teaspoon cayenne
    ¼ cup cooking oil
    1 cup chicken bouillon
    6 medium raw potatoes, peeled and quartered

Marinate meat in vinegar, onions, garlic, and seasoning for 2 hours or more. Place in top-stove casserole with oil and bouillon. (Sesame oil is used in western India, but any cooking oil will do.) Cook over medium heat for 20 minutes. Add potatoes and cook slowly, covered, about 40 minutes, or unitil they are tender. Add more bouillon if necessary. Makes 6 servings.

ROGAN GOSHT
[Lamb Curry]

An exceptionally rich dish of the Punjab, this type of lamb curry needs plain rice or *chapati* to go with it. It may also be made with beef.

    2 medium onions, chopped
    1 cup butter or margarine
    1 pound small white turnips, peeled and halved
    2 pounds lamb in large cubes
    1 tablespoon sugar
    1 cup plain yogurt
    1 tablespoon ground coriander
    ¼ to ½ teaspoon cayenne
    2 teaspoons salt
    ½ teaspoon each of ground cardamom, cloves, and
      saffron
      Hot water

Brown onions in butter. Add all other ingredients except saffron and hot water. Cook for 25 minutes, or until meat is browned. Add 1 cup hot water. Reduce heat and simmer, covered, for 45 minutes, or until meat is tender. Dissolve saffron in 1 tablespoon hot water and add just before serving. Makes 6 servings.

Chapati

Rogan Gosht

Pachadi

Gajar Halwa

Bhaji Malida Machli

CHANNA KARI
[Chick-Pea Curry]

This provides the vegetable protein required by many Indians who eat no meat. When you use canned rather than dried chick-peas, it is quick to prepare.

    1 tablespoon curry powder
    1 tablespoon minced garlic
    ½ cup chopped sweet green pepper
    ¼ cup cooking oil
    2 cans (each 1-pound 4 ounces) chick-peas
    1 teaspoon salt
    ¼ cup chopped fresh coriander or parsley

Sauté curry powder, garlic, and green pepper in oil. Add chick-peas and salt, stir, and heat through. Simmer for 5 minutes and serve sprinkled with coriander. Makes 6 servings.

MOONG KI DAL
[Mung Beans]

Another of India's best-known foods, rich in protein, this *dal* is made with either mung beans, the dark-green beans used for bean sprouts, or green split peas.

    1 cup mung beans or split peas
    2 tablespoons curry powder
    1 teaspoon salt
    2 whole hot green peppers
    2 medium onions, sliced
    ¼ cup cooking oil

Soak beans in water to cover for several hours. Bring to boil, add curry powder, salt and peppers, and cook for 1 to 2 hours, depending on desired texture of finished dish. Peppers will have lost their heat and may be given to anybody who wants them. Amount of water used will determine whether the result is a thick soup or a mush. Fry onions in oil until very brown and place on top of *dal* with the pan drippings when serving. Makes 6 servings.

PONGAL

This rice dish has the same name as the January harvest festival in South India. It can be made either hot or (as follows) sweet.

    ½ cup mung beans or green split peas
    ½ cup butter or margarine
      Water
    ¾ cup raw rice
    ⅔ cup sugar
    ½ cup cashew nuts
    ¼ cup raisins
      Pinch each ground cloves and cardamom

Fry beans in 1 tablespoon butter until lightly browned.

Bring to boil 3½ cups water, add beans and rice, and cook until very soft. Add 2 tablespoons water to sugar and boil to a syrup, about 10 minutes. Add cooked rice and beans to syrup and stir, adding remaining 7 tablespoons butter, nuts, and raisins. Serve hot, sprinkled with cloves and cardamom. Makes 6 servings.

DAHI BHATH
[Rice with Buttermilk]

This cold rice is made for picnics. Carry it in foil or eat it at home in hot weather.

    1½ cups cold cooked rice
    1 cup buttermilk
    1 teaspoon each minced garlic and hot green chili pepper
    ¼ cup chopped fresh coriander
      Salt to taste

Combine all ingredients. If rice does not hold together, add more buttermilk until desired stickiness is reached. Makes 4 servings.

GAJAR HALWA
[Carrot Dessert]

One of India's most delicious and nutritious desserts.

      Water
    1 can (14 ounces) sweetened condensed milk
    2 cups grated carrot
    1 cup cooking oil, butter, or margarine
    2 tablespoon each chopped blanched almonds and raisins
    ¼ teaspoon ground saffron
    1 tablespoon fresh lime juice, heated

Add 1 can of water to condensed milk and bring to boil. Add carrot and cook over low heat about 45 minutes, stirring occasionally. Add oil gradually. Cook until fat begins to separate. Then add almonds and raisins, and saffron dissolved in lime juice. May be eaten hot or cold. Makes 6 servings.

INVERT SUGAR—A mixture that results from the process used in making jelly, jam, candy, and frosting. With the use of heat and an acid, sugar is changed from sucrose to a mixture of glucose and fructose. Invert sugar keeps the sugar crystals small; therefore, the resulting product is creamier and smoother. The acid used may be vinegar, lemon juice, or cream of tartar. Heat alone can cause inversion of sugar but it occurs more quickly when an acid is added.

Acid in fruit juice also stops jellies and jams from recrystallizing; therefore, it keeps them clear and smooth.

IRISH COOKERY

by Maura Laverty

Plain boiled in its jacket is how we prefer our potato, the vegetable which is a "must" at least once a day in every home. It may be that there are four hundred ways of preparing potatoes, but I have yet to sample one which equals the flavor of the boiled Irish potato. Of course, we serve our potatoes in many other ways. Potato cakes dripping with butter may not be a weight reducer, but they are certainly a delight to the eye and to the palate. Boxty, the traditional dish eaten on Shrove Tuesday, is composed of grated raw potatoes and mashed cooked potatoes with a binding of flour. You may have your boxty baked on the griddle or fried in the pan, but whichever method you choose, you must never forget to stir into the mixture that all-important ring wrapped in paper which foretells an early marriage for the lucky finder.

Although the potato blight of Black '47 which decimated our population taught us not to place too much reliance on the "spud," we in Ireland still believe that a day without potatoes is a day without nourishment. In the West, no one used the cold term "potato field"; with affection they speak of "the potato garden." The very names of Irish potatoes are gastronomic poetry: Ulster Chieftan, Golden Wonder, Aran Banner, May Queen, Skerry Champion, etc.

According to the World Health Organization, we Irish rank high on the list of well-fed peoples. I have often wondered if this is not due mainly to the fact that forty-nine per cent of our population is agricultural, and that most of our farms are small holdings of from thirty to forty acres. Because of this, our farmers produce enough food for themselves and for town dwellers. And the short distances between towns and farms make us independent of processed and frozen food. "Plastic food," as we call it, and no one will ever convince us that it can be as flavorsome and nutritious as the food which comes straight from the good earth.

Long, long ago a poet sang, "A plenteous place is Ireland of hospitable cheer." Part of that cheer is the bread made in our own kitchens with our own grain and buttermilk. White bread, griddle bread, brown bread, potato bread, buns, scones, and potato cakes—the making of these is a daily ritual in most Irish homes. The eating of them is a thrice-daily delight whether served plain with golden butter or with our heather-scented honey or with the homemade jams of which we are proud. Sometimes, but not often enough, our bread is accompanied by cheese, for cheese making on an industrial scale is comparatively new in this pastoral land of ours.

Being gemmed with lakes and rivers, it is natural that Ireland should abound in fish. The lazy Suir, the tree-fringed Blackwater, the broad Boyne, and the lovely lakes of the Shannon—these are the principal sources of that noblest of fish, the gleaming salmon. I have stood on Galway Bridge and watched those arcs of silver take the leap with an indolence which bespoke their fatness.

Every lake and river in Ireland offers a wealth of trout, both brown and speckled. From the Liffey to the smallest lake in Connemara, you will find trout galore. So well stocked are our rivers and lakes with salmon and trout that these are among our chief exports to France and Britain where, no doubt, cooks have their own ways of preparing them. Here, at home, we like our salmon poached and served whole with melted butter and lemon: or cut into thick slices and simmered golden in butter. And I know of no better way with a good-size trout than to split it, remove the backbone, dip it into seasoned rolled oats, and fry it in butter. Some people like to add a little vinegar and mustard to the butter in which the trout has been fried.

As in so many other countries, Christmas is the great Irish feast. It commences on Christmas Eve with the lighting of the Christmas candle which is placed in the window of every house in the country as a sign to any homeless strangers who may be abroad that we are eager and willing to try to compensate for the cold welcome offered to Mary and Joseph on the first Christmas Eve. When midnight ends the Christmas Eve fast, there is a meal of spiced beef, corned brisket rich in spices, simmered to tenderness and served cold. For dinner on Christmas Day there is the special fattened fowl, a goose stuffed with sage-and-onion dressing, or a roast turkey ringed with golden sausages and bursting with parsley-and-thyme dressing. In either case, a boiled ham accompanies the fowl. The time-honored pudding on Christmas Day is, of course, a flaming plum pudding which may have been made for as long as six months in advance, since its brandied, fruity spiciness improves with keeping. The same is true of the cake of the year: every cook worth her salt makes a rich fruitcake well in advance. Layered with marzipan and coated with snowy icing, it is decorated to taste. In our house, for many years the choice has been a miniature crib.

BREADS

BASIC RECIPE FOR SODA BREAD

- 2 cups all-purpose flour
- 1½ teaspoons baking powder
- ¾ teaspoon salt
- ¼ teaspoon baking soda
- 1 cup buttermilk

Mix dry ingredients. Add buttermilk and stir to make a soft dough. Turn out on lightly floured board and knead for about 1 minute. Shape the dough into a round loaf about 8 inches in diameter. Put in a greased round pan or on a greased cookie sheet. With a sharp knife, cut a cross on the top. Bake in preheated moderate oven (350°F.) for 40 minutes, or until done. Bread is done if it sounds hollow when tapped with knuckles. Cool on its side before cutting. For a soft crust, wrap loaf in a tea towel and stand on its side to cool.

BOXTY-ON-THE-GRIDDLE

For this recipe I am indebted to Grannie Doyle of Lennox Street. Dublin, who told me. "Now I'll tell you how our boxty bread was baked. My mother took a couple of grated raw potatoes and a skillet of hot mashed potatoes, 3 or 4 handfuls of flour with a bit of butter rubbed in and a generous grain of salt—all mixed well and roled out on the board, cut into squares, and baked on a well-greased griddle to the tune of the children singing:

Three pans of boxty, baking all the day, What use is boxty without a cup of tay?

The children in those days got very little 'tay.' Each one got a nice tin porringer of milk and sat up to the table and ate hot buttered boxty to the fill—and we lived."

BOXTY-ON-THE-PAN

1 cup each grated raw potatoes, all-purpose flour, and mashed potatoes
2 teaspoons each baking powder and salt
2 eggs beaten
¼ cup milk (about)
Butter

Squeeze grated raw potatoes in a cloth to remove as much moisture as possible. Sift flour with baking powder and salt. Mix all potatoes and dry ingredients well together with beaten eggs; add sufficient milk to make a dropping batter. Drop by tablespoonfuls onto a hot buttered frying pan and cook over moderate heat, allowing about 4 minutes on each side. Serve hot and well buttered, with or without sugar. Makes 4 to 6 servings.

SOUPS

COCK-A-LEEKIE SOUP

When the Scottish planters came over the border and took over the rich Ulster farms, ordering their rightful owners "to Hell or to Connaught," they brought with them just one good thing: their cock-a-leekie soup.

1 elderly fowl (stewing chicken, about 4 pounds)
4 pounds boneless shin of beef
3 dozen leeks
3 quarts cold water
1 tablespoon salt
1 teaspoon pepper
1 cup pitted dried prunes

Truss the fowl as for boiling. Cut up beef into small pieces. Wash leeks, cut into thin slices, using as much as possible of the green part. Put all ingredients except prunes in a large pot. Simmer for 3 hours, then add prunes and simmer for 1 hour longer. Take up the fowl, remove the skin, gristle, and bones; chop the meat small and return to the pot. Correct seasoning. The prunes should be left in the soup. Makes 5 quarts.

PRIDE OF ERIN SOUP

1 green cabbage (about 1 pound)
2 tablespoons butter
3 tablespoons chopped onion
¼ cup chopped raw potato
½ teaspoon ground mace
2 tablespoons all-purpose flour
2½ cups milk
2½ cups water or chicken bouillon
Salt and pepper
¼ cup heavy cream, whipped
2 tablespoons chopped parsley
2 tablespoons grated cheese (Parmesan preferably)

Quarter the cabbage; cut away the hard stalk. Cover with boiling water and leave for 5 minutes. Drain, pat dry, and shred. Melt butter in heavy pan over low heat and simmer chopped onion until tender, but without browning. Add cabbage and potato and stir over low heat; add mace. Stir in flour to coat all ingredients, but do not brown. Add liquids, bring to a boil, and simmer for 20 minutes, or until vegetables are tender. Rub through a sieve. Reheat and add salt and pepper to taste. If soup is too thick, add a little boiling milk. Serve with a spoonful of whipped cream on each serving. Sprinkle parsley and grated cheese on cream. Makes about 7 cups.

FISH

LIFFEY TROUT WITH MUSHROOM SAUCE

I have known the delight of preparing and eating this dish after catching the trout myself in a leaf-dappled stretch of the Liffey. And, on the way home, I stopped at a field where cuppeens (little button mushrooms) nestled like fallen stars among the tufts of grass. There are few joys on earth to compare with gathering mushrooms in the early morning. Next best is to buy your trout and your mushrooms and to prepare the fish in this way:

4 small trout
6 tablespoons all-purpose flour
Salt and pepper
6 tablespoons butter
12 button mushrooms (about)
1 cup half cream and half milk
1 tablespoon chopped parsley

Clean, wash, and dry trout. Roll in ¼ cup flour seasoned with pepper and salt. Fry in ¼ cup butter. Drain, and keep hot. Wipe and slice the mushrooms and sauté in the same pan. Melt remaining 2 tablespoons butter in a small saucepan; stir in remaining 2 tablespoons flour. Add cream and milk and season to taste. Add mushrooms and reheat to serving point. Garnish trout with parsley and serve sauce separately. Makes 4 servings.

DINGLE MACKEREL

6 small mackerel
¼ cup white vinegar
¾ cup water
  Few grains of cayenne
6 peppercorns
1-inch piece of cinnamon stick
1 bay leaf
3 parsley sprigs
2 teaspoons salt

Cut off head and fins. Wash and clean mackerel, split, and remove backbones and tails. Roll up and place in a 1½-quart casserole. Bring vinegar, water, spices, and seasonings to boil and pour over fish. Cover and bake in preheated moderate oven (375°F.) for 45 minutes. Makes 6 servings.

MEAT AND POULTRY

STUFFED PORK FILLETS

2 fresh pork fillets or tenderloin
1 cup fine dry bread crumbs
1 parboiled onion, chopped
¼ teaspoon ground sage
  Butter
  Milk or chicken bouillon
  Salt and pepper
  Thick brown gravy
  Apple sauce

Split fillets lengthwise and flatten them well. Combine bread crumbs with onion, sage, 1 tablespoon melted butter, sufficient milk to bind, and salt and pepper to taste. Place one fourth of stuffing on each fillet piece; fold over each piece and secure in place by sewing or skewering. Weigh. Place in baking pan, dot with butter, and roast in preheated moderate oven (350°F.) allowing 40 minutes to the pound. Serve with brown gravy and apple sauce. Makes 4 servings.

BEEF-AND-KIDNEY PUDDING

  All-purpose flour
1 teaspoon baking powder
  Salt
1 cup finely chopped beef suet
1 cup fine stale-bread crumbs
  Water
¾ pound round steak, cut into small pieces
¼ pound beef kidney, cut into small pieces
¼ pound mushrooms, sliced
2 tablespoons chopped onion
1 tablespoon chopped parsley
¼ teaspoon pepper
⅔ cup beef bouillon or water

Sift 1 cup flour with baking powder and ½ teaspoon salt. Add suet and crumbs and mix well. Add enough water to make a stiff dough. Line a greased 1-quart casserole with half the dough. Put meats, mushrooms, onion, and parsley in layers in lined casserole, sprinkling each layer with 3 tablespoons flour, seasoned with 1 teaspoon salt and pepper. Add bouillon. Cover with remaining dough, moisten edges, and press together well. Cover with greased foil and steam for 3 hours. Makes 4 servings.

VEAL HOT POT

2 pounds lean veal
2 large onions
8 young carrots
¼ pound sliced bacon
¼ cup all-purpose flour
  Salt and pepper to taste
2 tablespoons dry sherry
1 cup chicken bouillon or water

Dice veal, peel and slice onions, wash and slice carrots, dice bacon. Mix flour with salt and pepper; combine sherry with bouillon. Put layer of onion and carrot in a greased 2-quart casserole; add a layer of bacon and veal. Repeat until all are used, sprinkle each layer with some seasoned flour. Add combined sherry and bouillon. Cover closely and cook in preheated very slow oven (275°F.) for about 2½ hours. Makes 4 to 6 servings.

BAKED LIMERICK HAM

Long ago a whole pig would have been baked in a pit lined with stones previously heated in the fire. Or it might have been cooked in one of the great bronze caldrons which were the most treasured possessions of well-to-do households. Pork was always the favorite meat of the Irish. Wasn't it as a swineherd that St. Patrick first came to us? When the meat was cooked the various cuts were served according to the social importance of the guests:

A thigh for a king and a poet;
A chine for a literary sage;
A leg for a young lord;
Heads for charioteers;
A haunch for a queen.

"The hero's morsel" was the choice tidbit reserved for the man who had performed the greatest or bravest exploit . . . and woe betide anyone who helped himself to it if he was not entitled to the honor. One of the biggest battles in Irish history occurred because a chieftain wrongfully appropriated "the hero's morsel."

1 Limerick ham (10 pounds)
  Water
1 tablespoon whole cloves
¾ cup honey
1 cup Madeira wine

Soak ham in cold water for 12 hours. Place in a pot, cover well with fresh water, and bring slowly to a boil; simmer for 2 hours. Place ham in a baking pan, remove the skin, and stick cloves over the entire surface. Pour honey mixed with Madeira wine over the ham and bake in preheated moderate oven (350°F.) for 2½ hours, or until the knuckle bone can be removed. Makes about 20 servings.

SEVENTEENTH-CENTURY BEEF POT ROAST

    1 cup very finely ground veal
    1 egg white
    3 pounds boneless beef (select a thick solid piece)
    4 slices of bacon
      Salt and pepper
    6 tablespoons all-purpose flour
    3 tablespoons beef drippings
 1½ cups water or beef bouillon
    1 cup red wine
    4 medium mushrooms, sliced

Mix veal and egg white. Make holes here and there in the beef and fill with veal mixture. Lay the strips of bacon on top and tie in place. Mix salt and pepper with 2 tablespoons flour; rub into the meat. In heavy pan sear meat quickly on all sides in smoking hot drippings. Add water, wine, and a sprinkling of salt and pepper. Cover and simmer until tender, about 3½ hours. When done, place meat on a platter, remove bacon and string, and keep the meat hot. Skim fat from the liquor and cook down until liquor measures about 2 cups. Add mushrooms, and thicken with remaining 4 tablespoons flour blended to a paste with a little cold water. Correct seasoning; serve the gravy separately. This beef is excellent cold. Makes 8 servings.

COCK OF THE NORTH

    1 capon, about 6 pounds
      Juice of 2 lemons
  ¼ cup all-purpose flour
      Salt and pepper
    1 cup butter
  ½ pound bacon, diced
    5 small yellow onions
  ¾ cup Irish whiskey
    1 garlic clove
  ½ teaspoons ground allspice
    1 cup dry red wine
    1 cup water
    2 egg yolks
    2 tablespoons light cream
    1 pound pearl onions
    1 pound mushrooms

Cut up capon as for fricassee. Dip pieces into lemon juice and then into 3 tablespoons flour, seasoned with salt and pepper. Brown in butter. Add bacon and small yellow onions; sprinkle with 1 tablespoon flour, and brown again. Flame capon with Irish whiskey. Add salt, pepper, garlic, and allspice. Cover with wine and water, and simmer gently for 45 to 60 minutes.

For the sauce make a broth with the neck and gib-lets. Strain off the liquor from the bird and add to the broth. Reduce to half by rapid boiling. Thicken with raw egg yolks beaten with cream; reheat but do not boil after adding egg.

Serve capon in a dish garnished with the pearl onions and mushrooms, each cooked separately in water and lemon juice. Pour part of the sauce over the capon and serve the remainder separately. Makes 8 to 10 servings.

IRISH STEW

The original Irish stew was made with spareribs. Today we make it with mutton.

    2 pounds neck of mutton or lamb
  ½ pound streaky bacon
    9 medium (3 pounds) raw potatoes, peeled
 10 to 12 small onions, sliced
      Salt and pepper
    2 cups cold water

Cut meat into ¾-inch cubes and trim away as much fat as possible. Remove rind from bacon and cut into 1-inch pieces. Place a layer of bacon, potatoes, and onions and sprinkle with seasoning. Repeat layers, finishing with potatoes. Add water, let it come slowly to a boil, remove any scum, cover, and simmer gently for 2½ hours. The potatoes should be cooked to a pulp. Makes 4 servings.

VEGETABLES

BRAISED CABBAGE

    1 medium Savoy cabbage
    2 tablespoons butter
  ¼ cup chopped onion
    2 large tomatoes, skinned, seeded, and chopped
    1 tablespoon all-purpose flour
    1 cup chicken bouillon
      Salt and pepper to taste
    2 teaspoons finely chopped parsley
  ¼ cup dairy sour cream

Quarter cabbage, remove most of stalk, cover with boiling water, and blanch for 10 minutes. Drain and pat dry in a towel. Place in greased glass baking dish. Melt butter over moderate heat and sauté onion until tender but not brown; add chopped tomatoes, stir in flour, add bouillon, and bring to a boil, stirring constantly. Add seasoning and parsley, mix well, and spoon the mixture over the quartered cabbage. Cook, covered, in preheated moderate oven (375°F.) for 30 minutes, basting occasionally. Stir several tablespoons of liquid from cabbage into sour cream. Pour over cabbage, and bake for 15 minutes longer. Makes 4 to 6 servings.

SLIEVE na mBAN CARROTS

The ruddy crest of *Slieve na mBan* (The Mountain of the Women) rising above its stole of milk-white mist gives its name to this dish of cream-wreathed carrots.

    12 young carrots
     3 tablespoons butter
    ½ cup milk
       Salt and pepper to taste
    ½ cup heavy cream
     2 egg yolks
     1 teaspoon finely chopped parsley

Halve carrots lengthwise. Melt butter over moderate heat, add milk, season with salt and pepper, add carrots, and cook gently until tender. Remove from heat, stir in cream and beaten egg yolks, and reheat but do not boil, stirring until eggs thicken. Correct seasoning and add parsley. Makes 4 servings.

POTATO COLLOPS

There is no denying that the best way of all to cook potatoes is to boil or bake them in their jackets. And, notwithstanding the advice of foreign cooks, the skins of potatoes should not be gashed when being put to cook. If the skins should burst slightly in the boiling and subsequently drying (boiled potatoes should always be shaken for a minute or two over low heat after being drained) it is all to the good: there is no more appetizing sight than the floury "grin" of a burst boiled potato.

Admittedly, during the weeks before the new potatoes are ready for digging, last season's potatoes begin to show their age and sometimes need dressing up. And I know of few better potato dishes than Collops ("collop," by the way, means a small portion of any foodstuff). Originally "collope," the 16th century Irish referred to our famous rashers and eggs as "collopes and eggs."

    3 medium raw potatoes
    1 large onion
      Salt and pepper to taste
    2 teaspoons chopped parsley
    ¼ pound bacon, diced (to be omitted on fast days)
    2 tablespoons butter
    1 cup milk, boiled
    3 tablespoons grated cheese

Pare potatoes and cut into very thin slices. Chop onion. Place a layer of vegetables in a greased baking dish. Sprinkle with seasonings, parsley, and diced bacon (rind removed), and dot with butter. Repeat layers until all ingredients are used, finishing with potatoes. Pour in milk and sprinkle top with grated cheese. Cover and bake in preheated moderate oven (350°F.) for 45 minutes. Uncover and continue cooking until potatoes are done and top layer is brown. Makes 4 servings.

COLCANNON

This delectable mixture of buttered greens and potatoes is yet another way of foretelling the future at Halloween.

A heaped portion is served on each plate. A well is made in the center of the heap to hold a generous amount of butter. The colcannon is eaten from around the outside of the heap, each person dipping his fork first into the colcannon and then into the melted butter. The perfect accompaniment is a glass of fresh buttermilk.

In the Midlands colcannon is called "Thump." In the North and West it is called "Champ." Here is a recipe for colcannon. Put the cooked potatoes through a sieve or ricer. Beat in a good lump of butter and enough hot cream or milk to make the mixture light and fluffy. Add to the potato mixture half its bulk of finely chopped cooked kale and 1 tablespoon minced onion. Add salt and pepper to taste, beat well, and reheat thoroughly. And don't forget the ring and that all-important silver coin.

HAGGERTY

    3 medium raw potatoes
    1 large onion
    2 tablespoons bacon fat
    ¾ cup grated Cheddar cheese
      Salt and pepper to taste

Wash and pare potatoes, cut into paper-thin slices, and pat dry in a towel. Slice onion very thin. Heat 1 tablespoon bacon fat in a heavy frying pan and fill pan with alternate layers of potatoes and onion and cheese, finishing with potatoes. Sprinkle each layer with salt and pepper. Dot the top layer of potatoes with remaining 1 tablespoon bacon fat. Cook over moderate heat until potatoes are almost tender. Turn the Haggerty carefully onto a platter, slip it, top side down, back into the pan, and continue cooking until done. To serve, cut into wedges. Makes 4 servings.

DESSERTS

APPLE PUDDENY-PIE

    4 medium cooking apples
    1 teaspoon ground cinnamon
    ½ teaspoon ground nutmeg
    ½ cup sugar
    ½ teaspoon salt
    ⅓ cup water
    1 teaspoon grated lemon rind
    2 teaspoons fresh lemon juice
    ½ teaspoon baking soda
    1 cup quick-cooking oats
    ⅓ cup butter

Pare and core apples. Cut in eighths and place in greased baking dish about 10 x 6 inches. Sprinkle with combined spices, sugar, and a little salt. Mix water, lemon rind and juice and pour over apples. Add baking soda and remaining salt to oats; work butter into this mixture until crumbly. Spread oatmeal mixture over apples and bake in preheated moderate oven (375°F.) for 40 minutes. Makes 4 to 6 servings.

LENTEN CAKE [EGGLESS]

½ cup butter
3 tablespoons molasses
1 cup milk
4 cups sifted all-purpose flour
¾ cup sugar
3 teaspoons ground allspice
2 teaspoons baking powder
1 teaspoon baking soda
½ teaspoon salt
½ cup seedless raisins

Melt butter, add molasses and milk, and cool. Sift together flour, sugar, allspice, baking powder, baking soda, and salt. Stir butter mixture into dry ingredients. Add raisins and mix well. Pour into buttered pan, 13 x 9 x 2 inches, and bake in preheated moderate oven (350°F.) for 30 minutes.

BARMBRACK

The term *barmbrack* for an Irish fruit loaf or cake does not derive from barm or leaven. It is a corruption of the Irish word *arán breac*, "speckled bread."

Halloween in Ireland would be unthinkable without barmbrack, the sweet and sticky-crusted loaf which foretells one's fortune for the coming year. Into the dough we knead (paper-wrapped to guard against choking or appendicitis) a ring for marriage, a silver coin for wealth, and a button for single blessedness.

7 cups sifted all-purpose flour
2 teaspoons ground allspice
1½ teaspoons salt
1 cup sugar
2 packages active dry yeast
1½ cups warm water
1½ cups warm milk
6 tablespoons butter
2½ cups seedless raisins
¾ cup dry currants
¾ cup chopped citrus peel
Paper-wrapped charms

Sift flour, allspice, salt, and sugar into a large bowl. Dissolve yeast in warm water (105°F. to 115°F.). Add yeast and warm milk to dry ingredients, and mix thoroughly. Knead into a ball and turn out on a floured board. Knead until the dough no longer feels sticky and comes away clean from the board. Wash and grease the bowl, place dough in bowl, cover, and let stand in a warm place until doubled in bulk, about 1½ hours. Turn the dough onto a floured board and flatten to a large round. Place butter, fruits, and peel in the middle, and work in these ingredients by squeezing and kneading until they are evenly incorporated in the dough. At this point, work in the paper-wrapped charms. Return the dough again to the greased bowl, cover, and leave to rise for about 45 minutes. Divide the dough into two parts and shape to fit 2 loaf pans, each 9 x 5 x 3 inches. Half fill the pans, cover, and leave in a warm place to rise to the top of pans. Bake in preheated hot oven (450°F.) about 50 minutes, reducing the heat to 425°F. for the last 15 minutes of baking. Five minutes before the barmbracks are done, brush with sugar and water in equal quantities. Makes 2 large barmbracks.

POTATO SEEDY CAKE

1½ cups sifted all-purpose flour
½ cup sugar
2 teaspoons baking powder
1 teaspoon salt
½ teaspoon ground allspice
¼ cup butter
1 teaspoon caraway seeds
½ cup dry currants
1 cup mashed potatoes
2 eggs, well beaten

Sift together flour, sugar, baking powder, salt, and allspice; rub in butter. Add caraway seeds. Add currants and mashed potatoes, mixing well. Add eggs. Place in a well-greased flat pan, 8 x 8 inches, and bake in preheated hot oven (425°F.) for 30 minutes. Cut into squares and serve hot. Makes 9 squares.

IRISH COFFEE

Pour 1 jigger Irish whiskey into a warmed goblet or coffee cup. Add 1 to 2 teaspoons sugar. Add hot strong coffee to within ½ inch of the top. Top with chilled sweetened whipped cream. Makes 1 serving.

IRISH MOSS or CARRAGEEN—A
species of small edible seaweed, varying in color from greenish yellow to purplish brown, named after Carragheen, Waterford County, Ireland. This seaweed is found along the coast of the British Isles, the rocky shores of continental Europe, and the eastern shores of the northern United States and Canada. The moss used domestically is obtained principally from New Hampshire and Massachusetts. The plants are washed in salt water and spread on the beach to dry and bleach, the process being repeated several times. The greater part of the supply is used for clarifying malt beverages. The remainder is retailed through druggists and health-food stores. It was formerly used in New England and still is, occasionally, to make a blancmange-type dessert.

IRISH MOSS BLANCMANGE

¾ cup Irish moss
4 cups milk
Dash of salt
½ teaspoon lemon or vanilla extract
Sugar and cream

Soak moss in cold water for 5 minutes. Then tie moss in cheesecloth and put in top part of double boiler with milk and salt. Put over boiling water and cook, covered, for 30 minutes. Remove cheesecloth bag and add flavoring to milk mixture. Pour into bowl and chill until firm. Serve with sugar and cream, or with fruit. Makes 4 servings.

ITALIAN COOKERY

Italian cuisine is divided into butter and oil cooking. Northern Italy, cooler and pastoral, produces and uses excellent butter. Central and Southern Italy produce and use oil and cured pork fats, which do not suffer from the heat. Within these two basic divisions, the variety in foods is also very great, for historical, geographical, and economic reasons.

Italy's history has been one of independent tribes, cities, duchies, and kingdoms until the country was united, in 1870, into one nation. After the second World War, the kingdom became a republic. In spite of the unification, an intensive local patriotism is part of the Italian character. Villages, towns, and regions askance at each other, as exemplified in the Italian proverb of *moglie e buoi dei paesi tuoi,* "wives and cattle from your own locality."

This regional feeling has produced an independent, nonstandardized people and an infinite variety of architecture, customs, products, and cooking. Verona and Venice, for instance, are only a few hours' train journey apart, but their food is quite different.

Throughout Italy the cooking is careful, with an instinctive feeling for flavor and texture combination. The laborer who eats his bread sprinkled with oil and chopped herbed tomatoes, the cook who can take a piece of cheese, put it between two slices of bread, fry it, and serve it with anchovy sauce, or transform a few little pieces of veal into dozens of delightful dishes are people who enjoy good food and are discriminating about it.

In Italy, it is always worthwhile to find out what foods and wines can be had locally, because many of them are not transported away from home, and many of them are strictly seasonal. Quite a number of dishes are made only in certain seasons or for certain holidays. Similar dishes turn up in many regions, but under various names and with their own special character. *Ravioli,* for instance, is called *ravioli* only in Piedmont and Genoa, and *tortellini, tortelli, agnolotti, anolini, cappelletti,* and *melfatti* in other places, and is everywhere filled with different stuffings.

No writing about Italian cookery would be complete without mention of Italian wines. All of Italy is a vineyard, and wine is part of the daily food, drunk at meals. The best-known Italian wine is red Chianti. But any Italian region, town, or village produces its own excellent wines, which should be savored by travelers in Italy.

APPETIZERS

ANTIPASTO MISTO
[Antipasto Plates]

The **antipasto** (meaning "before the meal") platters and plates can be a little salad or a meal in itself. The idea is to combine vegetables, meats, fish, and eggs in as colorful an assortment as possible. Great care is taken in arranging the foods in an attractive and orderly way.

Antipasto Combinations

Arrange the following on a platter or plate: slices of Italian salami; rolled-up prosciutto or other ham; tuna in olive oil; black and green olives; eggs sliced or stuffed and topped, in both cases, with a parsley sprig or 3 capers; pickled mushrooms; radish roses; tomato slices, strips of red pimientos, and green peppers marinated in olive oil; celery stuffed with mashed Gorgonzola or other blue-veined cheese; eggplant salad; artichoke hearts marinated in a mixture of olive oil, white wine, basil or other herb, and salt and pepper; rolled anchovies, sardines, and any relishes such as pickled peppers, cauliflower, and artichokes, labeled Italian style in food stores.
Cantaloupe or honeydew melon wedges wrapped in slices of prosciutto; pare chilled melon and cut into wedges; wrap with wafer-thin slices of prosciutto (allow 2 melon wedges for each person to be served); mushroom salad; anchovy-stuffed eggs; tomatoes; sliced fennel; slices of Italian salami; potato salad; pimiento marinated in olive oil; green olives; anchovies; sardines.
Meatless antipasto: overlapping slices of tomatoes and hard-cooked eggs, surrounded by chunks of tuna in olive oil and rolled anchovies, garnished with mayonnaise and decorated with parsley sprigs.

MEDAGLIONI DI MOZZARELLA
[Medallions of Mozzarella Cheese]

Cut medallions (diameter of fifty-cent piece and ½ inch thick) of Mozzarella or other cheese. Roll each piece of cheese in flour, well-beaten egg, and fine bread crumbs. Deep fry in ¼ inch of olive oil in skillet until golden-brown.

MELANZANE ALLA MARINARA
[Marinated Eggplant Appetizer]

- 1 large unpeeled eggplant, cut into 1-inch cubes
- ½ cup white vinegar (preferably wine vinegar)
- 1 teaspoon salt
- ½ teaspoon white pepper
- 1 garlic clove, minced
- 1 teaspoon dried oregano
- ½ teaspoon dried basil
- ¾ cup olive oil

Boil eggplant in boiling water to cover for 8 to 10 minutes; drain. Cubes should be soft but retain their shape. Mix other ingredients except oil. Place drained eggplant in large bowl and pour marinade over. Toss thoroughly. Marinate overnight, or for at least 8 hours. Before serving, toss with oil. This will keep about 1 week in the refrigerator. Makes 6 to 8 servings.

PROSCIUTTO WITH FRUITS

One of the most typical of Italian first courses for luncheon is the ham of Parma called prosciutto. This specially cured ham is eaten in thin slices. It is combined with various fruits and eaten with a little freshly ground black pepper and in some cases with a squeeze of lemon. These paper-thin slices of ham are always laid over the fruits they are to complement. Try them with:

Luscious ripe melon wedges
Quarters of peeled ripe pears

Prosciutto with Honeydew

Wedges of ripe pineapple
Whole ripe figs with ham slices wrapped around them cornucopia fashion
Crisp bread and fresh butter go with this exciting appetizer.

SOUPS

MINESTRONE MILANESE

¼ cup olive oil
1 garlic clove, minced
1 onion, minced
1 leek, diced (when in season)
1 tablespoon chopped parsley
1 teaspoon dried thyme
1 tablespoon tomato paste
¼ cup water
3 canned or fresh tomatoes, peeled, seeded, and chopped
3 celery stalks, chopped
2 carrots, diced
2 potatoes, diced
¼ small cabbage, shredded
2 zucchini, diced
6 cups hot water or bouillon
Salt to taste
½ teaspoon pepper
⅓ cup raw rice
1 to 1½ cups cooked and drained dried beans
Grated Parmesan cheese

Antipasto Misto

Put olive oil in large kettle. Add garlic, onion, leek, parsley, and thyme and cook until soft. Add tomato paste thinned with water and cook for 5 minutes. Add all remaining ingredients except rice, beans, and cheese. Simmer, covered, for 1 hour. Bring to boil, add rice, and cook until soft. Add beans; heat. Serve with cheese. Makes 3 quarts, or 6 servings.

NOTE: In this northern version of Italy's national soup, rice replaces pasta.

PAVESE
[Egg Consommé]

6 cups beef or chicken consommé
1 tablespoon minced parsley
3 eggs
3 tablespoons grated Parmesan cheese

Bring consommé to a boil. Beat parsley, eggs, and cheese together. Stir into consommé and cook, stirring, for a few seconds, or until eggs are set. Makes 1½ quarts, or 4 to 6 servings.

ZUPPA VENEZIANA DI PESCE
[Venetian Fish Soup]

3 pounds white-fleshed fish, including heads
3 cups water
1 onion, studded with 2 cloves
2 bay leaves
3 parsley sprigs
1 teaspoon salt
¼ teaspoon pepper
½ teaspoon dried marjoram
½ cup olive oil
1 garlic clove
½ cup dry white wine
1 cup stewed tomatoes

Trim fish and cut flesh into bite-size pieces. Reserve. Combine trimmings, including heads, water, onion, 1 bay leaf, parsley, salt, pepper, and ¼ teaspoon marjoram. Simmer, covered, for 30 to 40 minutes, stirring occasionally. Drain and reserve fish stock; there should be about 2 cups. Discard everything else. Fry fish pieces in the hot olive oil with remaining ¼ teaspoon marjoram, bay leaf and garlic. Add stock, wine, and tomatoes. Simmer, covered, for 15 minutes. Remove garlic. Makes 1½ quarts, or 4 to 6 servings.

NOTE: This fish soup is almost a stew.

MINESTRONE DI PASTA E FAGIUOLI
OR PASTA FAZULA
[Thick Soup of Macaroni and Beans]

Wash 1 pound dried pinto or navy beans and soak overnight in 2 quarts water. Cook beans in the same water. Prepare sauce. Sauté ½ cup chopped salt pork, bacon, or ham with 1 minced garlic clove or 2 tablespoons minced onion and a dash of chili pepper. Add to beans and cook until tender. Just before serving, add 1 pound

cooked and drained *ditalini* (macaroni) and let simmer for 5 minutes. Stir well, and serve topped with grated Romano cheese. Makes 8 to 10 servings.

FISH AND SEAFOOD

PESCE FRITTO
[Fried Fish Fillets, Italian Style]

4 medium fish fillets
½ cup all-purpose flour
½ cup olive oil
  Salt to taste
  Lemon wedges

Coat fillets with flour and fry in hot oil for about 8 minutes on each side. Drain on absorbent paper. Sprinkle with salt and serve with lemon wedges. Makes 4 servings.

NOTE: The olive oil gives fried fish a unique flavor.

Minestrone Milanese

PESCE LESSO
[Poached Fish, Italian Style]

2 tablespoons minced parsley
1 garlic clove, minced
3 tablespoons olive oil
1 cup hot water
1½ pounds flounder fillets
1 teaspoon salt
⅛ teaspoon pepper
Dash of dried oregano

Cook parsley and garlic in olive oil in skillet for 3 minutes. Add hot water and bring to boil. Add fish and seasonings. Cover, bring again to boil, and cook for 5 to 10 minutes. Serve with the liquid. Makes 4 servings.

PESCE ALLA SICILIANA
[Sicilian Fish]

4 slices of halibut or swordfish or other thick fish (1¾ to 2 pounds)
¼ cup olive oil
1 tablespoon chopped parsley
1 garlic clove, minced
½ cup white vinegar
2 pounds tomatoes, peeled, seeded, and chopped
Salt and pepper to taste
1 package (10 ounces) frozen peas, thawed

In skillet brown fish in hot oil. Add parsley, garlic, and vinegar. Cook until liquid has almost evaporated. Add tomatoes, salt, and pepper. Simmer, covered, for 5 minutes. Add peas. Simmer, covered, about 30 minutes. Put fish on hot platter and pour sauce over it. Makes 4 to 6 servings.

SCAMPI AI FERRI
[Garlic Broiled Shrimps]

2 pounds raw shrimps
½ cup olive oil
2 garlic cloves, minced
2 teaspoons salt
⅓ cup chopped parsley
Lemon wedges

Split shrimp shells with scissors. Remove shells and devein shrimps. Arrange shrimps in greased shallow baking pan. Sprinkle with olive oil, garlic, salt, and half of parsley. Broil about 4 inches from heat for 5 to 7 minutes on each side, depending on size of shrimps. Sprinkle with remaining parsley and serve with lemon wedges. Makes 4 servings.

MEAT AND POULTRY

SCALOPPINE DI VITELLO
[Veal Scaloppine]

1 pound veal scaloppine, cut very thin
Salt and pepper
⅓ cup all-purpose flour
6 tablespoons butter
¼ cup dry white wine

Coat scaloppine with seasoned flour. Sauté in hot butter about 3 minutes on each side. Add white wine. Simmer for 2 minutes longer. Serve at once. Makes 3 or 4 servings.

COSTOLETTE ALLA PARMIGIANA
[Veal Chops Parmigiana]

½ cup fine dry bread crumbs
½ cup grated Parmesan cheese
¾ teaspoon salt
¾ teaspoon paprika
4 large loin veal chops (2 to 2½ pounds)
1 egg, beaten
3 tablespoons butter
4 thin slices of Mozzarella cheese
2 cups well-seasoned tomato sauce

Mix crumbs, Parmesan, salt, and paprika. Dip chops into egg and roll in crumb mixture. Heat butter and brown chops on both sides. Cover each with a slice of Mozzarella. Pour tomato sauce over chops. Cover and simmer about 45 minutes. If sauce is too thick, add a little hot water. Makes 4 servings.

ARROSTO DI AGNELLO
[Roast Lamb]

Taking a leg of lamb or an entire baby lamb, rub it well with garlic, rosemary leaves, and salt and pepper. Pour ½ cup olive oil into the roaster. Set lamb in it and roast, uncovered, in preheated moderate oven (350°F.), turning occasionally until practically done, allowing 30 minutes to the pound. Place peeled tiny new spring potatoes around meat and continue roasting until they are tender.

NOTE: Lamb prepared with a blend of herbs is an Easter delicacy throughout Italy, as is turkey on Thanksgiving in America.

POLLO ALLA CACCIATORA
[Chicken Cacciatora]

¼ cup olive oil
1 chicken (2½ to 3 pounds), cut up
2 onions, sliced
2 garlic cloves, minced
1 can (1 pound) Italian tomatoes
1 can (8 ounces) tomato sauce
1 teaspoon salt
¼ teaspoon pepper
½ teaspoon celery seed
1 teaspoon crushed dried oregano
2 bay leaves
½ cup dry white wine

Heat oil in large deep skillet; brown chicken. Remove chicken and keep hot. Cook onions and garlic in oil in skillet until tender. Add other ingredients except wine, and blend. Cook for 5 minutes. Return chicken to skillet. Cover and simmer for 45 minutes. Add wine and cook, uncovered, about 15 minutes. Arrange on hot platter. Skim excess fat from sauce and remove bay leaves. Pour sauce over chicken. Serve on spaghetti or noodles with a sprinkling of cheese. Makes 4 to 6 servings.

SALSICCIE E FAGIOLI
[Italian Sausages with Beans]

1 pound sweet or hot Italian sausages
2 tablespoons olive oil
2 tablespoons tomato paste
¼ teaspoon salt
⅛ teaspoon pepper (omit if hot sausage is used)
4 cups drained cooked kidney beans
¼ cup bean liquid or water

Prick sausages and put in skillet with cold water to cover. Cook over moderate heat until water evaporates. Then cook for 20 minutes, allowing sausages to brown on all sides. Remove from pan and keep hot. Add oil to fat in pan. Stir in tomato paste, salt, and pepper. Cook for 5 minutes. Add kidney beans, liquid, and sausages to pan. Simmer for 15 minutes, stirring occasionally. Garnish with parsley, if desired. Makes 4 servings.
NOTE: Use the sweet or hot variety of sausage, according to taste.

FEGATINI DI POLLO ALLA SALVIA
[Chicken Livers with Sage]

Season chicken livers with salt and pepper and coat with chopped fresh or dried sage (about 1 tablespoon fresh sage or ½ teaspoon dried sage leaves, crumbled, per liver, depending on taste). Wrap chicken livers in strips of prosciutto or partly cooked lean bacon. Thread on small skewers. Broil over a campfire or an outdoor grill or a rotisserie or under the range broiler, turning occasionally. Allow about 8 to 10 minutes of broiling time. If livers are wrapped in prosciutto, baste with melted butter.

EGGS AND CHEESE

UOVA IN PURGATORIO
[Eggs in Purgatory]

¼ cup chopped onion
¼ cup minced parsley
  Salt and pepper to taste
1 tablespoon olive oil
2 cups chopped, peeled tomatoes (or canned)
8 eggs
4 slices of buttered toast

Sauté onion and parsley with salt and pepper in oil for 10 minutes. Add tomatoes and simmer for 30 minutes, stirring often. Bring to a boil, then carefully drop in eggs, one at a time, to poach. Serve on buttered toast with the sauce. Makes 4 servings, allowing 2 eggs for each portion.

Salsiccie e Fagioli

CROSTINI ALLA MOZZARELLA
[Italian Mozzarella Skewers]

Mozzarella originally came from the marshy farming districts around Naples, where buffaloes from India are used as beasts of burden. Their milk goes into cheese making. Our Mozzarella is more bland than the Italian and it is therefore a good idea to serve the *crostini* with anchovy butter.

Remove the crust from a loaf of French bread. Cut loaf into slices about ⅓ inch thick. Cut Mozzarella into slices the same size and thickness as bread. Place alternate slices of bread and cheese on a skewer until there are 3 of cheese and 4 of bread, beginning and ending with bread. Preheat baking dish and place skewers on it. Bake in a very hot oven (450°F. to 475°F.) just long enough for the cheese to melt and the bread to brown. Serve very hot with Anchovy Butter.

Anchovy Butter

Melt 1 cup butter. Chop 8 anchovy fillets and simmer in butter for 5 minutes. Pour sauce over each skewer serving.

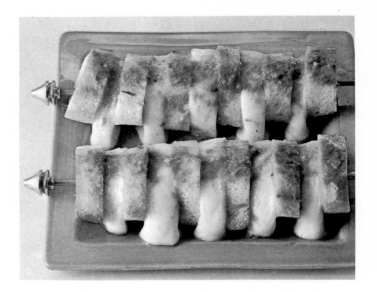

Parmesan Sauce

Melt 3 tablespoons butter; blend in 3 tablespoons all-purpose flour. Add 1½ cups light cream; cook, stirring, until thickened. Stir in ½ cup grated Parmesan cheese. Season.

PASTA, PANCAKES, AND RICE

CANNELLONI ALLA PARMIGIANA
[Stuffed Pancakes]

    Butter
1 cup milk
2 eggs, beaten
½ cup sifted all-purpose flour
1 teaspoon baking powder
½ teaspoon salt
    Sausage Stuffing
    Parmesan Sauce

Heat 2 tablespoons butter and the milk until butter is melted. Cool slightly. Add next 4 ingredients and mix until smooth. Drop by spoonfuls onto hot buttered skillet to form eighteen 3-inch pancakes. Fry until browned on both sides. Cool, and spread each with Sausage Stuffing. Roll up and put in greased broilerproof shallow baking dish. Cover with Parmesan Sauce. Broil for 5 minutes. Makes 6 servings.

Sausage Stuffing

½ pound sausage meat, cooked and drained
1 package (10 ounces) frozen spinach, cooked and chopped fine
1 cup finely chopped cooked chicken
¼ cup grated Romano cheese
⅛ teaspoon ground thyme
⅛ teaspoon pepper

Mix all ingredients together.

SPAGHETTI AL QUATTRO FORMAGGI
[Spaghetti with Four Cheeses]

½ cup butter
⅔ cup shredded Mozzarella cheese
⅔ cup grated Gouda or Edam cheese
⅔ cup grated imported Swiss cheese
⅔ cup grated Parmesan cheese
1 pound spaghetti
    Salt and pepper

Melt butter in top part of a double boiler; have cheeses ready. Cook spaghetti to your taste in boiling salted water. Drain well and turn into a chafing dish or electric skillet turned to low. Add Mozzarella and Gouda and toss well. Then add ¼ cup butter and Swiss cheese. Give it a thorough mixing and add freshly ground pepper. Finally add remaining ¼ cup butter and Parmesan cheese. Toss again and serve very hot. Makes 4 servings.

LASAGNE CON LE POLPETTINE
[Lasagna with Meatballs]

¾ pound ground lean beef
½ teaspoon salt
¼ teaspoon pepper
1 teaspoon grated lemon rind
2 tablespoons olive oil
3 cups favorite tomato sauce
1 pound lasagna, cooked and drained
1 pound ricotta or cottage cheese
1 pound Mozzarella cheese, cubed
1½ cups grated Parmesan cheese

Season beef with salt and pepper, add lemon rind, and shape into balls the size of a large marble. Brown in hot oil. Cover bottom of greased 2- to 3-inch-deep baking dish sparingly with tomato sauce. Line with lasagna. Dot with half of cheeses. Spread with half of remaining sauce; top with meat. Cover with remaining lasagna, sauce, and cheeses. Bake in preheated slow oven (325°F.) for about 45 minutes. Cool slightly. Makes 10 to 12 servings.

SPAGHETTI CON VONGOLE
[Spaghetti with Red Clam Sauce]

    1 garlic clove, crushed
    2 tablespoons vegetable oil
    2 tomatoes, peeled and chopped fine
    ½ cup minced parsley
      Salt
      Freshly ground black pepper to taste
    2 cans (7½ ounces each) minced clams
    8 ounces spaghettini
    ¼ cup sliced black olives
      Grated Parmesan cheese

In saucepan, cook garlic in oil just until soft, not browned. Add tomatoes, parsley, ½ teaspoon salt, pepper and liquid from clams. Heat gently. Meanwhile, cook and drain spaghetti. Add clams to tomato mixture, heat and toss with spaghetti. Put in serving dish and sprinkle with olives. Serve at once with cheese. Makes 4 servings.

PASTA AL PESTO
[Spinach Noodles with Genoa Green Sauce]

    1 or 2 garlic cloves
    1 tablespoon pine nuts or other bland nuts
    1 large bunch fresh basil leaves or 1 tablespoon dried
      basil
    1 bunch fresh parsley, stems removed
    6 tablespoons strong white Italian cheese (Pecorino or
      Parmesan)
      Salt
    ⅓ cup vegetable oil
    8 ounces spinach noodles
      Grated Parmesan cheese

To make sauce, grind fine, pound in mortar or whirl in blender garlic, nuts, basil, parsley and strong cheese. Add salt to taste. Then add oil, a small amount at a time, stirring, to form a creamy-thick sauce. Set aside at room temperature. Cook noodles in boiling salted water until just soft (al dente). Drain and serve hot in soup plates with the sauce. Serve grated cheese separately. Makes 4 servings.

SPAGHETTI CON LE POLPETTINE
[Spaghetti with Meatballs]

    1 can (1 pound 12 ounces) tomatoes
    3 cans (6 ounces each) tomato paste
    4 cups water
    1 onion, minced
    1 garlic clove, minced
    ¼ pound salt pork, minced
    2 tablespoons olive oil
    2 tablespoons chopped parsley
    2 teaspoons salt
    ½ teaspoon pepper
    1 teaspoon sugar
    ½ teaspoon dried oregano
    1 bay leaf, crushed
      Meatballs
    ¼ cup grated Parmesan or Romano cheese
      Hot cooked spaghetti

Combine tomatoes, tomato paste and water; bring to boil. Sauté onion, garlic, and salt pork in hot olive oil. Add to tomato mixture. Add remaining ingredients except meatballs, cheese and spaghetti; simmer, covered, about 1 hour, stirring frequently. Add meat balls to tomato sauce and simmer, covered, about 40 minutes, stirring occasionally. Before serving, stir in grated cheese. Pour over hot cooked spaghetti. Makes 6 servings.

Meatballs

    ½ pound each ground beef, veal, and pork
    2 eggs, beaten
    1 teaspoon salt
    ¼ teaspoon pepper
    ¼ teaspoon dried oregano
    ½ cup grated Parmesan cheese
    2 tablespoons chopped parsley
    2 teaspoons grated lemon rind
    ¼ cup fine dry bread crumbs

Combine all ingredients and mix thoroughly with hands. Shape into balls.

RISOTTO ALLA MILANESE
[Rice, Milan Style]

¼ cup butter
¼ cup chopped beef marrow or 2 tablespoons butter
1 onion, minced
2 cups raw rice
½ cup dry white wine
5 cups boiling chicken bouillon (about)
½ teaspoon ground saffron, steeped in a little chicken bouillon
  Salt to taste
½ teaspoon white pepper
⅔ cup grated Parmesan cheese

In heavy saucepan melt butter and beef marrow; sauté onion until soft but not brown. Add rice and cook for 3 or 4 minutes, stirring. The rice must be transparent but not brown. Stir in wine and cook for 3 minutes. Add ½ cup boiling bouillon. Cook until bouillon is absorbed, stirring. Add remaining bouillon by half cups, allowing it to become absorbed after each addition, and stirring constantly. The cooking time should be 20 to 25 minutes after the bouillon has been first added, depending on the kind of rice used and the degree of doneness desired. (Italians eat it *al dente*.) After about 15 minutes of cooking time, add saffron, salt, and pepper. When done, stir in cheese. Serve with more cheese. Rice can be served plain or with chicken livers or mushrooms. Makes 4 to 6 servings.

NOTE: The finished product should be moist and creamy, not dry.

MANICOTTI
[Stuffed Pancakes]

1 cup sifted all-purpose flour
1 cup water
  Salt
7 eggs
2 pounds ricotta cheese
  Grated Parmesan or Romano cheese
¼ teaspoon pepper
½ pound Mozzarella, cut into 12 strips
3 cans (8 ounces each) tomato sauce

To make pancakes combine flour, water, and ¼ teaspoon salt; beat until smooth. Beat in 4 eggs, one at a time. Heat a 5- to 6-inch skillet and grease with a few drops of oil. Put about 3 tablespoons batter in hot skillet and roll around pan to distribute evenly. Cook over low heat until firm; do not brown. Turn, and cook lightly on other side. Continue making pancakes until all batter is used. This amount will make 12 to 14 pancakes. Do not grease skillet a second time.

To make filling mix ½ teaspoon salt, 3 eggs, ricotta, ¼ cup Parmesan, and pepper. Put about 2 tablespoons filling and a strip of Mozzarella on each pancake and roll up. Pour 1 can tomato sauce into large shallow baking dish. Put pancakes, seam side down, in sauce. Cover

with remaining 2 cans sauce and sprinkle with ½ cup Parmesan. Bake in preheated moderate oven (350°F.) for 45 minutes. Makes 6 generous servings.

VEGETABLES

BEEF-STUFFED EGGPLANT SLICES

1 large eggplant (long, thin one is best)
  Salt
½ pound ground chuck
¾ cup fine soft bread crumbs
1 egg
  Grated Italian-type cheese
2 tablespoons chopped parsley
⅛ teaspoon pepper
10 pitted black olives, chopped
1 to 2 tablespoons milk
  Sauce

Cut unpeeled eggplant in ¼-inch slices. Spread slices out in order cut, so you can fit them back together later. Sprinkle each slice on both sides with salt. Put under a weight 2 to 3 hours. Drain, rinse and pat dry. Mix meat, crumbs, egg, 2 tablespoons cheese, parsley, ¾ teaspoon salt, pepper, olives and enough milk to hold mixture together. Make enough thin, flat patties of meat mixture to fit between eggplant slices. Put some sauce in 15 x 10 x 1-inch baking pan. Put patties between eggplant slices and arrange on the sauce. Cover with remaining sauce and sprinkle with cheese. Bake in preheated moderate oven (350°F.) 1 hour. Makes 6 servings.

Sauce. Cook 1 minced onion in ¼ cup olive oil until golden. Add 2 cans (8 ounces each) tomato sauce, 2 cups water, ½ teaspoon fennel seed, and salt and pepper to taste. Simmer, uncovered, over medium heat about 30 minutes.

BROCCOLI WITH MACARONI

1 box (10 ounces) frozen chopped broccoli
1 garlic clove
2 tablespoons olive oil
8 ounces elbow macaroni
  Salt and pepper to taste
  Grated Italian-type cheese

Cook broccoli as directed on the label, adding garlic and oil to the water. Remove garlic and drain. Cook and drain macaroni. Mix broccoli and macaroni and season with salt and pepper. Serve with the cheese. Makes 4 servings.

MELANZANE ALLA PARMIGIANA
[Eggplant Parmigiana]

- 2 cups olive oil (about)
- 1 garlic clove, minced
- 1 large onion, chopped
- 5 cups canned Italian-style tomatoes
- ½ teaspoon dried basil
- Salt and pepper to taste
- 1 cup all-purpose flour
- 2 eggs, beaten
- 1 cup milk
- 2 medium eggplants, cut into ½-inch slices
- 1 cup grated Parmesan cheese
- 8 ounces Mozzarella cheese, diced
- ¼ cup butter

Heat ¼ cup of oil in skillet; sauté garlic and onion until soft. Add tomatoes, basil, salt, and pepper. Cook, covered, stirring occasionally, for 30 minutes. Make batter with flour, eggs, and milk. Dip eggplant slices into batter and fry slices in hot shallow olive oil until just browned on both sides. Add more oil after each frying. Arrange alternate layers of eggplant, sauce, and cheeses in casserole, sprinkling each layer with salt and pepper; dot with butter. Bake in preheated moderate oven (350°F.) for 30 minutes. Makes 6 to 8 servings.

PISELLI E PASTA
[Peas and Shell Macaroni]

- ¼ cup butter
- ¼ cup olive oil
- 1 onion, minced
- 1 garlic clove, minced (optional)
- ½ pound shell macaroni, cooked and drained
- 3 cups cooked peas
- 1 cup chopped parsley
- ½ cup finely cooked ham (optional)
- Salt and pepper
- Grated Parmesan cheese

Heat butter and oil; sauté onion and garlic until onion is soft. Add next 4 ingredients and season to taste with salt and pepper. Simmer, covered, for 10 minutes. Serve with cheese. Makes 4 to 6 servings.
NOTE: This dish is also served without the cheese in Italy.

PEPERONI CON PATATE
[Peppers and Potatoes]

- 1 pound sweet peppers
- ¼ cup olive oil
- 1 garlic clove, minced
- 1 onion, minced
- 5 raw potatoes, peeled and sliced or cubed
- 1 cup tomato juice
- Salt and pepper to taste

Trim peppers and cut into strips lengthwise. Heat olive oil and sauté garlic and onion. Add peppers and all other ingredients. Cook, covered, over low heat, for 30 minutes, or until potatoes are tender. Stir occasionally and add a little more tomato juice if necessary. Makes 4 servings.
NOTE: Served with eggs, this makes a good luncheon dish.

ZUCCHINI FRITTE
[Fried Squash]

- 8 small zucchini, unpeeled
- Salt and pepper
- ½ cup all-purpose flour
- ½ cup olive oil

Wash zucchini, dry, and cut into ¼-inch rounds. Coat with seasoned flour. Fry in hot oil until crisp and golden. Drain on absorbent paper. Makes 4 to 6 servings.
NOTE: Wonderful with veal.

SAUCES

SALSA PARMIGIANA
[Basic Tomato Sauce]

- ¼ cup minced onion
- 1 garlic clove, minced (optional)
- ¼ cup olive oil
- ¼ cup minced raw carrot
- 1 cup minced celery
- ¼ cup minced sweet basil
- Salt and pepper to taste
- 3 cups canned tomato sauce or 2 cans (6 ounces each) tomato paste diluted with 3 cans water

Sauté onion and garlic (if used) in oil until golden-brown. Add carrot, celery, sweet basil and salt and pepper and continue cooking until vegetables are wilted. Add tomato sauce or paste and simmer for 45 minutes, until tasty and thick. Serve this sauce over your favorite cooked pasta. Makes about 2¾ cups.

SALSA ALLA MARINARA
[Mariner's Sauce]

- 3 garlic cloves, minced
- ¼ cup minced parsley
- ½ cup olice oil
- 2 cups chopped, peeled tomatoes
- 1 teaspoon dried oregano
- Salt and pepper to taste

Sauté garlic and parsley in oil. When garlic is delicately brown, add tomatoes, oregano, and salt and pepper, and simmer for 30 minutes, or until well blended and thick. Makes about 1½ cups.
NOTE: For noodle-dough recipes.

SALSA VERDE PICCANTE
[Piquant Green Sauce]

½ cup minced parsley
¼ cup chopped pine nuts
2 tablespoons drained capers, chopped
½ cup fine dry bread crumbs
6 pitted black olives, minced
3 tablespoons olive oil
1 tablespoon wine vinegar
  Salt and pepper
1 teaspoon crushed chili pepper
1 teaspoon minced chives, onion, or garlic

Mix all ingredients thoroughly. Serve with fish. Makes about 1 cup.

SALSA DI ALICI
[Anchovy Sauce]

¼ cup olive oil
¼ cup butter
4 garlic cloves, minced
2 cans (2 ounces each) flat anchovy fillets, drained
¼ cup chopped parsley

Heat oil and butter and add garlic. Cook until garlic is soft, stirring. Add anchovies and cook, stirring, until anchovies have disintegrated. Stir in parsley. For fried Mozzarella, pasta, and boiled-fish dishes. Makes about ¾ cup sauce.

SALSO DI VONGOLE
[White Clam Sauce]

3 tablespoons butter
1 garlic clove, minced
1 tablespoon all-purpose flour
2 cans (10½ ounces each) minced clams
¼ cup chopped parsley
  Salt and pepper to taste
¾ teaspoon dried thyme or basil

Heat butter and cook garlic for 1 minute. Blend in flour. Add other ingredients and simmer, covered, for about 10 minutes, stirring frequently. Serve over hot cooked spaghetti or linguine. Makes 3 cups sauce.

SALADS

INSALATA DI FAGIOLINI E PATATE
[Green-Bean and Potato Salad]

4 large raw potatoes
1 pound fresh green beans (Italian preferred)
2 medium-size onions, chopped
  Salt and pepper
  Olive oil and wine vinegar

Wash potatoes and boil until tender; drain, peel, and cool. Boil beans in salted water until tender but firm; drain and cool. Slice or dice potatoes into a large bowl. Add beans, onions and salt and pepper to taste and mix all carefully. Pour in about 3 tablespoons olive oil and 1 tablespoon wine vinegar, according to taste. Stir salad carefully; marinate in refrigerator at least 2 hours. Stir again just before serving. Makes 6 to 8 servings.

INSALATA BANDIERA
[Flag Salad]

Fresh tomatoes, sliced or diced
Green beans, cooked, drained, cooled
Chopped carrots, raw or cooked and cooled
Florets of cauliflower, cooked, drained, cooled
Potatoes, cooked, peeled, and diced with a bit of chopped green onion
Red beets, cooked, peeled, and sliced or diced
Finely cut endive or other greens

In preparing Flag Salad, make your own choice among the vegetables, parboiling, straining, and cooling each vegetable separately. (Drop it into rapidly boiling salted

Insalata Bandiera

water and leave it for just a few minutes, until cooked but firm.) Do not cook the tomatoes or members of the lettuce family (romaine, endive, chicory, escarole, dandelion). When each vegetable is cooled, sprinkle it with salt and pepper and salad dressing to taste. Toss well, and place in individual dishes of a Lazy Susan so that each dish is different from the others.

SWEETS AND DESSERTS

CASSATA NAPOLITANA
[Rich Dessert Cake]

  1 9- or 10-inch spongecake or 2 sponge layers
1½ pounds ricotta cheese
  ⅓ cup sugar
  ½ cup light cream
  1 teaspoon vanilla extract
  ¼ teaspoon almond extract
  1 square (1 ounce) semisweet chocolcate or ¼ cup semisweet chocolate pieces, chopped
  ¼ cup chopped toasted almonds
  ⅔ cup finely diced mixed candied fruit
  ¼ cup rum
    Frosting
    Candied cherries

If a whole cake is used, cut into 2 layers; chill. Combine ricotta, sugar, light cream, and flavorings and mix well. Rub through a sieve or whip until smooth. Add chocolate, almonds, and fruit. Chill. Place 1 cake layer on serving plate and spread with filling. Top with remaining layer. Sprinkle with rum. Chill until shortly before serving time; then frost top. Reserve some of the Frosting to tint pink and use it for decorative swirls on cake. Decorate with cherries.

Frosting

  1 egg white
  2 cups sifted confectioners' sugar
  1 teaspoon almond extract
  1 tablespoon fresh lemon juice

Mix all ingredients until smooth. If necessary, add a little water, ½ teaspoon at a time, to achieve right spreading consistency.

FRAGOLE ALL' ITALIANA
[Italian Strawberries]

  2 tablespoons sugar, or more, depending on berries
  4 cups washed and hulled strawberries
  ⅔ cup dry white wine or fresh orange juice

Sprinkle sugar over strawberries and cover with wine. Chill before serving. Makes 4 to 6 servings.

Cassata Napolitana

GROSTOLI
[Crisp Cookies]

  3 eggs, lightly beaten
  5 cups sifted all-purpose flour
  ½ cup granulated sugar
  1 teaspoon baking powder
  1 cup milk
  1 teaspoon salt
  1 grated lemon rind (optional)
  2 tablespoons (1 ounce) brandy
    Lard
    Confectioners' sugar

Mix first 8 ingredients into smooth noodle dough and roll thin as a dime. With pastry cutter, form rectangles 2 by 3 inches. Deep fry in pure lard. Drain, and dust with sifted confectioners' sugar. Makes about 8 dozen.

BUDINO DI RICOTTA
[Cream-Cheese Custard]

  ½ pound ricotta cheese
  ¼ cup grated milk chocolate
  ¼ cup finely chopped walnuts
  2 tablespoons heavy cream (about)

Cream ricotta; add chocolate and nuts and blend thoroughly. Add cream as needed for desired consistency. Serve in sherbet glasses. Makes 4 servings.
NOTE: This "custard" can also be used as a filling for many cakes and cookies.

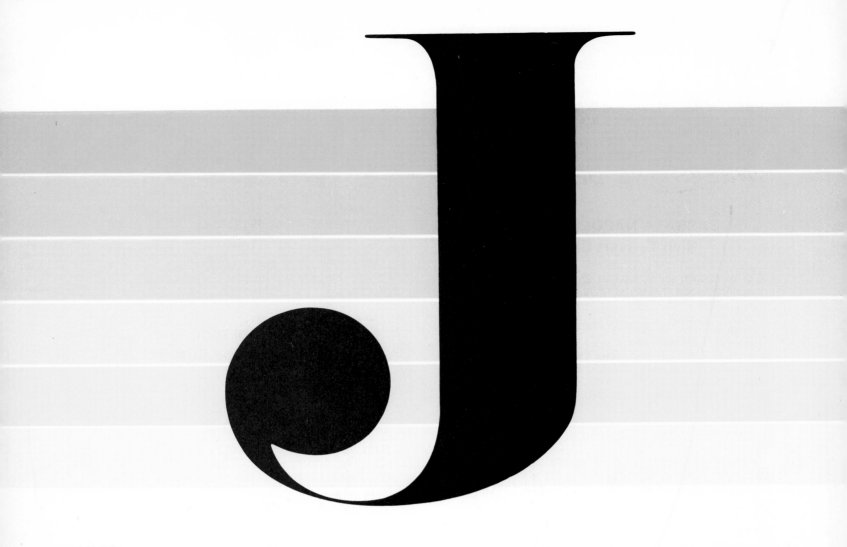

JAM—A preserve of fruit which is usually crushed, or may even be ground, cooked with sugar until thick, and stored in sterilized jars. The crushed particles of fruit remain in the finished product. The fruit used can be fresh, canned, frozen, or dried. Jam is sometimes made of fruits mixed with vegetables.

Making jam is one of the most satisfying branches of the ancient art of preserving foods. Before the general availability of canned and frozen foods and commercially made jams, homemade jams were the homemaker's pride and the joy of her family during many a long winter, when the jam's fragrance and sparkle brought summer sunshine to the cold dark season. Housewives slaved over hot stoves on many a summer day when the fruit was perfect for the purpose.

Success in jam making depends on the kind of fruit used, the cooking, handling, and storing. Because of the products available today, the homemaker has a choice of several methods for making jam:

Jam Made without Added Pectin—(Pectin is a water-soluble substance present in plant tissue. It yields a jelly when it is properly combined with acid and sugar.) Some fruits contain enough natural pectin to eliminate the necessity for adding commercial fruit pectin. These fruits include tart apples, blackberries, cranberries, currants, gooseberries, Concord grapes, quinces, and raspberries.

Even when using them, however, some underripe fruits (they contain more pectin than ripe ones) should be included with the ripe fruits to insure the presence of enough pectin for gelling.

Jams Made with Commercial Fruit Pectin—Liquid pectin is added to the cooked fruit and sugar after it is removed from the heat. Or powdered pectin is added to the unheated crushed fruit.

Jams Made without Cooking—Some fresh, canned, or frozen fruits can be used without cooking if liquid or powdered fruit pectin is added and a long storage life is not desired. These fruits include blackberries, raspberries, strawberries, cherries, and peaches. No-cook jams cannot be stored at room temperature. If kept in the freezer, they will last up to one year; in the refrigerator their storage life is three to four months.

TO MAKE JAM

Follow recipe directions for preparing and cooking fruit and for handling it after cooking.

Stir well during cooking to prevent sticking and scorching.

Remember that the mixture will thicken more as it cools. Jams made without added pectin take longer to cook than jams made with pectin, and it is more difficult to tell when the jam is finished. To determine this, use a candy and jelly thermometer, and cook mixture to 220°F. If you do not have a thermometer, you can use the spoon, or sheet, test (the old "jelly test") although it is not absolutely dependable: Dip a cool metal spoon into the boiling mixture. Then raise it at least 1 foot above the kettle, out of the steam, and turn the spoon so that the syrup runs off the side. If the syrup forms drops that flow together and fall off the spoon as one sheet, the jam should be done.

Prepare jars or glasses properly. Have them ready for use when jam is finished cooking. Jars and lids should be covered with hot, not boiling, water and brought to a boil. No further boiling is necessary. Keep hot in water or in a very slow oven until they are needed.

To Seal Jam—Jam which will not be kept more than two months does not need any special sealing. Jam which will be kept longer should be kept in canning jars or sealed with paraffin.

Canning jars, such as the new all-purpose jars with two-piece metal screw-top lids, should be filled to the top, the rim wiped, and the clean hot metal lids placed on the jar with sealing compound next to the glass. The metal band is screwed on firmly, the jar cooled on a metal rack or folded cloth; then labeled, and stored in a cool, dry place.

If using paraffin to seal glasses, the paraffin should be kept hot without overheating. A double boiler is good for this. As soon as jam is in the glasses, filled to within ½ inch of top, cover immediately with a ⅛-inch layer of paraffin. Be sure jam is completely covered by paraffin, and prick any air bubbles that may appear in the jam. A thin single layer of paraffin is preferable to either a thick or two thin layers as this gives a tighter seal with no chance for air bubbles.

JAMS MADE WITHOUT PECTIN

SPICED PEACH JAM

     4 cups peach pulp
     4 cups sugar
     3 or 4 peach pits
     1 tablespoon whole gingerroot
     ¾ tablespoon whole allspice
     ½ tablespoon whole cloves
     1 cinnamon stick
       Juice of ½ lemon

Chop peach pulp; mix with sugar in preserving kettle. Crack peach pits; remove kernels and add to peach pulp. Add spices tied in a bag. Simmer until clear and thick, stirring occasionally to prevent sticking. Remove spice bag and add lemon juice. Fill hot sterilized jars; seal. Makes about four ½-pint glasses.

SPICED BLACKBERRY JAM

     4 cups canned blackberry pulp
     1 teaspoon ground allspice or combination of ground
       spices
     1¼ cups sugar*
     2½ cups corn syrup
     1 tablespoon fresh lemon juice

Bring pulp to boil in heavy 6-quart kettle. Boil hard for 15 minutes. Add spice, sugar, and syrup. Boil rapidly until jam forms thick jellied drops that adhere to edge of spoon, about 45 minutes. Add lemon juice. Cool slightly; stir; pour into sterilized glasses and seal. Makes four or five ½-pint jars.
*Or use 3 cups sugar, omitting syrup.

CRANBERRY AND FIG JAM

     3 cups dried figs
     3 cups water
       Grated rind of 1 orange
     4 cups cranberries
     3 cups sugar
     ¼ teaspoon salt

Wash figs and remove the hard stem ends. Put through food chopper, using medium blade. Add water and boil for 30 minutes, stirring frequently. Add rind, cranberries, sugar, and salt and boil for another 30 minutes. Stir often to prevent burning. Pour into hot sterilized glasses and seal. Makes six ½-pint jars.

CRANBERRY, ORANGE, AND HONEY JAM

     4 cups cranberries
     2 cups boiling water
       Grated rind of 1 orange
     1 cup sugar
     ¾ cup strained honey

Pick over, wash, and drain cranberries. Add water and orange rind; boil for 20 minutes. Force cranberries through a fine sieve. Bring to rapid boil and add sugar and honey, stirring until thoroughly mixed. Boil for 3 minutes longer. Pour into hot sterilized glasses or small molds and seal. Makes about four ½-pint jars.

SPICED GRAPE JAM

     1½ pounds stemmed Concord grapes
       (2½ cups pulp and skins)
       Grated rind of 1 orange
     ½ cup water
     2¼ cups sugar
     ½ teaspoon each ground cloves and cinnamon

Wash grapes and slip skins from pulp. Heat pulp to boiling and rub through a coarse sieve to remove seeds. Add orange rind and water and cook for 10 minutes. Add grape skins, bring to boil, and add sugar and spices. Cook until thickened. Pour in hot sterilized jars and seal. Makes four or five ½-pint jars.

GOLDEN JAM

2 large oranges
6 cups diced rhubarb
3 cups ground raw carrots
3 cups light corn syrup
2 cups sugar*

Remove seeds and grind oranges. Combine with remaining ingredients and let stand overnight. Bring to a boil and cook slowly until rhubarb is transparent and mixture is thickened. Pour into hot sterilized jars and seal. Makes ten ½-pint jars.
*Or use 4 cups sugar, omitting corn syrup.

OLD-COUNTRY STRAWBERRY JAM

6 cups hulled strawberries
3 cups sugar

Put strawberries in a large heavy saucepan and mash. Cook over moderate heat until fairly thick, stirring frequently. Gradually add sugar; stir constantly over low heat until sugar is dissolved. Bring to boil and boil rapidly for 15 to 20 minutes, or until juice sheets from spoon, stirring occasionally to prevent sticking. Skim, and pour into hot sterilized jars. Seal. Makes four ½-pint jars.

TOMATO-APRICOT JAM

1 package (12 ounces) dried apricots
2 cans (1 pound 12 ounces) tomatoes
1 teaspoon whole cloves
3 cinnamon sticks
1 teaspoon salt
7 cups sugar
  Juice of ½ lemon

Soak apricots overnight in tomatoes. Add spices, tied in a bag, and salt. Bring to boil and cook for 15 minutes. Add sugar and cook until clear and of consistency of marmalade. Remove spice bag; add lemon juice. Pour into hot sterilized jars and seal. Makes about five ½-pint jars.

RASPBERRY CURRANT JAM

2 cups currant pulp
2 cups crushed raspberries
3 cups sugar

To prepare currant pulp, cook currants (about 3 cups) until soft, press through a sieve or food mill. Measure pulp. Combine currant pulp, raspberries, and sugar. Bring slowly to boil, stirring occasionally until sugar dissolves. Cook rapidly to jellying point, about 30 minutes. As mixture thickens, stir frequently to prevent sticking. Pour, boiling hot, into sterilized jars and seal. Makes four ½-pint jars.

JAMS MADE WITH PECTIN

THREE-MINUTE STRAWBERRY JAM

2 cups mashed or sieved strawberries
4 cups sugar
1 box (1¾ ounces) powdered fruit pectin
1 cup water

Combine berries and sugar. Let stand for about 20 minutes, stirring occasionally. Stir pectin into water; bring to boil and boil rapidly for 1 minute, stirring constantly. Remove from heat, add berries, and stir constantly about 2 minutes. Pour into sterilized jars; cover and let stand at room temperature for 48 hours, or until gelled. Seal and store in freezer, where jam will keep well for several months. Or it will keep for 6 to 8 weeks stored in refrigerator. Makes five ½-pint jars.
NOTE: To use liquid fruit pectin for this jam, omit powdered pectin and water and use ½ bottle liquid pectin (½ cup). It is not necessary to heat liquid pectin; just stir strawberry-sugar mixture into it and proceed as directed above.

TOMATO JAM

Scald, peel, and chop about 2¼ pounds ripe tomatoes. Bring to boil and simmer for 10 minutes. Measure 3 cups into large saucepan. Add 1½ teaspoons grated lemon rind, ¼ cup fresh lemon juice, and 6 cups sugar. Mix well and bring to a full rolling boil. Boil hard for 1 minute, stirring. Remove from heat and at once stir in 1 bottle (6 ounces) liquid pectin. Skim, then stir and skim by turns for 5 minutes. Ladle into hot sterilized jars and seal. Serve with any cold meat. Makes about seven ½-pint jars.

BERRY JAM

2 quarts blackerries, boysenberries, dewberries, strawberries, or youngberries or any mixture of these
7 cups sugar
½ bottle (6 ounces) liquid pectin or 1 box (1¾ ounces) powdered pectin

Wash berries and crush. If berries are very seedy, sieve half of berries to remove part of seeds. Combine 4 cups crushed berries and sugar in saucepan. Mix well and bring to a full rolling boil. Boil for 1 minute, stirring constantly. Remove from heat and stir in pectin. Skim off foam and stir and skim alternately for 5 minutes. Fill hot sterilized jars and seal. Makes about eight ½-pint jars.
NOTE: If berries are lacking in tartness, substitute ¼ cup fresh lemon juice for ¼ cup of the fruit.

Loganberry or Red Raspberry Jam
Follow Berry Jam recipe, but use only 6½ cups sugar.

RED-PEPPER JAM

Wash and seed 1 dozen large sweet red peppers. Force through medium blade of food chopper. Add 1 tablespoon salt and let stand overnight. Drain well, pressing out all liquid. Put in kettle with 2 cups white vinegar and 3 cups sugar. Cook, uncovered, for 45 minutes, or until of marmalade consistency, stirring frequently. Pour into hot sterilized jars and seal. Makes four or five ½-pint jars.

QUINCE AND PEAR JAM

    3 cups quince pulp
    2 cups pear pulp
 3½ cups sugar
      Salt
    1 cup water

Wash and cut quinces; cover with water and cook until tender and mushy. Drain and use liquid for making Quince Jelly. Meanwhile wash and cut up pears, cover with water, and cook until tender. Put through food mill, and measure. Put quinces through food mill to remove seeds and cores, and measure. Put measured pulp purée into kettle with sugar, salt, and water, and cook until thick, stirring to prevent scorching. Pour into hot sterilized jars and seal. Makes four ½-pint jars.
NOTE: This is sometimes called Quince and Pear Honey.

PEACH JAM

    3 cups canned sliced peaches
    1 jar (8 ounces) maraschino cherries
    1 large lemon
 7½ cups sugar
    1 cup liquid pectin

Drain peaches before measuring, then chop them. Add cherries, cut into quarters, juice from cherries, and lemon juice. Add peach syrup if necessary to make 4 cups of fruit mixture. Combine with sugar, bring to boiling point, and boil hard for 2 minutes. Stir constantly during the cooking. Remove from heat, stir in pectin, and let stand for 5 minutes, stirring frequently. Turn into hot sterilized jars and seal. Makes about six ½-pint jars.

BLUEBERRY JAM

Wash and pick over 1½ quarts ripe berries and crush; there should be 4½ cups. Combine in kettle with 2 tablespoons fresh lemon juice and 7 cups sugar; mix well. Bring to full rolling boil over high heat; boil hard for 1 minute, stirring. Remove from heat and stir in 1 bottle (6 ounces) liquid pectin. Skim off foam. Continue stirring and skimming for 5 minutes to prevent floating fruit. Ladle into hot sterilized jars and seal. Makes nine ½-pint jars.

SOUR CHERRY JAM

    1 quart ripe sour cherries (about)
    4 cups sugar
  ¾ cup water
    1 box (1¾ ounces) powdered fruit pectin

Pit and grind the cherries and measure 2 cups into large bowl or pan. Add sugar to fruit, mix well, and let stand. Mix water and pectin in small saucepan. Bring to a boil and boil for 1 minute, stirring constantly. Stir into fruit mixture. Continue stirring about 3 minutes. There will be a few remaining sugar crystals. Ladle quickly into glasses. Cover at once with tight lids. When jam will be used within 2 or 3 weeks, it may be stored in refrigerator. Makes about seven ½-pint jars.

PINEAPPLE-MINT JAM

    1 can (1 pound 13 ounces) crushed pineapple
  ¾ cup water
      Juice of 2 lemons
 7½ cups sugar
    1 bottle (6 ounces) liquid pectin
    1 teaspoon peppermint extract
      Green food coloring

Mix first 4 ingredients. Bring to a boil, stirring. Boil for 2 minutes. Add pectin, peppermint, and coloring. Stir and skim for 5 minutes. Pour into hot sterilized jars and seal. Makes nine ½-pint jars.

PEAR-RASPBERRY JAM

Thaw 1 package (10 ounces) frozen raspberries. Peel and core about 2 pounds fully ripe pears and force them through medium blade of food chopper. Measure raspberries and enough ground pears to make 4 cups fruit. Put in kettle with ¼ cup fresh lemon juice, 1 tablespoon grated orange rind, and 6 cups sugar. Bring to full rolling boil over high heat; boil hard for 1 minute, stirring. Remove from heat and stir in half of 6-ounce bottle of liquid pectin. Skim off foam. Continue stirring and skimming for 5 minutes to prevent floating fruit. Ladle into hot sterilized jars and seal. Makes seven or eight ½-pint jars.

JAMS MADE WITHOUT COOKING

NO-COOK BLACKBERRY JAM

    1 quart fully ripe blackberries
    4 cups sugar
    2 tablespoons fresh lemon juice
    ½ bottle liquid pectin

Crush berries to make 2 cups. (*For a less seedy jam, allow 1 more cup berries; strain half the berries and discard this seedy half of the pulp.) Put fruit in large bowl and add sugar. Mix well. Combine lemon juice and pectin, and add to fruit. Continue stirring for 3 minutes. If a few sugar crystals remain they will do no harm. Pour into glasses or freezer jars. Cover with tight lids and let stand 24 hours to set. Store in freezer or for up to 3 weeks in refrigerator. Makes six ½-pint jars.

No-Cook Red-Raspberry Jam

Substitute red raspberries for blackberries in recipe above. Makes about six ½-pint jars.

No-Cook Strawberry Jam

Substitute 1¾ cups crushed strawberries for 2 cups berries in No-Cook Blackberry Jam recipe. Makes about five ½-pint jars.

No-Cook Peach Jam

    2¼ pounds ripe peaches
    6½ cups sugar
    ⅓ cup fresh lemon juice
    1 bottle liquid pectin

Peel, pit and grind peaches to make 2¾ cups. Proceed as in No-Cook Blackberry Jam recipe. Makes about nine ½-pint jars.

No-Cook Sour Cherry Jam

    1 quart sour cherries
    4 cups sugar
    ¼ cup fresh lemon juice
    ½ bottle liquid pectin

Pit and grind cherries to make 1¾ cups. Proceed as in No-Cook Blackberry Jam recipe. Makes about five ½-pint jars.

JAMAICAN SOUPS by Leila Hadley

—Hearty and deliciously different, these soups capture the flavor of one of the loveliest islands in the Caribbean. Admittedly, there is something in my nature that finds much of the Caribbean cuisine unappealing. Roasted breadfruit sings no siren song for me. I have no truck with peanut stew, and I turn a rich shade of antique green when confronted with curried goat. Sweet-potato pone makes my teeth scream with anguish. To my notion, the best cooking is simply the best there is, but not necessarily the strangest or the most complicated or the most original.

And so, on coming to live in Jamaica, it was a matter of pure joy to find that no matter how disturbingly sweet and glutinous their pudding desserts, nor how scaringly seasoned their meat curries, the Jamaicans are masters at the preparation of fish and soup.

When fish and soup come together in a chowder, the combination is delectable and soul-warming. If you don't want to cope with anything more than a one-dish meal, yet feel like something more inventive than chicken, more delicate than steak, a fish chowder such as the one I'm about to describe is the perfect solution. At lunch or supper, accompanied by a green salad, hot buttered popovers, some fruit, or perhaps lemon sherbet with an extra tang of grated lemon, it makes a thoroughly delicious and satisfying meal. Jamaicans are connoisseurs of fish, and savor their fish bright-eyed and firm-fleshed, fresh from the sea. So in the morning, when the fishermen return in their dugout canoes, we go down to the beach to do our marketing. No matter how early we go, the higglers are there before us. The higglers (a polite corruption of the word hagglers) are the local peddlers. Traditionally, the fish higglers are women whose speech, colorful as their bright-printed cotton skirts, is shot through with startling endearments. "My darlin'," one of the women says, bargaining with a fisherman straight from his boat with a basket of fish, "you greedy as a old hog for make me pay such a price. Man, you two-face like a star-apple leaf. You is a real terrible t'ief for true."

She walks away, her hips penduluming with indignation, but the round wicker basket she balances on her head is nevertheless filled with fish. Purple doctorfish with curious smiling mouths, groupers, parrot fish—turquoise and shining—and red-spotted butterfish. After doing a little higgling myself, I buy shrimps, a lively lobster, a mirror-smooth kingfish, and a snapper the color of a pink sunset, all carefully weighed on a battered brasspan scale.

Back home again in the kitchen, Miss Gladys, our cook, sets the final seal on my shopping pleasure by saying, "Them didn't rob you. Everything them lovely for true, Mistress." So now we are ready to make the chowder. By the way, if you live inland where fresh lobster and shrimps aren't available, there's no reason why you shouldn't use frozen seafood. Don't let the long list of ingredients put you off. The recipe is actually simpler than it looks.

Another house specialty of ours is a Jamaican Pepperpot, and I'm sure that somewhere in the pot is a touch of white magic. For after that first spoonful has spread its influence on tongue and· palate, strong taciturn men, previously all too plainly impervious to my charms as a temptress, have indicated in giddy phrases that I am the moon of all delight. Women, who would just as soon shred me into pieces and clap me into a Saratoga trunk, dimple at me sweetly, kowtow with fitting humility, and beg me to give them the recipe.

This Jamaican soup is an island specialty, and although there are innumerable ways of making it, this is the way it is prepared at the Myrtle Bank, the oldest hotel in Kingston, justly famed for its charm and comfort. In the evening, the tourists, unburdened of their complex of cameras, raffia-embroidered straw hats and baskets, souvenir shells and bundles of duty-free merchandise, sit out in the cool of the broad hotel veranda, listening to the palm trees clacking in the wind. Down by the bar, the band strikes up a Jamaican *meto*, or work song, soft and pleasing, and then sends out an animated Trinidadian calypso. A departing liner gives a resonant farewell hoot. The fireflies in the moonlit garden flash mating signals to each other. In a pleasantly lazy, calypso-collapse mood, you go in to dinner and, with a certain well-bred greediness, you wait for the pepperpot soup to appear.

JAMAICAN SPLIT-PEA SOUP

2 cups split peas
2 onions, coarsely chopped
6 cups water
3 cups chicken or beef bouillon or consommé
Salt and pepper
4 strips of bacon, cooked and crumbled
Croutons

Boil split peas and onions in water for 30 minutes. Then simmer for 1½ hours. Whirl this purée in a blender for a few seconds. Return to pot and add bouillon. Season to taste. Garnish with crumbled bacon and croutons. Makes about 6 servings.

CHICKEN SOUP WITH SHERRY

Bones and scraps of 1 chicken
2 onions, chopped
2 teaspoons salt
½ teaspoon ground ginger
8 cups water
3 tablespoons sherry

Put chicken bones and scraps, onions, salt, and ginger in the pot with cold water and quickly bring to a boil. Reduce heat and simmer for 1½ hours. Add sherry and simmer for another 30 minutes. Strain, and serve. Very easy and very good. Makes about 6 servings.

MYRTLE BANK JAMAICAN PEPPERPOT SOUP

2 pounds spinach (locally known by the fetching name of Callaloo!) or 2 packages (10 ounces each) frozen spinach, thawed
2 pounds beef, cut into 1-inch cubes
½ pound diced salt pork
3 onions, coarsely chopped
4 cups water
½ teaspoon dried thyme
3 scallions or chives, minced
1 seeded green pepper, minced
1 bay leaf
2 tomatoes, sliced
2 teaspoons salt
⅛ teaspoon cayenne or ½ teaspoon freshly ground black pepper
12 okras, stemmed
Butter
½ cup heavy cream
Paprika

Wash spinach, drain thoroughly, then chop coarsely. Put in large soup pot and add beef, salt pork, onions, and water. Bring these ingredients to the boiling point and then let simmer gently for 1 hour. Add thyme, scallions, green pepper, bay leaf, tomatoes, salt, and cayenne; simmer about 30 minutes. Slice okras into rings and sauté gently in butter. They mustn't brown but must absorb the butter as flowers absorb the sun. Add them to soup for last 10 minutes of cooking time. Just before serving, add cream. Sprinkle each serving with a wisp of paprika. Makes about 6 servings.

JAMAICAN CONGO-PEA OR KIDNEY-BEAN SOUP

4 cups water
½ cup Congo peas (pigeon peas) or kidney beans
¼ pound salt pork or a ham bone with meat
1 bay leaf
4 peppercorns
Milk or light cream
Croutons
Chopped parsley

Bring water to a rapid boil. Drop peas in slowly so as not to lower boiling point. When last pea has been added, add meat, bay leaf, and peppercorns; simmer about 2½ hours, or until peas are soft. Remove meat and mince finely. Whirl soup in a blender and return to the pot. Return meat. Thin soup as desired with milk. Garnish with croutons and parsley. Makes about 6 servings.

JAMAICAN ONION SOUP
WITH CHEESE

2 tablespoons soft butter
2 egg yolks
2 cups milk
1 can (10½ ounces) condensed consommé
⅔ cup water
1 cup coarsely chopped onions, sautéed
½ cup grated Gruyère cheese
Salt and pepper

Beat butter with egg yolks. When thoroughly mixed, add milk and consommé. Bring to boiling point, stirring as you go. Reduce heat. Add onions, cheese, and salt and pepper to taste. Serve piping hot. Makes about 6 servings.

KINGSTON POTATO SOUP

6 tablespoons butter
6 leeks, sliced
2 onions, sliced
6 large potatoes, sliced
6 cups chicken bouillon
½ cup cooked green peas
Dash of cayenne
1½ teaspoons salt
1 cup milk
1 avocado, peeled and sliced

Melt butter in saucepan; add leeks and onions and sauté until golden-brown. Add potatoes and bouillon and simmer for 30 to 40 minutes. When potatoes are well done, put soup through a sieve or whirl in a blender. Return to saucepan, add peas, cayenne, and salt, and cook for 5 minutes longer. Thin with heated milk. Place a slice or two of avocado in each soup plate and pour over hot soup. Serve very hot. Makes about 6 servings.

JAMAICAN FISH CHOWDER

Fish

1 large or 2 small lobsters
1 pound shrimps
2 pounds fish fillets (cod or haddock)

Fish Stock

8 cups water
1 carrot, coarsely chopped
1 onion, coarsely chopped
1 celery stalk, coarsely chopped
1 garlic clove
1 bay leaf
1½ tablespoons salt
6 peppercorns
2 whole cloves
½ lemon

Chowder

½ cup olive oil
¾ cup sliced onions
1 tablespoon minced garlic
¼ cup parsley leaves
½ teaspoon dried basil
1 bay leaf
3 peppercorns
1 can (1 pound) solid-pack tomatoes
½ teaspoon salt
Dash of ground saffron
¼ teaspoon grated lemon rind
1 cup dry white wine, or more

Garnish

3 tablespoons minced parsley

If you have brought home a live lobster, start by plunging it into enough boiling water to cover it generously. Add 2 tablespoons salt for each quart of water. When the water has returned to a rollicking boil, count the cooking time from this minute and allow 5 minutes for each pound of lobster. Remove the lobster from the water with kitchen tongs. When it is cool enough to handle, clip out the hard sac near the head, remove the dark intestinal vein, and draw out the meat from the shell. Cut the meat into serving pieces. If you've brought home a cooked lobster, all you have to do is remove the meat from the shell, discard the intestinal vein and the hard sac near the head, and cut the meat into serving pieces. Cover the chunks and put them in the refrigerator. Don't save the water in which the lobster was boiled in the hope you can use it for the stock. Take my word for it, you can't.

Now on to the shrimps, the fish, and the fish stock. Wash, shell, and devein raw shrimps. Set aside. Cut the filleted fish into 2-inch cubes, wrap cubes in wax paper, and refrigerate until needed. Next step is to simmer for 10 to 15 minutes all the ingredients listed under Fish Stock. Then add the fish scraps, if you had a whole fish, and shrimps. Let these simmer for 10 minutes. Let the shrimps cool in the stock. Remove shrimps and store them, covered, in the refrigerator until needed. Strain the stock and set aside.

Now then, get out a large soup pot. Pour in olive oil and place the pot over medium heat. Add sliced onions, minced garlic, and parsley leaves. Cook and stir until these are lightly browned. Then add basil, bay leaf, peppercorns, tomatoes, salt, and saffron. Simmer these ingredients, covered, for 30 minutes. You may want to place a slice of toast in each soup plate, and, if so, now is a good time to make the toast. Some people prefer plain crackers with the chowder, but others prefer the chowder ladled over a slice of toast plus a liberal offering of popovers. After the soup has simmered for 30 minutes, add stock. Stir. Then add fish cubes, and do give these a last-minute pinch to find any bones that might have remained. Let fish simmer for 10 minutes. Then add lobster, shrimps, and lemon rind, and let this supreme concoction simmer for 5 more minutes. Add white wine, ladle the chowder into soup plates, garnish with minced parsley, and bring to the table at once! Makes about 6 servings.

PUMPKIN SOUP

Scooped-out chunks and pulp of a large pumpkin
2 onions, coarsely chopped
2 teaspoons salt
⅛ teaspoon cayenne
4 cups chicken bouillon
1 teaspoon grated onion
½ cup heavy cream, whipped
Pepper

Remove the seeds and strings from pumpkin. Add pumpkin, coarsely chopped onions, and salt and cayenne to bouillon and simmer until pumpkin is tender. Put soup through a sieve or whirl in a blender. Reheat to boiling point, but do not allow to boil. Just before serving, add grated onion. Top each serving with whipped cream and a grating of freshly ground black pepper. Makes 6 servings.

JAMBALAYA—A New Orleans Creole dish,
made with combinations of ham, sausage, fowl, shrimps, oysters, tomatoes, onions, garlic, and other seasonings.

The origin of the dish is obscure, although it is evidently based upon elements of French and Spanish cooking. The Spanish *paella,* a mixture of rice, meat, and seafood, is a close relative. The origin of the name is obscure, too. It may derive from the French word for "ham," *jambon,* or it may come more directly from a Provençal word, *jambalaia* meaning "a dish of rice and fowl."

Jambalayas make excellent party dishes since they can be prepared beforehand. For a party, cook the jambalaya until it is almost done, refrigerate, and finish cooking just before serving. A green salad is a good accompaniment, and a creamy bland dessert provides a pleasant flavor contrast to the well-seasoned jambalaya.

CREOLE JAMBALAYA

2 tablespoons butter
1 pound raw smoked ham, coarsely diced
2 large onions, chopped
2 garlic cloves, minced
1 medium green pepper, cut up
2 cans (1 pound 3 ounces each) tomatoes
3 cups meat broth or 2 chicken cubes and 3 cups water
1 bay leaf, crushed
½ teaspoon dried thyme
½ teaspoon chili powder
¼ teaspoon pepper
2 cups raw long-grain rice
1 pound fresh shrimps, cooked, shelled, and cleaned or 1 package (12 ounces) frozen shelled cleaned shrimps, cooked

Melt butter in top-of-stove casserole or Dutch oven. Add ham, onion, and garlic; cook until lightly browned. Add remaining ingredients except rice and shrimps and bring to boil. Gradually stir in rice. Cover and simmer for 30 minutes, or until rice is tender and liquid is absorbed. Add shrimps, and more seasoning if desired. Makes 6 servings.

Menus

50 Menus to help you plan more varied meals

BREAKFASTS OR BRUNCHES

Grapefruit Sections
Crisp Sausage Links
Huckleberry Griddle Cakes
Whipped Cream Cheese
Honey

Applesauce
Sonkas Palacsinta (Pancakes
Layered with Minced Ham)
Fried Tomatoes

Sliced Oranges
with Cranberry Sauce
Broiled Kippered Herring
Mamaliga (Cornmeal Mush)
Butter

Pears Stewed in Grape Juice
Crisp Bacon
Pecan Waffles
Honey Topping

Pineapple Juice
Baked Hominy Grits
Broiled Ham Slice
Coffee

Stewed Dried Fruit
Creamed Dried Beef
on Toast Points
Hazelnut Cinnamon Buns

Spiced Tomato Juice
French Omelet with Parsley
Irish Soda Bread
Pineapple-Strawberry Jam

Fresh Figs with Cream
Cheese Omelet
Brown and Serve Sausages
Espresso

LUNCHES OR SUPPERS

Pavese (Egg Consomme)
Insalata di Fagiolini et Patate
(Green-Bean and Potato Salad)
Assorted Crisp Breads
Orange Sherbet

Jamaican Congo-Pea
or Kidney-Bean Soup
Crabmeat Salad
Cracked Wheat Toast
Plum-Orange Jam

Grilled Frankfurters
or Hamburgers
Buttery Garlic Grits
Tomato Lettuce Salad
Apple and Grape-Juice Ice

Ham and Swiss Cheese Pie
Insalata Bandiera (Flag Salad)
Chocolate Fudge Brownies

Rollmops
Jellied Vegetable Salad
Pumpernickel Bread
Sweet Butter
Honey-Date Bars

Tuna Salad with Sour-Cream
Horseradish Sauce
Dill Pickles   Cherry Tomatoes
Crackers
Honey-Orange-Almond Cake

Honeydew Rings
with Shrimp Salad
Hominy Puffs
Hot Chocolate or Coffee
Ice Cream Sodas

Kingston Potato Soup
Toasted Cheese Sandwich
Strawberries à la Mode
Iced Tea

Kidney Beans with Green Peppers
Broiled Polish Sausages
Sliced Celery and Shredded
Cabbage Salad
Squash Muffins
Orange Ice

Sliced Corned Beef
Corn Fritters
Pineapple Coleslaw
Brown-Sugar Hermits

Green Pea Soup with
Frankfurter Pennies
Nut Bread and Cream Cheese
Sandwiches
Instant Blender Lemon Ice

Macaroni Salad with
Cheese Cubes
Chicken-Salad Sandwiches
Marinated Green Beans
Nutmeg Sundae

Melon and Berries in Cream
Grilled English Herring
Home-Fried Potatoes
Crumpets
Tomato Jam

Minestrone Milanese
Toasted Italian Bread
Banana Splits

Welsh Rabbit on
Toast Triangles
Broiled Tomato Halves
Mixed Green Salad with
Black Olives
Fresh Coconut Ice

Creamed Chicken with Pimientos
Chow-Mein Noodles
Summer Squash
Sweet-Sour Cucumbers
Sponge Dessert Shells with
Pineapple Ice Cream

DINNERS

Chicken-Liver Pâté
Crisp Rye Wafers
Broiled Fish Fillets
New Potatoes with Peas
Huckleberry Cottage Pudding
with Lemon Hard Sauce

Jamaican Onion Soup
with Cheese
Crisp Buttered Toast Points
Waldorf Salad
Hickory Crescents

Roast Fresh Ham Shoulder
Succotash
Winter Squash Baked in Shells
Red Cabbage Slaw
Pocketbook Rolls
Chocolate-Rum Sundae

Grapefruit Avocado Cup
Stuffed Ham Slices
Corn Pudding
Buttered Green Lima Beans
Hot Biscuits
Cranberry and Fig Jam
Mocha Parfait

Melanzane alla Marinara
Marinated Eggplant Appetizer
Pollo alla Cacciatora
(Chicken Cacciatora)
Spaghetti with Parmesan Cheese
Bread Sticks
Watermelon Granité

Magyar Gulyás
(Hungarian Goulash)
Buttered Noodles
with Caraway Seeds
Honeyed Beets
Celery Hearts
Rum-Raisin Ice Cream

Polynesian Watercress Soup
Haddock Baked in Butter
Deviled Eggs on Lettuce
Sliced Tomatoes
Szilvás Gombóc
(Plum Dumplings)

Sarson Bhara Kekda
(Shrimps with Mustard)
Murgha Kari (Chicken Curry
with Tomatoes)
Rice   Raw Cauliflower
Salad with Sesame Seed
Banana Ice Cream

Tongue with Horseradish Sauce
Cabbage Strudel
Waldorf Salad
Chocolate Ice-Cream Roll

Bárány Pörkölt Árpakásával
(Lamb and Barley Stew)
Squash Casserole
Green Bean Salad
Sour Rye Bread
Applesauce
Huszarcsok (Hussar's Kisses)

Broiled Haddock Fillets with
Fresh Grapefruit Sections
Peperoni con Patate
(Peppers and Potatoes)
Watercress-Radish Salad
Jelly-Roll Sandwiches with
Ice Cream and Jam

Head Cheese
Sweet Pickles
Mellanzane alla Parmigiana
(Eggplant Parmigiana)
Chicory and Romaine Salad
Italian Bread Sticks
Fresh or Stewed Figs in
Tokay Wine

Watercress Soup
Braised Stuffed Veal Breast
Vegetables
Zeller Salata (Celery-Root
Salad) on Greens
Pumpernickel Toast
Nut Strudel

Petto di Vitello
(Veal Breast)
Vermicelli with Ricotta
Marinated Tomatoes and
Cucumbers
Fresh Fruit Cup
Italian Cookies

Turkey Hash
Shoestring Potatoes
Broccoli with Hollandaise Sauce
Tomato Aspic on Lettuce
Seeded Hard Rolls
Chocolate Diamonds with
Hazelnuts

Tomato-Avocado Hors-d'Oeuvre
Dingle Mackerel
Slieve na mBan Carrots
Hard Rolls   Butter
Honey-Nut-Apple Pie

Pumpkin Soup
Pork Fricassee Filipino
Curried Rice
Banana and Macadamia
Nut Salad
Coconut Cake

Meatballs with Mushrooms
and Noodles
Zucchine Fritte (Fried Squash)
Green Pepper, Pimiento and
Cabbage Salad
Plum Ice   Poundcake

Danish Veal Hearts
Hominy au Gratin
Panned Mixed Greens
Radishes   Green Onions
Strawberry Ice
Vanilla Wafers

Melon Wedges Wrapped in
Prosciutto
Lasagne con le Polpettine
(Lasagna with Meatballs)
Tossed Green Salad with
Ripe Olives
Lemon Frappe

Broiled Cod Steaks with
Salsa Verde Piccante
(Piquant Green Sauce)
Shoestring Potatoes
Orange and Grapefruit Salad
Toasted Italian Bread
Hazelnut Cream

Ham Baked in Claret
Succotash   Baked Yams
Spinach Red-Onion Salad
Huckleberry Cream-Cheese Pie

Barbecued Tenderized Round
Steak
New Potatoes in Cream
Peas and Mushrooms
Grape and Orange Salad
Buttered Parkerhouse Rolls
Harlequin Crinkle Cups

Maiale Affogato
Stewed Pork with Celery
Whipped Potatoes
Marinated Carrots and Peas
on Lettuce
Seeded Hard Rolls
Cassata Napolitana
(Rich Dessert Cake)

Crab Bisque
Liffey Trout with Mushroom
Sauce
Duchess Potatoes
Coleslaw
Blueberry Ice Cream
Molasses Hermits

Clam Pastries
Creamed Hamburger and Cabbage
French-Fried Potatoes
Celery and Cucumber Sticks
Fresh Pineapple Ice
Honey-Date Bars

Table of Equivalents

few grains = less than 1/8 teaspoon (tsp.)

3 tsp. = 1 Tablespoon (Tb.)

4 Tb. = ¼ cup

8 Tb. = ½ cup

5 Tb. plus 1 tsp. = ⅓ cup

16 Tb. = 1 cup

1 cup = ½ pint (pt.)

2 cups = 1 pt.

4 cups = 1 quart (qt.)

4 qts. = 1 gallon

16 ounces (oz.) = 1 pound (dry weight)

16 oz. = 1 pt. (liquid measure)